All That Jazz

All That Jazz

The Life and Times of the Musical Chicago

Ethan Mordden

OXFORD
UNIVERSITY PRESS

OXFORD
UNIVERSITY PRESS

Oxford University Press is a department of the University of Oxford.
It furthers the University's objective of excellence in research, scholarship,
and education by publishing worldwide. Oxford is a registered trade mark of
Oxford University Press in the UK and certain other countries.

Published in the United States of America by Oxford University Press
198 Madison Avenue, New York, NY 10016, United States of America.

Library of Congress Cataloging-in-Publication Data
Names: Mordden, Ethan, author.
Title: All that jazz : the life and times of the musical Chicago /
Ethan Mordden.
Description: New York, NY : Oxford University Press, [2018] |
Includes bibliographical references and index.
Identifiers: LCCN 2017031337 (print) | LCCN 2017032526 (ebook) |
ISBN 9780190651800 (updf) | ISBN 9780190651817 (epub) |
ISBN 9780190651794 (alk. paper)
Subjects: LCSH: Kander, John. Chicago. | Chicago (Ill.)—Drama—History and
criticism. | Musicals—United States—History and criticism.
Classification: LCC ML410.K163 (ebook) | LCC ML410.K163 M67 2018 (print) |
DDC 792.6/42—dc23
LC record available at https://lccn.loc.gov/2017031337

Illustrations courtesy of Photofest; Billy Rose Theatre Collection, New York
Public Library for the Performing Arts, Astor, Lenox, and Tilden
Foundations; and private collections.

Two short passages in Chapter 8 first appeared in the
Wall Street Journal, October 15, 2016.

1 3 5 7 9 8 6 4 2

Printed by Sheridan Books, Inc., United States of America

CONTENTS

ACKNOWLEDGMENTS

To my wise agents Joe Spieler and Kent Wolf; at the Library of Congress, to Raymond White and Janet S. McKinney; for the Gershwin Trusts, to Michael Owen; at Photofest, to Howard Mandelbaum; to the Herbert von Karajan of the West End, Gareth Valentine; to my fellow historians Jon Cronwell and Ken Mandelbaum; to Ian Marshall Fisher, as helpful and diplomatic as ever in his own smooth way; and, at Oxford, to Benjamin Sears, Joellyn Ausanka, and my excellent editor, Norman Hirschy.

All That Jazz

Introduction

It's about more than the musical *Chicago*, actually. Because there is an entire *Chicago* saga—a play, a silent film, a talkie, and only then the musical, followed by a revival that turned a mere Broadway success into a global phenomenon, leading to a Best Picture movie musical.

Yet there's more, because this too easily underestimated show—underestimated as mere crazy fun, and everyone knows crazy fun has no intellectual content—carries with it the rich content of two of America's great myths, that of Chicago itself, the industrial, cultural, and geographic metropolis at the center of the American continent; and that of the 1920s, the first decade in our history that every educated American can "place" by its events, from the introduction of Prohibition to the Wall Street Crash.

So we have something of a panorama to investigate. *Chicago* is a tight show, fleet and ruthless. Yet it is filled with allusions to our show-biz past, the musical's favorite metaphor for American life from *Show Boat* to *Follies*. We need to take in all the elements of the *Chicago* saga to understand how resonant a form the American musical really is.

I feel it necessary to give the reader this little prelude, so he or she will be prepared for the unexpected. It happens that a friend, learning I was working on "*Chicago* the musical," envisioned Bob Fosse hectoring his dancers like those directors in Hollywood backstagers who keep shouting for more energy no matter how hard everyone is working.

"Meanwhile," he went on, "Gwen and Chita are fighting over who gets 'My Own Best Friend,' and one of the chorus boys recites a daring limerick about the musical director, but he overhears even as Mary McCarty gets into it with one of those long-legged Fosse beauties. That's how it starts, right?"

I shook my head.

"No? Then what does it start with?"

"Indians," I replied.

1

٭

The City

Unregulated Capitalism

It was the best of sites, it was the worst of sites: a low-lying swamp of mud and water pockets with a thick grass cover impeding drainage, all this cut up by a sluggish river. The watercourse came down from the north and up from the south alike, to meet and drag itself eastward to drip into a gigantic lake, though its right-of-way was blocked by a reef of sand and gravel. To build a city on this mud-hole would create a sewage problem, which, emptying into the lake, would create a drinking-water problem and a cholera problem. And that reef limited water traffic to the very lightest craft, useless in conveying trade goods in any serious economy.

However, by the time Chicago was officially founded, in 1833, its location commanded the southwestern sector of a seaway running through other lakes to the east right into the already functioning Erie Canal and thus through New York State down to New York City, the greatest harbor in the world. Once Chicago built a canal to connect its eponymous river to the suite of watercourses feeding the Mississippi River, Chicago could become the hub of a trading operation uniting New York with New Orleans, effectively homogenizing the commercial forces of much of what was then the settled United States. Then, too, Chicago, the capital of what used to be called "the northwest," commanded the colonization of the western half of the continent. Chicago's chief industries, in lumber, grain, and livestock, would open up Louisiana Purchase land to the pioneer and, after him, the farmer, banker, and tradesman. As for that reef at the mouth of the Chicago River, a canal broke through it and, finally, it was scooped up as though a giant had intervened. The railroad, too, found a welcome, making Chicago the nation's midpoint depot. It was the worst of sites but the best of destinies, and Chicago became the fastest-growing and most abundantly thriving city in history.

The area's first inhabitants, of course, were Indians, mainly Potawotami, though they seem not to have pitched their camps just where the yet to be named Chicago River met Lake Michigan, the geographical point at which Chicago first took shape. The Indians named it, though: Chigagou, French fur-trappers' corruption of the local term meaning, more or less, "Where the wild garlic grows."

But the Indians couldn't hold on to it—not against the might of whites' ever-westward expansion. Treaties were signed in which Indians ceded territory, but they never truly understood the white concept of land ownership. To the Indian, owning land was like owning the rain or the moon. Nature preceded, defied, and outlasted ownership. A man might stake a claim to a rifle or beaver pelts. But how could a man cut his name onto a forest glade or a river or the weather that came along with them? No wonder there were no Indian metropolises: cities are based on the proprietorship and development of the earth.

Thus, it was tragic but inevitable that the white man remove the Indian, because whites were not only going to trade in the land around Chigagou: they were going to remodel it. They went ahead and built that canal to bond Lake Michigan with the Mississippi. They tunneled under the lake bed to draw their drink from a purer source farther out in the water, away from the industrial waste befouling the river. And when that wasn't enough, they built a second canal, dredging so deeply into the ground that it actually reversed the river's course, changing its eastward flow to run to the west.

And they finally solved the drainage problem by building a sewer network and literally *raising the entire city*. From shacks to hotels and office hives, buildings were painstakingly cranked upward, inch by inch. It took twenty years to accomplish, and a few modest houses refused to take part, creating sudden lurches in the sidewalk grades. Some landlords simply moved their property, and citizens grew used to seeing buildings majestically sailing down boulevards on their way to a restful plot in the suburbs. Chicago, declared Robert Herrick, in his novel *The Gospel of Freedom* (1898), was "a stupendous piece of blasphemy against nature. Once within its circle, the heart must forget that the earth [itself] is beautiful."

We need to look in on the growth of Chicago to understand why *Chicago* the musical occupies so unusual a spot in the history of American art. For one thing, while there is an undeniable excitement to Chicago the city, it has thrown off few classic works in literature or theatre. There are Chicago novels, certainly—the one of Herrick's mentioned above, Theodore Dreiser's *Sister Carrie*, John O'Hara's *Pal Joey* stories, or, most recently, Veronica Roth's very popular series on life in post-apocalyptic Chicago, the *Divergent* trilogy. True, James T. Farrell's remarkable *Studs Lonigan* books, another trilogy, capture the vernacular of Irish working-class Chicago to an astonishing degree. Nevertheless, there is no classic Chicago fiction rich in the map and spirit of the place comparable to *Ulysses'* revelation of Dublin, Balzac's Paris, or Dickens' London.

The American stage, too, always preferred New York as the most useful urban setting. Was there something in the very meaning of Chicago that felt too resonant and cumbersome to serve the needs of playwrights who use location as a prefabricated meme? The south is a racial crucible. Boston is prim. The countryside is as simple as a psalm. But Chicago is . . . what?

All our great cities have thrown off a myth. New York was the cultural capital, the place of wit and sophistication. Los Angeles was the "company town," run by the movies, and San Francisco styled nonconformism as its default setting. Chicago entered the lists for crime, especially the Prohibition gangsterism of the 1920s. An immortal New Yorker is Dorothy Parker, an Angeleno is Clark Gable, a San Franciscan is Harvey Milk. But mention Chicago and the name that springs to mind is Al Capone.

Yet Chicago is renowned also for its pantheon of architects—
Louis Sullivan, Frank Lloyd Wright, partners Daniel Burnham and
John Wellborn Root—and their astonishing agglomeration of sky-
scrapers in the concentrated business section known as The Loop
(after the public transportation line that ringed it). There is the
Great Fire of 1871, the most destructive conflagration in American
history, bound into legend because of a false tale that Catherine
O'Leary's cow kicked over a lantern in her hay-filled milk barn (and
referenced in *Chicago* the musical's cut number "Loopin' the Loop").
And there is Chicago the city of jazz, when the Great Migration of
the 1910s and 1920s brought a huge black population up from the
south, with King Oliver, Jelly Roll Morton, and Louis Armstrong
disseminating the new music of New Orleans.

Above all, Chicago was the can-do city, mixing its engineering
marvels with an obsessive love of commercial activity. Cyrus Hall
McCormick, who invented the harvesting reaper that revolution-
ized grain agriculture, had no life outside of his business. Even on
his deathbed, he longed to get dressed and go down to the factory,
feebly crying, "Work! Work!," his last words on earth. No other city
concentrated its industries so centrally, with the mini-metropolises
of the lumber yards, stockyards, and grain elevators not far outside
The Loop itself. Put simply, Chicago looked like money—"so proud
to be alive," its native son and poet laureate Carl Sandburg wrote,
"and coarse and strong and cunning."

But then, Chicagoans loved hearing how tough and ruthless the
city seemed to outsiders, tough as a prizefighter and ruthless as a
millionaire, capitalism's city of the plain or, to knock it down to
Americanspeak, "City of the big shoulders," in Sandburg's phrase.
The natives were called "boosters," because they loved even its flaws,
no doubt thrilling to the words of the unsuccessful mayoral candidate of 1911, Charles E. Merriam: "Chicago is unique. It is the only
completely corrupt city in America."

It didn't have to be the best, but it had to be the most. Lincoln
Steffens, the most famous of the muckrakers of the early 1900s who
uncovered the flaws in American civic life in stinging magazine ar-
ticles, thought Chicago "first in violence, deepest in dirt," and—

here's the insult—"an overgrown gawk of a village." Especially gall-
ing to booster sentiment was A. J. Liebling's three-part profile of
Chicago in *The New Yorker*, in 1952. Liebling saw The Loop as not the
dazzling core of an urban sprawl with its own unique tang but as the
only part of Chicago that *was* urban: "like Times Square and Radio
City set down in the middle of a vast Canarsie." The low-slung buildings and industrial plants of Chicago at large suggested "an endless
succession of factory-town main streets." Then came The Loop, all
of a sudden, as if one were "entering a walled city."

Mark Twain, however, saw it as an American Arabian Night, "where
they are always rubbing a lamp, and fetching up the genii...and
achieving new impossibilities." And, finally, James Bryce, author of
the de Tocquevillesque book *The American Commonwealth* and the
English ambassador to the United States in the years around 1910,
thought Chicago "perhaps the most typically American place in
America."

Why? Because of all the technical ingenuity combined with a certain human arrogance—reversing the course of a river!—and the
emphasis on the free and unregulated market of buying and selling.
For two generations in the middle of the nineteenth century,
Chicago (and St. Louis, its at times bitter rival) marked the western
edge of America's calendar of cities, the embarkation point for continental development. Chicago gives us a *concentration* of energies. The
Indians thought the land owns the people, but those who seized
that land used it as a platform for the infrastructure of a civilization:
new ways to erect buildings ever higher, to amortize the cost of
realty in The Loop and its temples of money-changers; the eventual
founding of arts institutions, to keep beauty handy; the sorting out
of civic responsibilities, to reckon just how much corruption to
allow; and what to do about sex.

Because of its explosive growth,[1] Chicago became a metropolis while
it was still a frontier town, with all the license and chaos of innocents
and opportunists pouring in from everywhere. Law enforcement

---

1. On its legal emergence, in 1833, Chicago counted fewer than 500 residents. Four
years later, when it officially incorporated as a city, its population was 4,000.

was often helpless to keep order. "We are beset on every side," the *Chicago Journey* observed, "by a gang of desperate villains!" The place was known as "the wickedest city in America"—and this was before the criminal bands of the 1920s, with their getaway cars and Thompson sub-machine guns and St. Valentine's Day Massacre.

However, Chicago was as well the great immigrants' city, where the Germans and then the Irish formed substantial sub-cultures; in the 1870s, over half the population had been born in Europe. In *Gem of the Prairie* (later republished as *The Gangs of Chicago*), Herbert Asbury revealed that by 1890 Chicago had become the fifth largest German city in the world, the third largest Swedish city, and the second largest Bohemian city, behind only Prague in its Czech population.

And Chicago was the great merchants' city, that "Work! Work!" of Cyrus McCormick often tweaked into "Sell! Sell!" In McCormick's case, he created something that hadn't existed before and sold it to those with a genuine need for it: the grain reaper that enabled farmers to harvest their entire crop within the very narrow window between ripeness and spoilage. However, one might also sell what no one needed (as we'll presently see), till, ultimately, almost anything could be sold, including crime. This is what Maurine Watkins' 1926 play—the original *Chicago*—and its four adaptations are about.

Another aspect of Chicago the city that is typically American is its profusion of eccentrics, for this nation has a strange fondness for colorful characters that we don't find in other cultures. Indeed, Chicago's pride of gaudy gangsters of Prohibition's beer wars, robbing banks unmasked or murdering one another with exhibitionistic flair on main streets, both in broad daylight, inspired Chester Gould's comic strip *Dick Tracy*, which first appeared in 1931. A native of Oklahoma before it was a state, Gould had moved to Chicago to study at Northwestern University, but from the start he had—as he told Herb Galewitz in an interview for a 1970 *Dick Tracy* anthology—"the intent of getting on the [*Chicago*] *Tribune*" as a comic-strip artist.

Gould tried out numerous ephemeral ideas—*Radio Cats*, *Fillum Fables* (a spoof of movie serials), *The Girl Friends*. "Then," Gould tells us, "it suddenly dawned on me that perhaps we ought to have a detective in this country that would hunt these [gangsters] up and shoot 'em down."

It would be a rough justice, in contrast to what was happening in both Chicago the city and *Chicago* the play, where the guilty get off. But Tracy's antagonists are very unlike the casual "I killed him, so what?" murderesses we see in *Chicago*'s narrative. More and more as the strip developed, Gould introduced fantastical career criminals— The Blank; tiny Jerome Trohs, who rides around on a dog named Tip; The Mole; Little Face Finny; the suavely homicidal band leader 88 Keyes. It was as though Gould had transmogrified the brazen lawlessness of Chicago's outlaw class into physical deformities.

And this may have led to *Batman*, developed by artist Bob Kane and writer Bill Finger and introduced in *Detective Comics #27*, in 1939. Batman's most famous foes—the Joker, the Penguin, Two-Face—were more flamboyant than Dick Tracy's, and they were insistently recurring nemeses, never more than temporarily defeated. So Batman's world is a kind of Chicago, where lawbreaking is an accepted element of the status quo.

In fact, when *Batman* began, Kane and Finger set it in the northeast. An early episode showing the hero leaping from rooftop to rooftop is captioned with "Through the dark of a New York night...," and even when when Batman's place of business was quietly renamed Gotham City, it seemed based in "New York below Fourteenth Street after eleven o'clock at night," according to Denny O'Neil, one of the many editors who assumed control of the character in later years.

Even so, the feeling of a Chicago-like town where the underworld behaves as if it were the overworld is inescapable in the *Batman* saga. Many of Chicago's worst citizens were as celebrated as its mayors and theatre stars; its champion defense attorney Clarence Darrow; its "directa" (as she liked to term it) of the local opera, fascinating Mary Garden. The Mickey Finn knockout drink is actually named for a notorious pickpocket, fence, and, finally, proprietor of and chief bartender at the Lone Star Saloon and Palm Garden, which opened in 1896. (The Garden—as Herbert Asbury tells us in *Gem of the Prairie*—was no more than "a back room decorated with a scrawny little palm tree in a pot.") From "a Negro voodoo doctor...who sold love potions and charms to the inmates of the bawdy houses" along with cocaine and morphine, Finn got a bottle of something Asbury believed to be "hydrate of chloral." A sign on the wall urged the Saloon's customers to "try a Mickey Finn Special," and those who did were stripped down to their money belt and then tossed into a back alley.

There is no counting the victims of operations like Finn's, from slumming gentlemen to college boys on a lark to farmers making their first trip to the Big City. Once they entered the vice district well south of The Loop, they were all but doomed to be the victims of criminals well-practiced in the arts of con games, sudden surprises, or simply a physical attack. Bordellos were often fitted up as "panel houses," with fake walls in rooms of assignation to allow a third party access to a man's belongings while he was erotically distracted. "Beware! O sportive young gentlemen in search of a little diversion," cries a little handbook of 1893, *Chicago By Day and Night: The Pleasure Seeker's Guide To the Paris of America*. "While the interview between the more or less affectionate lovers is in progress, a panel in the wall slides back...and...the male confederate of the damsel slinks through it into the apartment" to take the john's watch and wallet.

Chicago By Day and Night warns also of the badger game, by which an assignation is interrupted as the woman's "husband" suddenly crashes into the room. Naturally, his offended honor must be bought off lest blood be shed. It is bemusing to read Herbert Asbury's deadpan recitation of the limits of Chicago's vice district, because it didn't seem to have any. The neighborhoods include Mother Conley's Patch, Shinbone Alley, Little Cheyenne, the Black Hole, The Bad Lands, Satan's Mile, Hell's Half-Acre, and Dead Man's Alley, among others, and the list of streets of the depraved runs from Franklin, Jackson, Wells, Clark, and State to Fourth, Blue Island, and Chicago Avenues—twenty major thoroughfares in all, and Asbury quotes a police detective calling "the whole stretch of Clark Street" as "about as tough and vicious a place as there was on the face of the earth." One judge dismissed charges against two thieving prostitutes, reasoning that any man who set foot in an area so infamous as Chicago's viceland deserved what he got.

Women were victimized as well, especially naive young girls out on their own. No place was safe; on the contrary, the library, an ice-cream parlor, or a theatre matinee were all perilous. A more or less dashing gentleman or sympathetic older woman—a "rope," in underworld parlance—would strike up a conversation, win the target's confidence, and if the rope could somehow lure the mark out of public view (and these expert procurers knew all the somehows), the young victim would end up cut off from friends and family as a sex slave in a bordello. While this could theoretically happen anywhere in the world,[2] it would seem to have happened in Chicago especially. In *Gem of the Prairie*, Herbert Asbury tells us "during a period of about nine months in 1907 and 1908," the law caught up with 157 ropes and rescued 329 of their victims. This is why, in both the play and musical *Chicago*, lawyer Billy Flynn so casually plans murderess Roxie Hart's ghosted newspaper "autobiography" under the title "From Convent To Jail": many a daughter of the middle class, through no fault of her own, became trapped in the bad world of Chicago wickedness, and everyone in town knew it.

A very few simply chose The Life, to master it as a vocational opportunity. Every American city had its Tenderloin district, but Chicago gloried in it; this town had an outlaw's quartier before it had a sewage system or adequate drinking water. Karen Abbott's *Sin in the Second City* tells us that as early as 1935, when Chicago was little more than a settlement of buildings clustered around the mouth of the Chicago River, the city fathers had already assessed a penalty of $25 for opening a brothel, a disincentive that had absolutely no effect on the sex business.

---

2. The American opera singer Frederica von Stade told me that, aged nineteen, in Paris, she knew a fellow American girl who was riding in a packed elevator when she suddenly felt she was losing consciousness. Immediately, she loudly exclaimed, in French, "I am alone! I am not with anyone! Please call the police! Do not let anyone take me away!" She had suspected that a modern-day rope had given her a shot of something. Luckily, someone did protect her, the gendarmes arrived, and she woke up in the hospital. There the story ended—happily, in this case though not others.

Abbott's book is actually a biography of the Everleigh sisters, Minna and Ada, who were to Chicago's underworld what Mrs. Potter Palmer, the wife of the city's millionaire department-store-and-hotel magnate, was to Chicago Society. Like so many famous Chicagoans, the Everleighs came from somewhere else, in this case Kentucky via Omaha, at the very end of the nineteenth century. They had it in mind to cater to an elite clientele in a place where a common-sense acceptance of the human appetite kept reformers at bay with a combination of luxe and style. Not a bordello. *The* bordello, for the plutocrat of taste.

And Chicago was the perfect place for them, for its Red Light District was not only flourishing, but run by and for riffraff, so there was an opening for the Everleighs. Taking over adjoining houses at 2131–2133 South Dearborn Street, the sisters set up an elegant shop, overdecorated in the style of the day but an outfit of finesse, with, Abbott notes, three orchestras and a dinner menu that ran from Supreme of Guinea-fowl to Spinach Cups with Creamed Peas and Parmesan Potato Cubes. The Everleighs' block of Dearborn was lined with bagnios—Madame Leo's, Monahan's, French Em's—and one block to the north lay no less than eight bawdy houses in a row, from the Frenchman's to Dago Frank's. But the Everleigh Club was *the* Chicago club, to the competition's fury: since when was a bordello supposed to be a place of refinement? Clearly, the managers of the cheap dives didn't know the First Rule of American business: you have to spend big to earn big.

As madams, the Everleighs fit right into Chicago's system of bribing the police—there actually were set prices to pay throughout the vice world, depending on how many Commandments one was shattering—and suavely began playing hostesses to the great and near-great of the tony North Side. It was the perfection of hypocrisy. As with the politicians who voted for Prohibition while maintaining an account with a bootlegger, the heavy Names of Chicago's merchant class talked family values but walked the adulterer's option. And the Everleigh Club, so discreet and protected, was the ideal resort.

The sisters felt so comfortable in their status as entrepreneurs of The Life that they openly circulated a promotional booklet complete with photographs of the pleasure suites on offer at their club. So everyone seemed to know about the brochure, and not only in Chicago. Another Everleigh biographer, Charles Washburn, tells us that the city's popular mayor Carter Harrison II, off on a junket just when the Everleighs' circular was enjoying renown, was greeted by a young man with "Pretty snappy town yours, isn't it?," in a tone that dripped with inside knowledge.

Though the brochure itself infuriated Harrison, he was generally tolerant of Chicago's sex industry, because there was no way not to be. Reform administrations, occasionally voted in, were immediately voted out, because the citizenry wanted freedom and reformers wanted to take it away. Further, while the play *Chicago* exposes collusion between the guilty and the press, and the musical *Chicago* reveals an even larger infrastructure of profit among disruptive forces, no play or movie in the saga of Watkins' heroine, Roxie Hart, bothers to show us reformers—and they didn't have much impact in the city of Chicago, either, even if the Woman's Christian Temperance Union, forerunner of the Anti-Saloon League that forced Prohibition into national law, had its headquarters in Chicago.

The system by which vice and payoffs formed an all but "legal" bond was so secure that one of its most apparent archons was another of Chicago's flamboyant characters, "Bathhouse" John J. Coughlin, his nickname drawn from early employment in a Turkish bath. In his prime, Coughlin was an alderman of the First Ward, the central district of the city, running from the eastern branch of the river through The Loop all the way down to Twenty-Ninth Street and the choice cut of the Tenderloin known as the Levee. This was deep Chicago: City Hall, the Board of Trade, the major office buildings and department stores, the theatres and restaurants...and then the bordellos, gambling dens, and anything-goes saloons with their back rooms of surprise and delight. It was the tourist's Chicago, the adventurer's Chicago, the Chicago of the powers that be: dishes of taste for Coughlin's own personal banquet.

Historians invariably lump Coughlin with his fellow First Ward alderman Michael "Hinky Dink" Kenna, but Kenna was careful and businesslike, physically short in a world of rowdy giants. Meeting him, one encountered little more than a grey suit.

No, it was Bathhouse John who was the Chicago Character, big in style with a waxed walrus mustache, the kind of politician who thought public life incomplete unless one wrote a sentimental ballad—both words and music, if the publication credit be believed—called "Dear Midnight of Love." Herbert Asbury said the lyrics bore "all the literary quality of a first-grade essay on 'Oh, See the Cat,'" but as with "Will You Love Me in December As You Do in May," whose lyrics were the work of New York's future mayor James J. Walker, it's not about quality: it's about versatility. A sentimental ballad shows your heart, always useful when the public knows you're up to your haircut in conspiracy and graft.

But Chicago's topsy-turvy view of morality didn't simply tolerate its Coughlins. It reveled in them. "The good-citizen majority looked on the wrongdoers as a sort of vaudeville," Ben Hecht observed in *Gaily, Gaily,* his reminiscences of his first days as a reporter in Chicago. The moral life was righteous but dull. "It was pleasant, in a way," Hecht explains, "to know that outside their windows, the devil was still capering in a flare of brimstone."

Thus, the burial of gangster "Big Jim" Colosimo, in 1920, came off virtually as a state funeral, with wagon after wagon of flowers, a vast crowd lining the route to the cemetery, and a pallbearer count that—says Herbert Asbury—included "three judges, an Assistant State's Attorney, a member of Congress, a state Representative and nine [city] aldermen, marching side by side with . . . notorious white-slavers, thugs, thieves, and gangsters." After another such cortège, the usual temporary reform mayor, William E. Dever, cried, "Are we living by the [right-is-might] code of the Dark Ages?" Only in Chicago were the authorities and evildoers bonded in such an overt—a nakedly insolent—way.

Coughlin himself didn't think the goo-goos (the popular derogation for those who tried to impose "good government" on corrupt administrations) were genuine. "When I see a reformer," he said, "I put a hand on my watch." He wasn't thought clever—Hinky Dink was the brains of the outfit—but at least Coughlin looked the part of the shameless crook, affecting couture you could see from Michigan, across the lake. The helpful Herbert Asbury pictures him for us: "silk hat, pink gloves, yellow shoes, a swallow-tail coat of bottle green, lavender pants, and a cream-colored vest blazing with diamond studs and embroidered with roses and carnations." Pink gloves would shock the eye in any age—but note an odd coincidence in that yellow shoes will become significant in the career of *Chicago*'s songwriters, John Kander and Fred Ebb, for their use in *The Visit*.

Such odd Characters as the Everleighs, Coughlin, and Kenna were more or less popular, but Charles Tyson Yerkes was not. A Philadelphian who had gone to prison for embezzlement and abandoned his wife and six children, Yerkes arrived in Illinois in the 1880s, managing to alienate all classes and ethnic groups as the "traction king" who replaced the horse-drawn streetcar with cable cars, able to cover long distances in vastly shorter time spans, meanwhile employing disused tunnels to avoid the waits at the swing bridges over the river.[3]

Yerkes' contribution to Chicago's well-being was incalculable, for while The Loop's buildings rose straight up to the sky, the rest of town was spread out over tremendous distances, making sheer physical communication very time-consuming. Using Yerkes' cable cars, everyone got together with everyone else with ease, a wonderful advance over those poky old horsecars—but Yerkes laid out his transportation system through bullying and cheating and back-room dealing. It was crony capitalism with a big stick, yet Yerkes loved being a public figure, warts and all. He dared you to disapprove, spending money like a drunken sailor who is also a multi-millionaire: he actually owned his own art gallery and slept in a bed that cost $8,000, once the property of the King of Belgium.

Oddly, Yerkes never cultivated Chicago's one percent, and, unlike the typical robber baron, he never pretended he was anything but a crook. "The secret of success in my business," he observed, "is to buy old junk, fix it up a little, and unload it upon other fellows." Or even:

---

3. These bridges connected Chicago's main avenues from the South Side to the North and from the East to the West while giving passage to water traffic. But they couldn't do both at once, because the bridges stood at grade level, blocking all but the smallest boats. So each bridge would serve as an artery for foot and wheel traffic, then "swing" out, parallel with the river line to allow water craft to pass, then move back to reconnect the two halves of the avenue again, and so on. They drove everybody crazy.

"Whatever I do, I do . . . to satisfy myself." Yes, of course—but you're not supposed to say so. In the end, Yerkes was more or less run out of town, and he went to London to build its subway system, the Underground.

This atmosphere of all but unopposed criminality had to throw up a saint somehow or other, and Chicago's was Jane Addams. Hearing of an experimental "settlement house" in London's East End, Addams crossed the ocean to see the experiment for herself: an imposing residence tucked away in the slums where Oxford alumni lectured and taught and coached local people in the arts and sciences. Inspired, Addams returned to her native Illinois to create something similar in Chicago. She and her partner in the venture, Ellen Gates Starr, took up residence in certain rooms in a disused mansion on the Near West Side, in 1889. When new, the building had been the country home of one Charles Hull; so swiftly had the expanding city gobbled up the surrounding geography that what had been a rural retreat now stood in the middle of a teeming slum, inhabited almost entirely by immigrants. Bit by bit, Addams' project, called Hull-House,[4] expanded too, till it took up all of Hull's former property and the rest of the block as well. The intent was to bring beauty and information to people who were struggling even for bare subsistence: to brighten their lives. Yet it was intensely practical, too; as most of Addams' neighbors lacked English skills, she programmed language classes and opened a library along with the art shows and music instruction.

It sounds like a low-key outfit, to be known strictly by folk of the Nineteenth Ward; on the contrary, Hull-House's success made Addams famous, and her focus was on national as well as local issues. As her biographer Louise W. Knight observes, Addams "worked to end child labor, support unions and workers' rights, protect free speech and civil rights, respect all cultures, achieve women's suffrage and women's freedom, and promote . . . the spread of peace." Knight likens Addams' influence to that of Eleanor Roosevelt, and there even were, Knight

---

4. The name of the building is spelled with or without the hyphen, even in biographies of Addams. But the first edition (in 1911) of Addams' own *Twenty Years At Hull-House* spells it thus throughout.

says, "wistful discussions of [Addams'] running for president." Yet Chicago's official Heroine Character lived ascetically, quite without the trappings of a Great Name. Knight quotes a writer for a Christian newspaper who says, "I don't quite understand her religious position. She seems to be a Christian without religion."

Or even a Chicagoan without Chicago: uncompromised. Some may see a parallel between Jane Addams and the "sob sister" reporter Mary Sunshine in the *Chicago* play and musical, but Sunshine is silly and credulous. Addams' salient quality was her bottomless well of common sense. On the subject of the many people harmed by Prohibition—imprisoned, sometimes on "life for a pint [of liquor sold]" sentences; poisoned; or shot—Addams said, "What the Prohibition situation needs first of all is disarmament."

On the lighter side, Chicago had Characters working in the popular arts, and Joseph E. Howard was one of the most prominent, an author of musicals written specifically for local production, first at the La Salle Theatre, then at the Princess. A transplanted New Yorker, born in 1878, Howard wrote book, lyrics, and music, but he was most familiar as the composer to wordsmiths Will M. Hough and Frank R. Adams. Their shows were the thrill of the midwest theatrical loop, though not all of them tried Broadway and none that did succeeded, not even *The Time, The Place and the Girl* (1906), a 400-performance smash in Chicago.

But then, the Howard shows were extremely derivative, respecting the corniest clichés of the day, and theirs were the songs that Irving Berlin and Jerome Kern swept away when Broadway's musical revolution took off, in the 1910s. Howard, Hough, and Adams' *The Isle of Bong-Bong* (1904), about a sultan in a fabulous palace on an island that floats around the Pacific Ocean, is typical, with its ethnic piece, "Heap Love, Indian Serenade"; its satiric number, "Diplomacy"; its Bowery waltz with comic observations, "If I Were the Man in the Moon." One verse tells of a cop who never seems to make an arrest, so the moon reveals the consequences of lazy policing:

> He would show why timid thugs
> Live in flats with Turkish rugs...

Pretty feeble, no? But Howard did manage to turn out a few hit tunes—"Hello Ma Baby," a black ragtime number; "I Wonder Who's Kissing Her Now"; and "Goodbye, My Lady Love," another ragtime number, interpolated into *Show Boat*'s Trocadero night-club scene to capture period authenticity. A tenor with an old-fashioned sound, half barbershop-top-line and half John McCormack, Howard eventually concentrated on performing, yet never evolved out of his Gilded Age mentality. Incredibly, he lasted long enough to host and perform on a very early television show, *The Gay Nineties Revue*, featuring absurdly antique acts—a trio of violinists that stunt-played their instruments (two of them bow a single fiddle at the same time, for instance), an operetta soprano, the inevitable barbershop four, and Howard himself in tails at seventy years of age to sing of walking "hand in hand in blyu-bird land." At one point Howard goes into an intensely Jurassic strut such as we might have seen on the stage of the La Salle Theatre when you and I were young, Maggie: moving slowly, tightly, one tiny yet showy step after another, demanding applause.

It's oddly confident for a performer capping a career of very little distinction. Worse, one year earlier, Hollywood filmed a Howard bio, using (as was traditional) one of the subject's hit tunes as its title, in this case *I Wonder Who's Kissing Her Now*. But then the song's true composer stepped forward. It was Harold Orlob, from whom Howard had bought the melody. This is like learning that Bambi was actually a weasel.

Howard interests us because he exemplifies an odd quality of the musical: few of them are set in Chicago, even though it has always been America's "second" city. We expect Howard's shows, written in Chicago for Chicago, to prove an exception, but, on the contrary, his musicals took place in New York or the countryside. At least *The Isle of Bong-Bong*'s "My Illinois," a homesick lament, does refer to a few sights familiar to Chicagoans. And, moving beyond Howard, *The Wizard of Oz* (1902; NY 1903), a Chicago production based on the famous fairy tale, did make the Wizard a "Dutch" comic (from *deutsch*, meaning "German," and referring to a stereotype character speaking fractured English with a German accent), to appeal to

Chicago's vast German sub-population. When the show traveled to Broadway the following year, the Wizard became an Irish comic, a more popular stereotype among New Yorkers.

It may be that Chicago's image simply didn't comport with the worldview of the musical. Chicago had baggage; there was too much questionable *there* in it for light entertainment to bear. Straight plays could tackle the Chicago mystique—this very saga begins with *Chicago* the play, in 1926. But even there, the theme is the show biz of crime, not the utter corruption of the municipality.

Still, we expect to see this corrupt Chicago in artwork that is set there. Consider this bit of Brian De Palma's movie *The Untouchables*, as unimportant old cop Sean Connery explains how things are to Kevin Costner's Eliot Ness:

> CONNERY: How come I'm walking the beat at my age? . . . Well, maybe I'm that whore with a heart of gold—or the one good cop in a bad town.

But it wasn't just the crime of Chicago: it was the *business* of Chicago, as if the two were united. A stickup artist is just a crook. But a man operating a huge business that underpays and overworks his employees and gouges his customers is a Prince of Commerce. "It was unregulated capitalism," says historian Donald I. Miller, "that created nineteenth-century Chicago." Business without brakes made a cesspool of the river, recklessly dumping waste in it till the waters bubbled like witch's brew. An industrial haze known as "the smoke horror" hung over the city, begriming buildings, clothing—everything—in a sooty film. In the neighborhood known as Back of the Yards (the plebes' quarter south of the stockyards), the residents learned to distinguish several different kinds of noxious odors.

This was Bertolt Brecht's idea of America, an Emerald City of Mammon, where all life is money. You breathe money, eat and drink money, fuck money. Brecht and Kurt Weill's opera *Rise and Fall of Mahagonny City* seems to be set in Florida, but everyone knows it's really Chicago, a "city of nets"—so one of its founders calls it—to fleece visitors of their property. As a reporter in Maurine Watkins' play puts it. "Chicago—the city of opportunity!" Mahagonny is little more than a clip joint with its own zip code, but in another Brecht work, *The Resistible Rise of Arturo Ui*, Hitler is seen as a kind of Al Capone and Chicago as a fascist state.

Actually, Chicago was just the opposite: a totally free state, with a population that ignored the authorities—the law, even—when it wasn't rebelling against them. Mushrooming from trading post to township to city and next to metropolis, Chicago moved too fast to remember to become civilized. A business energy drove it; it ran on the sheer liberty of the profit motive. Thus, when the Great Fire of 1871 destroyed most of the city's center (survivors, wandering the grid-plan streets in a daze, couldn't tell where they were because everything was gone), the rebuilding began while the earth was still smoking. More than any other town, Chicago was America's crucible of commerce. Grain, lumber, and livestock, yes. But also liquor, gambling, and sex. In Chicago, everything was a commodity.

And this fantastical emporium of life could not be tamed even when the wives of the first batch of Chicago millionaires pressed their husbands to beautify and uplift the place. More opera, less grunge. And, true enough, in those bygone times city fathers had the power to moralize disturbing elements of municipal life. They were the shadow authorities, well above the mayor, the police chief, and the crony capitalists, so Old Testament in their influence they didn't need cronies. Here was the one percent of the one percent, and what they wanted to happen was what would happen. Chicago's cornucopia of saloons, pleasure dens, and street crime meant nothing to them. As long as the banks were open and the trash was collected, they were content.

These éminences grises had but one problem: the workers. They suffered appalling conditions—an unnaturally shortened life-span for wages so low that children were forced out of school into jobs to keep a family alive—and sought relief in unionization. But the bosses crushed strike after strike, using the desperate unemployed as scabs under the protection of the police, state militia, and Pinkerton guards.

America saw many a strike in the late nineteenth century, but Chicago truly seethed with labor unrest, a place where a European kind of revolution might break out. During America's Great Railroad

Strike of 1877, the newspapers were filled with recollections of the Paris Commune of six years earlier, and Chicago itself exploded in riots. Thirty were killed, some two hundred wounded, and the mayor, correctly declaring it the "Battle of Chicago," took the unusual step of closing the saloons, the lifeblood of the city but also the social clubs of the men of the working class. It is no accident that Chicago was where the first international labor union, the Industrial Workers of the World, was formed, and likewise no accident that America's worst political violence, the Haymarket Bombing, of 1886, occurred in Chicago. The city, says Donald L. Miller, was "the capital of American radicalism."

All this brings us well beyond the world of the theatre, true enough, even if such a musical as *The Cradle Will Rock* (1937) treats labor unrest and management-goon terrorism and *Les Misérables* (Paris 1980; New York 1987) treats revolution. Still, *Chicago*'s view of a town tolerant of outlaws and their infrastructure of *Presto! Changeo!* justice wedded to the Pinocchio press complements this cross-section of all-powerful bosses and powerless workers. It's the Morlocks against the Eloi, the cannibals and their dinner—which is what you get when society rejects morality for absolute liberty. Why should any citizen respect laws when so many public figures, from police officials to gangsters, do not?

Indeed, looking at it from a Chicagoan's point of view, were the lords of the business world all that different from any who prey on the weak? Consider Upton Sinclair's novel of 1906, *The Jungle*, dedicated "To the workingmen of America," a *J'accuse* aimed at Chicago's business class in its depiction of a worker whose life is destroyed by overwork and low wages. Of having no freedom in the world's capital of freedom. Jurgis Rudkus, a Lithuanian immigrant, is blacklisted when he attacks his wife's boss, who molested her; loses his house; loses his wife in childbirth; then loses their baby, who drowns in the typical Chicago flooded street, a remnant of the city's swampy origins.

Even today, there are those who ridicule Sinclair's storyline as outrageous exaggeration. The events with which he oppresses his hero all but anticipate the sequence in Fritz Lang's film *Metropolis* (1927) in which the "energy" machine is seen as Moloch, its mouth agape and blazing with a greed for human sacrifice, as bound workers are dragged up a huge stairway to be hurled into the flames. In *The Jungle's* most chilling passage, a young boy is locked in a cellar and devoured by rats—and Sinclair includes a mention here and there of the collusion between the law and crime that we have noted throughout this chapter. It is this view of society as corrupt from top to bottom that gives *Chicago*—play, movies, and musical—its richly ironic flavor. "The police captain," Sinclair writes, "would own the brothel he pretended to raid, and the politician would [make] his headquarters in his saloon."

The Jungle ends with Jurgis at a meeting of revolutionaries, the final line a shouted "CHICAGO WILL BE OURS!" However, Sinclair found his readers less interested in his politics than in his description of the terror of the unregulated meatpacking industry, with its blithe marketing of diseased cattle covered in boils and sausage made from not only pork but rat carcasses, rat droppings, and rat poison. Everything on the packing floor went into the hoppers, including the remnants of men who had fallen into the cooking vats. *The Jungle* certainly was a teaching moment—not of the bosses' abuse of workers but of the vile practices of the food-processing interests. This actually resulted in national legislation to protect consumers.

There was one palliative oasis for the late-nineteenth-century Chicago worker—or was there? "Visitors to Pullman," Donald Miller tells us, "often arrived after touring the stockyards the previous day, and the contrast could not have been more startling." George Pullman, who designed and manufactured the railroad sleeping car that reinvented long-distance travel, founded his very own company town in 1881, this same Pullman, Illinois. He built it twelve miles south of The Loop, on the shores of Lake Calumet, near the southern tip of Lake Michigan. This planned community, the very opposite of the slums that most of Chicago's workers dwelled in, became an international sensation. *Harper's New Monthly Magazine* ran a profile of the place in 1885, when its population was about eight thousand, and the piece came complete with a city plan showing the orderly streets of workers' red-and-black-brick houses and the Arcade building containing bank, theatre, library, school, and shops. There was a playground and even the Hotel Florence, named for Pullman's favorite daughter, for when you're that rich you don't have to be nice to people you don't care about, including your family. You can have a favorite child, and all Chicago can know about it.

The *Harper's* article, by Richard T. Ely, was not a puff piece. It turned out that Pullman had designed his demesne as much for Control as for comfort. Women had virtually no work opportunities, and the men had no access to saloon or restaurant, for Pullman wanted them either laboring in his factories or inside their homes. These could be invaded without warning by Pullman staff for inspections, repair work, or painting. Those who balked could be evicted, on ten days' notice.

And everything in Pullman cost money, from your rent to the unwanted painting and even library use. George Pullman was not a philanthropist. Pullman was an overlord of slaves. "Not one single resident," Ely wrote, "dare speak his opinion about the town in which he lives." There wasn't even a newspaper. Ely called Pullman "a well-wishing feudalism," but it really was a fascism. And like so many other Chicago industries, it suffered a grievous strike, when the Panic of 1893 contracted Pullman's business and he passed his losses on to his helpless workers, firing some and cutting the survivors' wages (but not their rent bill) by 30 percent. Worse, the rent was creamed off the top of their salary before they got it, leaving them and their families starving. Of course there was a strike; of course it failed. But it cost Pullman—says Donald Miller—"his reputation, his town, and, some said, his life," for he died three years later.

Gangsters and robber barons, grafters and bordello madams: is that Chicago? How do people fight back? With a defiance of reason and fairness because that's how the authorities live? With impulsive acts committed without the slightest thought of what the consequences might be? Watch how Maurine Watkins' Roxie reacts when, after the murder, the police tell her to pack a bag and come with them to the cop shop. Suddenly, only now, does she realize that there may be punishment after crime:

ROXIE (chattering): O God…God…Don't let 'em hang me— don't…Why, I'd…*die*!

Yes, it's a laugh line; Watkins framed her lecture as a comedy. Still, it's all very real to Roxie:

ROXIE (shrieking):   Jail! *Jail!* O God!

Yes, right, *now* you think of that?

As we noted when discussing Joseph Howard's shows, the musical genre has largely avoided using Chicago, because the place comes loaded with so many memes and signifiers that they threaten to overwhelm plot and characters unless the setting is purged of its reality. In the end, Chicago really is a show in itself.

2

࿊

The Era

"Be Nonchalant... Light a Murad"

To repeat: the 1920s give us the first decade in American history that most educated people can place ontologically: Prohibition; Charles Lindbergh's flight to Paris; Al Jolson's popularizing of sound in the movies; the Wall Street boom and crash.

Most relevant to us here is Prohibition, because it, too, pitted hypocritical authority—a bizarre alignment of progressives, feminists, the Ku Klux Klan, and the usual professional busybodies—against a populace in revolt against the Rule of Fathers, skipping church to sass elders and adopt provocative lifestyles.

It was a religious thing. The Woman's Christian Temperance Union had been agitating for a national abolition of liquor for decades, but by January 17, 1920, when Prohibition became the law of the land, the WCTU seemed hopelessly nineteenth century, and the fiercer Anti-Saloon League had taken over the fight. And the ASL's motto was "The Church in Action Against the Saloon": a holy war.

But it was also a nativist thing, staid village Protestants resenting the influx of boisterous immigrants who flocked to the cities, those theme parks of the devil: a culture war. The Klan, which officially hated black and Jewish people and Catholics, terrorized as well anyone who didn't conform to local attitudes, behavior, beliefs. So it was also a totalitarian thing. It was even a gender thing, as

Prohibition's early leaders were almost all women (many of them apparently lesbians), seeking the vote not only as a civil right but to control men, who did most of the drinking.

And yet as popularly perceived it was a Chicago thing, as bootlegging gangs fought over turf through ever more colorful slayings. Prohibition created such turf wars everywhere, but it was Chicago that made international headlines for them; Chicago where the Thompson sub-machine gun marked the true criminal artiste; Chicago that claimed the outstanding gangster of the day, Al Capone; Chicago where Capone could take over the suburb of Cicero and turn it into a carnival of outlawry, twenty-four hours a day, all week. "We never close" could have been the town motto, though most people preferred the locals' grim joke: "If you smell gunpowder, you're in Cicero."

It was Chicago, literally the world's capital of saloon culture, where the battle of the wets and the drys was most conspicuously fought during the thirteen years till Repeal. Democracy trains people to choose their lives, for good or ill, and a sumptuary law—whether banning colorful dress or lavish banquets in bygone times or, as here, closing the combination social club and neighborhood message center that was the local saloon—virtually forces a free people to rebel.

This was a rebellion decade generally. Women were not only newly enfranchised but sought—demanded—more sheer livability. Academia and the professions were opening up. The movies were teaching villager America about life among sophisticates, who made their own rules. Radio introduced folks to music they had never heard before and ideas from beyond their borders, making them less easy for the cleric, the teacher, the doctor, the parent to control.

And of course there was jazz, the greatest portmanteau concept in the history of the American language. "Jazz" meant everything that was new, dangerous, delicious, liberating. Jazz was the opposite of the ice-cream social and the sermon. Yes, it was music, but, even more, it appeared to be anything community leaders warned would bring down society. It was blasphemy. It was speed. It was sex. It was Everything is available if you know whom to ask.

So jazz was the ideal accompaniment to speakeasy culture: city music, the Broadway Melody itself. It was rebellion against . . . well, everything, which is why "jazz" is a meme in the *Chicago* play, its reporters utterly in love with the way it thrills and appalls their readers. Roxie Hart is the "Jazz Slayer," partly because a louche song is playing on the Victrola during the murder but also because "jazz" relates Roxie's crime to the generally hedonistic air of Chicago.

Thus "All That Jazz," the musical *Chicago*'s opening number, is a celebration of guilty pleasures. The actual Jazz Age's version of the number is "Red Hot Chicago," from the De Sylva, Brown, and Henderson musical *Flying High* (1930) and introduced by Kate Smith, a pop contralto who fielded a wonderful blend of the majestic and the casual at once. Listening to her sing was like going to high school with Aida.

"Red Hot Chicago" was Smith's big uptune and *Flying High*'s big first-act finale, as Smith charged into the vocal, the Gale Quadruplets (actually two sets of twins but sisters all the same) led the dance break, and the ensemble then built the tune into an anthem for the curtain. Note, however, that the song's theme is not Chicago the place of lawbreaking but Chicago the hub of jazz. First, De Sylva, Brown, and Henderson establish a haunting after-hours-in-the-cabaret feeling with a verse in the minor key. The refrain, in the major and bristling with syncopation, identifies the soldiers in this war music that divides the generations and defiles the Sabbath as "Blue singers, those heartwringers who sob ballads to the nation" and "Musicians with ambitions to warm up an orchestration."

Granted, this is less than penetrating analysis; the lyric references "jazz Chicago" the way the old ethnic-stereotype numbers used "the Blarney Stone" in Irish songs or "Mr. Johnson" (anyone from an interfering cop to an ex-boy friend) in black songs: as imagery for automatic writing. At that, "Red Hot Chicago"'s music is no more than pleasing, though Smith surely made it resonate. The point is that the 1920s finally bring the musical into something like the form we recognize as modern.

We have only to go back to, for example, *The Wizard of Oz* to look in on the primitive version. At one point, a certain Cynthia Cynch is about to be tossed into a river, for the usual flimsy musical-comedy reasons. But hold:

CYNTHIA: I've been taking swimming lessons from a banker.

A MUNCHKIN: (repeating the set-up, in hoary show-biz practice, to be certain the audience gets the joke) Swimming lessons from a banker?

CYNTHIA: Yes (and here's the payoff:) He taught me how to float a loan.

Egad, those risible puns! But this one's almost cute:

WIZARD: What's this? Strangers here?

SCARECROW: Yes, little Dottie.

WIZARD: (surveying Dorothy's companions—an animated straw man, another man made of tin, and a fey, mute lion) You all look a little dotty.

The road to Kander, Ebb, and Fosse's *Chicago* encapsulates the history of the modern musical as it breaks away from *Wizard* shows in order to treat a story and characters like *Chicago*'s—to deal with the political reality of the municipal chaos Maurine Watkins was focusing on. Some of the present book's questions are: When was the American musical grown up enough to do that? And when did it become aware of the times it lived in? When did it develop the satiric power to reveal a justice system virtually run by the press corps? When did songwriters learn how to dramatize seriocultural ironies, such as the "innocence" of murder?

A key advance in the musical's growing sophistication was the development of wisecrack comedy, introduced into the culture generally around 1920—and, most important to us, the very fabric of the language Maurine Watkins chose for her *Chicago* characters. Thus, at the crime scene, a press photographer, taking in the attractive Roxie, says, "Keep them r.s.v.p. eyes off of *me*, sister; I'm a married man."

That's the tone of wisecrack, often favoring the grammar of the uneducated. Wisecrack's content, however, takes us deeper into the American psyche, as its adherents are the politically helpless, with a know-it-all attitude and a cynicism about the way the fates apportion their favors. We can sum this up in a pop song of 1921:

> There's nothing surer,
> The rich get rich and the poor get children.

In other words, the odds favored the house—the Establishment, with its crony favoritism, its secret deals, its contempt for the populace at large. Today, the wisecrack style is associated with the talkies of the 1930s, especially in the world of Warner Bros. Paramount was bon ton, MGM family-friendly, and Universal all for horror monsters, but Warner Bros. told of mean streets and just getting by, and wisecrack was the soundtrack of that way of life. Order corned beef hash from Eats waitress Joan Blondell and she calls out to the kitchen, "Plate of mystery for one!" Or swipe your neighbor's milk (in the days when the milkman left your bottle outside your apartment door) and Aline MacMahon excuses it with "The farmer stole it from a cow."

Wisecrack humor allowed ordinary folk to let off steam; the style became a political tool. And it made an ideal replacement for the puns we quoted in *The Wizard of Oz*—so musical comedy started speaking wisecrack as a rule. Twenties operetta dwelled elsewhere, such as the fifteenth-century Paris of *The Vagabond King*, with its tavern scene, its Tambourine Ballet, its "Only a Rose [I gi-i-ive you]." Hark as the hero cues it in with "My song is nothing—but that rose is you."

On the other hand, musical comedy[1] leaped past operetta's roses to explore wisecrackers' contentious attitude. In *Girl Crazy* (1930), a New York cab driver named Gieber Goldfarb takes a fare to Arizona, where Gieber keeps the plot humming by getting into all sorts of mischief. At one point he passes himself off as an Indian, "Big Chief Push-in-the-Face," but then he meets a real Indian, Eaglerock. So of course:

---

1. Throughout this book, distinctions will be drawn between musical comedy (an essentially zany and lightweight entertainment, such as *No, No, Nanette*) and operetta/ the musical play (more romantic and serious, such as *Carousel*). The two forms, obviously antagonistic, nonetheless share attributes, more and more as time goes on, till a work such as *Candide* seems an amalgam, very crazy yet musically most eloquent. And *Chicago*, when we get to it, will prove to be a musical comedy of very commentative worldview, zany yet not lightweight at all.

EAGLEROCK: What the hell kind of an Indian are you?
GIEBER: I'm Sioux Indian.
EAGLEROCK: Sioux Indian?
GIEBER: Yes. You sue me? I sue *you!*

Of course, the very sound of wisecrack, with its faulty grammar and salty observations, makes those who speak it sound raffish and even—here it is again—lawless. This is exactly why it serves Maurine Watkins so well: it is a lawless world that she wants to unveil. However, the widespread use of wisecrack in musicals tended to turn many of them into what the producing team of Cy Feuer and Ernest H. Martin termed "mug shows."

Guys and Dolls (1950), a Feuer and Martin offering, is the classic mug show, with its touts and gamblers and nightclub showgirls. But the form actually runs back through the historically imposing partnerships of Weber and Fields (in early burlesque) and Harrigan and Hart (in the farce-with-songs genre, centering on New York working-class Irish life) all the way to the very beginning of musical theatre in the all-rogue cast of *The Beggar's Opera*, in London in 1728. And of course our ultimate destination, the musical *Chicago*, is even more a mug show than *Guys and Dolls*, which at least balances its sinners with the Salvation Army. *Chicago* is mugs from top to toe.

Along with the new wisecrack libretto of the 1920s came the new music, from the generation led by Jerome Kern and Irving Berlin and taking in such followers as the Gershwins, Vincent Youmans, and Rodgers and Hart. Truth to tell, the real pioneer in the new music, the first of them all chronologically, was George M. Cohan—but Cohan, a composer-lyricist, was a slightly dowdy composer and a quaint rather than witty lyricist.

No, the new music demanded new lyrics, smart and worldly, conversational yet poetic. Remember Cole Porter's risqué "Let's Do It"? He was already flouting the sumptuary cautions as early as in the revue *Hitchy Koo 1919*, in "When I Had a Uniform On." The lament of a war veteran, this aggressive march hasn't a trace of jazz. But note the accentuating orchestral downbeat and sexy double meaning in the last line:

And in those days of glory I was the beau
Of every doggone musical show.
Each night you'd see me supping somewhere
With a dainty little star upon my [*BOOM!*] Croix de Guerre.

Why had so much in American life changed after World War I? In *Only Yesterday*, published in 1931, Frederick Lewis Allen offered a number of effects due to a single cause: the war itself. Facing one's possible mortality on the battlefields of Europe, men and the women associated with them, from wives to sweethearts, caught the non-conformist fever. There were, says Allen, "abrupt war marriages" and "less conventional liaisons" to challenge the stately old process of nuptial engagements produced by commanding elders and performed by obedient youngsters. Then, too, our boys in France (and American girls serving there as nurses) "had come under the influence of continental manners and standards." As another song of 1919 put it, "How 'Ya Gonna Keep 'Em Down on the Farm (After They've Seen Paree)?":

> Imagine Reuben when he meets his pa,
> He'll kiss his cheek and holler "oo-la-la!

The popular sobriquet for a farm boy, "Reuben," is no longer in use thus, but it gave birth to a word still with us, "rube." The song itself is silly, but its subtext is serious: how could young men from a narrow cultural background return to it when their perspective has been expanded by their experiences overseas? How were they now to defer to "the moral dicta of elders," Allen asks, "living in a Pollyanna land of rosy ideals which the war had killed for them?"

It may be that wisecrack comedy, soon to be the lingua franca of both Broadway and Hollywood, stemmed from this attitude that Allen discerned in the younger generation of the war era. And when, in the years following the Wall Street Crash of 1929, the Great Depression descended, wisecrack took on a distinctly political tone. It was the way those at the bottom of the political hierarchy commiserated with one another—prosecuting, so to say, those at the top who failed to raise the economic siege.

Again, none of this is overt in Watkins' play and its later versions: yet the air of sarcasm and snark, so twenties in tone, pervades the scene. To an extent, the saga of *Chicago* opens up an epic tale of what is possible in our lively arts and how they interact with what is occurring in the culture at large.

For instance, the social realities of the 1920s invented a host of new character types that would prove useful to musical comedy, a form devoted to youth: the sheik and the flapper, icons of the youngest generation. The **sheik** was to an extent a hangover from previous eras: athletic and (this was optional) playful, middle- or upper-class, collegiate or at least intelligent, and observant of an old-fashioned moral code. Some may think of him as the football hero, but in those days the alpha male gravitated also to the debate club, because a resourceful and front-footed opinion-maker was seen as extremely masculine. Further, the sheik carried new character baggage because of the war: he smoked cigarettes (previously thought effeminate) and wore a wrist watch (a novelty introduced to facilitate precise execution of battle plans), instead of a pocket watch on a chain.

Visually, the sheik became a national figure in the work of two artists, J. C. Leyendecker and John Held Jr. Leyendecker was a romantic and Held a satirist; because our modern view of the 1920s sees the time as absurd, Held is more often revived than Leyendecker when an art director needs a drawing to conjure up the age.

But Leyendecker was the house artist of the *Saturday Evening Post*, the most popular magazine in America—and Leyendecker's cover art, running from the comic to the epic, from grandmothers to New Year's cherubs, could be called the billboards of American culture. Leyendecker's men were not only handsome but dashing, the sort of whom hometown folks would say, "He ought to go to Hollywood." Leyendecker's oil painting titled "Couple in Boat" (1922) shows *him* commanding at the tiller and *her* lolling happily over the gunwale, both all in white with a tie each, their clothing seemingly made of some amazing plastic fabric in which the creases are like the sculpture of heaven. (Amusingly, the model for the male was Charles A. Beach, Leyendecker's lifelong love. So now we know, America.)

The sheik's opposite was the **flapper**, a total transformation of gender. The flapper threw off her corset, raised her hemline, cut her hair short, and even drank, preferably from a flask hidden somewhere intimate. Abandoning the confining corset suggests a liberation; it really had more to do with popularity control. All the influential girls were doing it—and boys called corseted maidens "Old Ironsides" and avoided dancing with them.

So the flapper was an apolitical development: a cultural twist, not an ideological one. The heroine of *No, No, Nanette* (1925) is rebellious, yes, but she just wants everyone to stop pushing her around. "He tried to cross me!" she sings to the chorus boys in the title song, about her boy friend. "He tried to boss me!" And when Nanette comes into a bit of spending money, he cries, "No good [changed to 'decent' in the current revision] woman *has* two hundred dollars!"

It's chaos!—exactly the devolution that, society's elders had been warning, would lead to the world *Chicago* describes. But then, those elders' supports had lost their power. "The family was in trouble," says Paula S. Fass in *The Damned and the Beautiful*, and "The church was in ruins."

The reason why was sex—or, as they called it then, "It." Elinor Glyn coined the term, though she really meant something like "charisma." It, she insisted, "can be a quality of the mind as well as a physical attraction." But nobody cared about charisma and everybody cared about sex.

Glyn was a British novelist who became a Hollywood screenwriter and general eminence, and, under Glyn's tutelage, Hollywood had an It Girl, Clara Bow. A sensation of the day and an ideal Roxie Hart if only her studio, Paramount, had locked up the rights, Bow was enchantingly mercurial: she moved the way the movies moved, a story ceaselessly activated by how it looked. "It, hell," Dorothy Parker wrote, "she had Those."

F. Scott Fitzgerald, the flapper's poet, saw her in all her versions, from chaste to racy, and some are both at once, like Sally Carrol (her Christian name) in the short story "The Ice Palace." There's two sides to me," she tells a beau, "the sleepy old side you love…and the feelin' that makes me do wild things." Because wild was the style.

When, in "Bernice Bobs Her Hair," the heroine mentions *Little Women*, her cousin Marjorie scoffs with "What modern girl could live like those inane females?"

Curiously, the English-speaking musical had been in alignment with this attitude since its inception. Way back in 1728, the women of *The Beggar's Opera*—heroine Polly Peachum, her mother, and Polly's rival, Lucy Lockit—are all strong-willed characters. They need but are not dominated by men, and as we move to America we find comparable pre-feminism feminist characters. Even the Cinderella figure was independent and resourceful. In *Irene* (1919), she's a spunky working-class Irish lass captivating High Socì, and in *Sally* (1920) she sings, "I wish I could be like Joan of Arc," to a military strain. The heroine of *Dearest Enemy* (1925) makes her entrance clad in nothing but a barrel—she has been swimming and lost her clothes. The setting is New York in the Revolutionary War, but this was flapper behavior, the "feelin' that makes me do wild things" mixed with a touch of eros. Again, this book is about more than *Chicago*: it tells how the musical developed the characterological and thematic methodology to observe and comment on American life.

And all of that really takes form in the 1920s. F. Scott Fitzgerald is our window on the era, recreating for us not the many gangsters, crooked politicians, and prostitutes we've met in the city of Chicago but the middle class of sheiks and flappers. The girls are well-intentioned (if daring), so it is titillating that Fitzgerald's story "Diamond Dick and the First Law of Woman" begins, "When Diana Dickey came back from France in the spring of 1919, her parents considered that she had atoned for her nefarious past." Like all flappers, Diana pulls gamy pranks because women are finally allowed to want things. Not jewelry or clothes. *Life*. Diana doesn't wait to be kissed, because sheiks are fumbly. She *asks* to be kissed—and then she goes after her man at his current girl friend's apartment *with a .44 in her purse.*

So we're closer to *Chicago* than ever before, and the **salesman** brings us closer yet. This is not the traveling man who meets the farmer's daughter, but rather the guy who cons you into buying what he has to sell. His spiel was advertising copy, whose intent was to rouse a buying public for something it would be better off without.

Smoking, for example. Murad cigarettes ran a series of magazine ads called "Embarrassing Moments," in which John Held Jr.–like figures illustrated a tense moment eased by . . . what else? Smoking. Thus, we see couples on the dance floor, one pair clearly not in on the fun, and the copy reads, "If your dancing partner chooses to fix her garter . . . *be nonchalant* . . . LIGHT A MURAD."

Here's another: we see three people. Two are obviously uncomfortable. "When you bring two delightful acquaintances together and find they divorced each other five years ago . . . *be nonchalant* . . . LIGHT A MURAD."

Who were these salesmen? They were **babbitts**, the term drawn from Sinclair Lewis' 1922 novel about a man of some interesting quirks who suppresses them to conform. And of course like everyone else in America, George Follansbee Babbitt was a merchant. Says Lewis, "He made nothing in particular, neither butter nor shoes nor poetry, but he was nimble in the calling of selling houses for more than people could afford to pay." A bit later, we learn that he was "scholarly in Salesmanship" and an acolyte of "the God of Progress."

The babbitt was everywhere in the 1920s. We even had a babbitt president, Warren G. Harding, a conformist who favored Prohibition, the good old values, and an ascetic government but who, on the sly, was a drinker, an adulterer with an illegitimate daughter, and a crony capitalist who left behind the federal oil-lands swindle known as "Teapot Dome," the biggest presidential scandal till Watergate.

Some of my readers may wonder if Roxie Hart's nondescript husband, Amos, is a babbitt. He isn't. Far from nondescript, the babbitt is a personality trying to seem vacuous. Lewis' point is that the American bourgeoisie is suspicious of anything quixotic or individual. The babbitt inhabits a Stepford world, supervised by the other babbitts and their wives with the mandate of stamping out, by intimidation or shunning, all nonconformist behavior. Thus, there can be no babbitts in *Chicago*, because its setting is the place that refuses to obey. In a strange way, Roxie Hart is a kind of anarchist, the perfect Chicagoan, because she fights with everyone about everything. You're either a fighter or a salesman in *Chicago* (some are both), but then almost everyone was a seller of something in twenties America. Even God.

That last revelation comes to us in one of the most forgotten Zeitgeist best-sellers of all time, the work of an advertising executive named Bruce Barton. Entitled *The Man Nobody Knows* (1925), it took a look at the Christ as the equivalent of an advertising executive, presciently employing the strategies of the guys who got you hooked on cigarettes in those Murad ads.

Interestingly, those who thought the book blasphemous were offended mainly by Barton's characterization of the Savior as a go-getter forging a path through masculine dominance and take-no-prisoners zeal. This contradicted His standard ID as a "soft" personality, sympathizing, healing, and passively submitting to the most momentous fate in Western history. "There was, in his [*sic*] eyes," writes Barton, "a flaming moral purpose; and greed and oppression have always shriveled before such fire."

True, we don't normally think of Jesus as a firebrand. The softness is meant to hide Him, to respect Christian mystery. In William Wyler's *Ben-Hur* (1959), Christ was Claude Heater, an opera tenor who was tall, handsome, and so gymmed-up he actually looked like the Siegfried he often sang in Wagner on the opera stages of Germany. Yet Wyler carefully kept Heater from direct head-on view, as if believing in a powerful figure while fearful of presenting one.

Still, where Barton more truly offends is in dragging a champion foe of profiteering into the world of profiteering itself. The epigraph of *The Man Nobody Knows* is " 'Wist ye not that I must be about my Father's *business*?' " Yes, that's Luke 2:49—but the italics are Barton's, deliberately changing the meaning of the sentence. That Father is not in commerce, and such chapter titles as "The Executive" and "His Advertisements" turn Christ into a babbitt of the Nazareth Rotary Club.

"He would not neglect the market-place [*sic*]," Barton assures us. "Few of his sermons were delivered in synagogues." And no doubt it is true, as Barton contends, that "the present-day [for 1925] marketplace is the newspaper and the magazine. Printed columns are the modern thoroughfares." And surely it is harmlessly picturesque when Barton translates Matthew 9:9 and 9:10 into headlines:

PROMINENT TAX COLLECTOR JOINS
NAZARETH FORCES
MATTHEW ABANDONS BUSINESS TO PROMOTE
NEW CULT
* * *

GIVES LARGE LUNCHEON

because that *is* what happens in Matthew 9:9 and 9:10. But it is risible to draw a parallel between the teachings of Christ and Barton's profession. Jesus "overthrew the tables of the moneychangers" in the temple. He didn't join forces with them.

Still, commerce was the romance of the 1920s—as was crime. And crime gives us the last of the Chicago personality type, the **wanton killer**, acting out of not self-defense, passion, revenge, or for gain but simply because "I felt like it." Charlotte, North Carolina, was the nation's murder capital, followed by Miami and New Orleans. But everyone thought Chicago held the title, partly because so many of its murders were so random, as when college buddies Nathan Leopold and Richard Loeb kill teenaged Bobby Franks for a "thrill." "I know I should be sorry," Loeb said at the time, "but I just don't feel it."

In *Gaily, Gaily*, Ben Hecht recalled an automobile salesman who bashed a reluctant customer's head in with a baseball bat, "a disappointed bridegroom who tried to dissolve his mate in . . . acid," and a "moral reformer who tilted at Sodom and Gomorrah by exploding a bomb in a movie palace," killing four women. We must note as well the case of H. H. Holmes, in the late nineteenth century. In his derby and handlebar mustache, he looked like any other Chicagoan. But he was unique, living in a fortress-like house filled with traps and secrets where he may have snuffed out well over a hundred souls.

And this brings us at last to the first of the *Chicago*s, Maurine Watkins' play, for her anti-heroine, Roxie Hart, kills because her will has been thwarted. Or she's offended. Or something. There actually was a Roxie, one Beulah Annan, and Watkins, a crime reporter for the *Chicago Tribune*, was covering the case. She could tell that Annan was guilty of sheer senseless murder and saw how her attorneys were staging a defense with all the integrity of a jumble sale, portraying a willful, destructive solipsist as a naive innocent, blithely skating over the fact that Annan's two statements to the police and then her testimony in court all contradicted one another. Watkins saw them as salesmen of the 1920s, salesmen of phony innocence. Chicago was stuffed with murderesses, and, unless they were physically un- attractive or non-English-speaking, the all-male juries of the day tended to acquit them. Only men are guilty. Women are...weak. The poor dears.

Watkins hated that, all of it. But she found it fascinating, too. And Watkins really wasn't a reporter by vocation; she was a story- teller, an incipient playwright. And she found a play in Beulah Annan, a scathingly cynical wisecrack comedy that would allow Watkins to rip open the lies and hypocrisy...and the show busi- ness!...of the Beulah Annan murder case.

But Watkins' play was more than that. It was about how every- thing in American life tends to exhibitionistic narratives bearing little relationship to the truth. It was about her adopted home town, because, like so many others, Maurine Watkins sensed that the gem of the prairie at the very center of the nation's seaway and railroad trade routes was a miniature America, with all its greatness and de- fects and individuality and quirky longings.

And that's why the play is called *Chicago*.

CHICAGO:
A PICTURE ESSAY

First, a classic shot of Gwen Verdon in her title song, "Roxie": ambitious yet carefree, the complete sociopath. Her costume (by Patricia Zipprodt) typifies the mixture of the realistic and the fantastical in Bob Fosse's musical-comedy version of life, sharp and clear, with all niceties and incidentals smudged out. All honesty, too. Seek not for justice in *Chicago*.

The City

Opposite page, top: Chicago in 1820, little more than Fort Dearborn (at center) and the home of John Kinzie (right), one of the so-called Fathers of Chicago. The south (left) and the north (right) forks of the Chicago River meet and flow into Lake Michigan. *Opposite, bottom*: Some seventy years later, the place is now the metropolis of the Midwest, with the sand bar removed and a great harbor created. Heavy industry—livestock, lumber, grain—is parked amid residential areas, for the business of Chicago is business. The city teems with it, as we see in Norman Jewison's movie *Gaily, Gaily* (*above*), with Beau Bridges (standing, left of three big white cylinders) as cub reporter Ben Hecht.

Early *Chicago*s

Above, the original Roxie, Francine Larrimore, in Maurine Watkins' drama that started it all, in 1926, modeling the dress she wears for her murder trial. "A nun," Watkins tells us, "would envy its chastity." Tradition demanded Roxie have a romance with the available hunk, Jake the reporter, played by Charles Bickford, seen here with Greta Garbo in MGM's *Anna Christie* (*opposite, top*), but Watkins wanted no distraction from her sermon on Justice. *Opposite, below*, Cecil B. DeMille's silent *Chicago*, in 1927, gave Roxie a marriage. But even breakfast in bed, lovingly prepared by Amos (Victor Varconi), can't soothe impatient, suspicious Roxie (Phyllis Haver).

The Talkie *Chicago*

Above, Ginger Rogers poses for "cheesecake," with Nigel Bruce (her agent) and George Montgomery (her future boy friend) at left and Phil Silvers (in beret) on the floor. It's twenties salesmanship, as with the ad *at right*: hyping tobacco but showing what was known as "it."

Above, lawyer Adolphe Menjou advises his client, now in jail. But in this version, she's innocent; so who dunnit? *Below*, the cops collar Amos (George Chandler) as press and public look on. Is he the guilty party?

Musical Satires Before *Chicago*

Above, *I'd Rather Be Right* (1937) was the first to concentrate on spoofing a sitting administration, putting onstage the president himself, FDR (George M. Cohan, center). His mother (Marie Louise Dana) hands him a friend's traffic ticket she wants fixed, and FDR's Republican presidential opponent in 1936, Alfred Landon (Joseph Allen), is now the Roosevelt family butler, carrying a cake for FDR's birthday ball. Mrs. Roosevelt is a doting mother, as when she meets the show's sweethearts:

> MRS. ROOSEVELT: What do you think of my son
>   being President of the United States?
> ROOSEVELT: Now, mother.
> MRS. ROOSEVELT: Twice, too.

Finian's Rainbow (1947), a fantasy, took on racism, capitalism, and consumerism, as sharecroppers (*below*) buy dream destinies on credit. *Left*, Anita Alvarez is mute and David Wayne a leprechaun, slowly turning mortal and horny, because everything in America that isn't about money is about sex.

Bob Fosse

All choreographers start as dancers. *Above*, Fosse steps out with Tommy Rall in the Columbia film *My Sister Eileen* (1953). Over twenty years later, when Fosse made the autobiographical *All That Jazz*, also for Columbia, the studio wanted a marquee name for the lead. Fosse (*opposite, top*) held out for Roy Scheider (*opposite, bottom*): because Scheider was as close to Fosse as Fosse could get. He wanted *All That Jazz* to serve as a kind of artistic epitaph, a movie *à clef*; its strange combination of buoyancy and bitterness is a key to not only Fosse's volatile personality but the personality of the musical *Chicago* itself.

Another Fosse movie: *Cabaret* (1972), with Emcee Joel Grey at center and Liza Minnelli, a mere ensemble attraction, second from right in the second row. Is there a link between the aesthetics of *Cabaret* and *Chicago*? Hal Prince, who directed the stage *Cabaret*, thought Fosse borrowed heavily from his show, and writers have discerned a certain resemblance. However, the format of a story show containing commentative numbers dates back to Kurt Weill and Alan Jay Lerner's *Love Life* (1948).

Gwen Verdon

Before her Broadway breakthrough in *Can-Can* (1953), Verdon danced in Hollywood musicals. Here, in the Danny Kaye vehicle *On the Riviera* (1951), Verdon worked with choreographer Jack Cole, her dancing mentor till she teamed up with Bob Fosse to conjoin art and love. Did Verdon owe Fosse everything, or was it vice versa?

The Musical *Chicago*

Verdon in the "Helen Morgan" icon number, "Funny Honey," awkwardly climbing onto Morgan's trademark upright piano, as Fosse wanted his Morgan vulgarized rather than worshiped. *Opposite, right*, *Chicago*'s finale in the Philadelphia tryout costumes, traded in New York . . .

. . . for the less salacious tasseled skirts. *Below*, the 1996 *Chicago* revival, with Ruthie Henshall and her boys in the "Roxie" number.

The Movie *Chicago*

Above, our third view of the "Roxie" number, with a strutting Renée Zellweger and her oddly mature "boys." *Below*, in turnabout, she must feign saintly tenderness on the advice of counsel Richard Gere. And that's justice in *Chicago*.

3

⌒⋎⌒

The Play

"Like Hell You're Through!"

Maurine Watkins' profile suggests a breakaway personality. She left home and family to try for a writing career, competing with men as a reporter on a fast-and-furious big-city newspaper and generally going after what she wanted with a resolve unusual in those steeped in small-scale township values and a religious upbringing.

Yet Watkins was not a flapper. In fact, her life completely upends the twenties stereotype of the insurgent maiden slicing away at received notions of womanhood with the new ultra-skinny look, hip flask at the ready. Watkins' hair was bobbed, yes—and she had her own way of doing things, no matter what men told her. But she compacted with no new gods and made no rumpus in the temples. Here was a true individual: even her nonconformism was nonconformist.

Watkins was born at the very end of the nineteenth century, in a family home in Louisville, Kentucky, and raised in Crawfordsville, Indiana, by stoutly religious parents. They belonged to the little-known Protestant sect of the Disciples of Christ, and young Watkins enthusiastically adopted its worldview, especially its love of Bible study. The Disciples of Christ are hard to categorize, as each congregation tends to make its own way through the spiritual life. However, reading and discovering the Bible from the viewpoint of the first followers, when Christianity was a Jewish heresy and the Word of

God absolute in the fulfillment of one's time on earth, was the oc-
cupation of every member of the church.

This is signicant, because Watkins' later life, when Broadway was
eager to musicalize *Chicago* and she kept saying no, has been misper-
ceived as an aberrant explosion of newly acquired religious fervor.
We are meant to believe that Watkins felt guilty about celebrating
evil. On the contrary, Watkins had been devout all her life, and her
play does not celebrate anything. Rather, it exposes the corruption
of justice, which pays the pretty, in league as it is with the toxins of
genderism, sensationalism in the media, and the babbitty buying
and selling of moral certainties. Again, her play's title doesn't really
mean "Chicago." It means "American life."

It all started when Watkins, a student at Radcliffe, got into the
famous course in playwrighting that George Pierce Baker taught at
Harvard. Celebrated as the first playwrighting seminar ever set up
on the college level, Baker's English 47 was founded in 1912—more
or less over Harvard's dead body—and counted among its alumni
such future boldface names as Edward Sheldon, Sidney Howard,
Philip Barry, S. N. Behrman, and even The One, Eugene O'Neill. True,
O'Neill found Baker's habit of teaching dramatic structure off of the
"well-made" plays of the nineteenth century offensively passéiste.
At some point, someone (apparently not Baker himself) "started
charting an Augustus Thomas[1] play on the blackboard to show how
it was built," O'Neill later recalled, "and I got up and left the room."
All the same, O'Neill appreciated Baker's driving encouragement of
his students, and though O'Neill left the course in 1915, he remained
on good terms with Baker till the professor's death, twenty years later.

Thomas Wolfe, another of Baker's students, reinvented him in
the novel *Of Time and the River* (1935) as one James Graves Hatcher.
Said Wolfe, "He was a man whose professional career had been made

---

1. Thomas was one of the better known playwrights before the 1920s, when O'Neill's
generation tore up the Standard Handbook in terms of content, genre, and language.
A typical Thomas hit was *The Copperhead* (1918), about a Civil War–era Illinois farmer
(played by Lionel Barrymore) thought to be a Confederate sympathizer. Stoically refusing to deny or explain for four acts, he finally reveals that he was working for the North
and produces as evidence a thank-you note... from President Lincoln. It was probably
the contrived plot more than anything else that offended O'Neill.

difficult by two circumstances: all the professors thought he looked like an actor and all the actors thought he looked like a professor." Actually, he looked like your doting and somewhat intellectual uncle, with those glasses that sit on the nose without ear handles and a wonderful way of getting you away from your desk and out into the world to find material. Balzac used to wander through Paris streets eavesdropping; Watkins went to Chicago to become a reporter. Not an etiquette adviser or an anthologist of recipes, as women writing for newspapers almost invariably were. Watkins became a seeker of news, sub-section: crime. She might have gone to any big city, but she wanted to see the place where the 1920s were playing, the Zeitgeist city of post–World War I America. The room where it happens.

So Watkins *was* a flapper? No—the flapper was a neighborhood phenomenon, a local cut-up who, at most, became the talk of the village gossips. Watkins traveled and achieved. We see her leaving home for Harvard and then Chicago, on her own in the masculine world of chasing scoops and fighting with the rewrite men. The flapper was a dissenter in the social sphere, while Watkins' dissent was moral, bound to expose society's sins. The acquittal of criminals—of either gender—not only incensed her: it ran against common sense, against ethics, against Biblical exhortation. It was more of that jazz, that louche whatever-it-was that, failing any absolute definition, could be thought of as the accompaniment to the dance of anarchy.

In a way, we can view Maurine Watkins as the antidote to Bruce Barton and his salesman-Jesus. God is not a salesman. God precedes salesmanship, so His word, Watkins knew, was being perverted by . . . well, everything. Watkins seems a bit like Joan of Arc, but—just to complicate the case for us—her high-school yearbook dubbed her the "prettiest girl in the senior class."

But why would Watkins choose to work for a newspaper, the very driver of all her outrage? Because that's where one reached one's audience. Ours is the age of social media; hers was the age of the newspaper. American journalism was, in fact, the wonder of the Western world, for though it had had to battle for the right to free expression in colonial days, after the Revolution it was the only truly outspoken press in Christianity. European visitors in the early nineteenth century were scandalized by the vituperative tone of the political press—and the "penny paper" model gave access to virtually every citizen. There was no equivalent in Europe.

All the same, the "selling" concept of the 1920s led the news outlets to become commercials by other means, anticipating the partisan propaganda of today's Pinocchio press. Thus, the plays of the 1920s—and, immediately after, their movie versions—looked at reporters and editors as scoundrels, eager merchants of not just sleaze but lying sleaze.

Even the figure of the intrepid war correspondent, a sort of sheik with binoculars and a sidearm, a hero of earlier generations, was deconstructed in Sam and Bella Spewack's *Clear All Wires!* (1932; filmed 1933). Their antihero, Buckley Joyce Thomas, seemed based on at least the name of Richard Harding Davis, bold and dashing and even glamorously married (to Bessie McCoy, a beloved Broadway musical star). To top this off, Davis was dead at an early age, like Adonis. The Spewacks' mock-up of the Davis figure, however, is a duplicitous finagler manipulating everyone in sight in Soviet Russia. Thomas Mitchell played him on stage, but in MGM's adaptation he's Lee Tracy, the era's epitome of the brash journalist, with his sneaky grin and the emptily jovial *ha-ha!* with which he peppers his dialogue. All Tracy cares about is scoops and banner headlines. When someone dismisses a Tracy interview subject as "a nut," Tracy snaps back, "Nuts make news." And to warn us how crooked Tracy is, he works for the (imaginary) *Chicago Globe*.

One wonders if Maurine Watkins entertained misgivings about establishing her byline on a Chicago paper, for, obviously, she was wholly unlike the Lee Tracy prototype, who was essentially a parasite. Tracy played a gossip columnist in Warner Bros.' *Blessed Event* (1932), his writing style modeled very closely on that of Walter Winchell and his taste in art very narrow. The Warners used *Blessed Event* to launch Dick Powell as a singing sweetheart; Tracy hates him. Why?

TRACY: He's a crooner, ain't he?
TRACY'S SECRETARY: Yeah.
TRACY: (Q.E.D.) Ain't that enough?

Ubiquitous in these roles for about five years, Tracy—anti-authoritarian and a hard drinker to boot—sabotaged his career when, on location for MGM's *Viva Villa!*, he (supposedly) urinated off his hotel balcony onto cadets of the passing Mexican Army. L. B. Mayer immediately exiled Tracy to other studios' B pictures and rebooted the reporter avatar in the persona of Clark Gable, with intense masculine charm and a crazy yet admirable moral code that brought the newsman figure back to heroic Richard Harding Davis territory.

But we lost a vital character in that trade—a kind of libertarian scofflaw who is above all aware of how the greedy run everything to enrich themselves. As we'll see, Maurine Watkins made particular use of this character, a reporter probably very like the ones she worked with on the *Chicago Tribune*—shrewd, eternally sarcastic, and with a rakish, mean-streets appeal and a ton of bad grammar. That "ain't" we just saw Lee Tracy flinging around is almost political in tone—again, it's the communication of the disenfranchised. Ironically, the authors of these wisecrack scripts were not only educated but cultured, and they couldn't resist writing *up* every now and then. *Blessed Event* (with a screenplay by Howard J. Green, from a play by others) actually gets a joke out of the length of *The Brook*, which no one can understand without a knowledge of Alfred Tennyson *and* English romantic poetry.

Of all the plays about the press, the most scathing denunciation was *Five Star Final* (1930; filmed 1931), which brings us yet closer to Watkins' viewpoint: the yellow press will not only tweak murder cases toward either a conviction or acquittal (depending on which direction will sell more papers), but it will even create a murder case where none exists. Journalism is the Chicago of professions, it seems: it does whatever the hell it wants to.

Five Star Final is based on an actual happening, the 1922 Hall-Mills case, in which an Episcopalian priest and a member of his church choir were found murdered side by side under the New Jersey sky, their adulterous love letters scattered around them. The likely suspects—his widow and her two brothers—could not be indicted for lack of evidence, but pressure from the tabloids demanded a trial, and it became one of the first modern-day media events, complete with a surprise witness straight from Bizarroland, the so-called "pig woman" (because she raised hogs), littered into court on her hospital bed to unleash a spectacularly unbelievable testimony, capped by a hysterical outburst aimed at the defendants (who were exonerated in the end).

It was all so dramatic that it had to be a play and a film, and even with the details changed, the essential accusation is unmistakable: the gutter press turns everything into trash and terror, victimizing a decent family with a murder scandal hidden away in its past. In Worthington Miner's clever staging on Broadway, *Five Star Final* had three playing areas, the main one flanked by two wing spots for transitional scenes. This gave the show the fast pace that was just then becoming the norm in advanced theatre production, an air of drive and focus that would be especially useful to *Chicago*. If George Pierce Baker was still teaching from outdated melodrama, his students were writing in a sleeker, more naturalized style—exactly what you need when, like Watkins, you intend to comment on contemporary mores rather than simply spin a yarn.

None of *Five Star Final*'s stage actors' names means anything today, but Warner Bros.' film starred Edward G. Robinson as the editor who hates what he does yet continues to do it. The movie helps us understand how *Chicago* might have played on stage, for, under Mervyn LeRoy's direction, the victims of Robinson's paper (the good guys) are completely stagey and mannered, while Robinson's crew (the bad guys) are vital and individualized to the point of eccentricity. In particular, Boris Karloff, just two months before he played Frankenstein's monster, pulls off a marvelous, oily study in Pecksniffian mode as a fake reverend manipulating the good guys into giving up their secrets for publication. He even tricks them into lending him a photograph, to authenticate the exposé that will destroy them.

Robinson, Karloff, and the other actors making louche journalism vivid for us are what *Chicago*'s cast must have been like, because realistic playwrighting encourages realistic acting (and vice versa). Again, the decade of *Chicago* is the great transitional age in American life, with its snake-oil salesman the advertising man; the talkie and its influence on spoken American; the jumpy miscellany of radio, from music to guest-star "ad libs" to comedy spots; the cult of "bunk" and "debunking"—meaning, respectively, the survival of the old false gods and the new wisecracking rejection of them.

Above all, there was the fleet new playwrighting style mentioned above. The more adroit authors were now dashing through the old-fashioned slooooowwww exposition to cut right to the development, and Maurine Watkins raised *Chicago*'s curtain on a mad wingding of a start: in a bedroom, to the accompaniment of a sexy 78 on the Victrola, a woman is watching a man getting into his overcoat. She suddenly screams, "You damned tightwad!" and "Like *hell* you're through!," and, reaching into a dresser drawer, she pulls out what Watkins calls "the latest necessity of milady's boudoir: a pearl-handled .32 revolver." She shoots the man, he falls, and, as the music on the Victrola ends, children are heard playing outside. A cuckoo clock sounds the hour. And, as a startled public gapes at the stage, the curtain falls.

It was perhaps the most shocking opening minute in Broadway history, but it didn't represent a flight of Maurine Watkins' fancy. It had really happened. In fact, much of the play *Chicago* was drawn from a pair of murder trials that Watkins reported on in the spring of 1924. Each of the killers was a woman enjoying an adulterous affair with a man she slew when he told her he was moving on.

The first of the two was Belva Gaertner, a former nightclub singer who shot her much younger boy friend while they were sitting in her automobile. Indeed, they had first met when he sold her the car, and their romance had been punctuated by her threats to end his life if he ever dared break up with her. Didn't he know what was coming? Then, when the police entered the picture, Gaertner claimed ignorance. "We got drunk and he got killed" was her story. "I don't know how."

Watkins used Gaertner as the model for *Chicago*'s second woman lead, renaming her simply Velma and billing her in the cast list as a "stylish divorcée." When George Pierce Baker urged his students to go out and find their plots in the public domain of real life, did he advise them also to include all the real-life details? Because Watkins left out the juiciest bit of the Gaertner case: Belva and her husband had hired detectives to keep an eye on each other. He brought in the first one, she countered with the second, he raised her with a third, she saw him with a fourth, and so it went till there were eight detectives trailing the two Gaertners like the folk in the Grimm Brothers' tale of "The Golden Goose."

But Gaertner was very quotable, in literally the worst way. "No woman can love a man enough to kill him," she explains. "They aren't worth it, because there are always plenty more." And here's Gaertner assessing the coroner's jury that indicted her: "They were narrow minded old birds," she observes. "Bet they never heard a jazz band in their lives." She prefers a panel of "worldly men" who "get out a bit. Why, no one like that would convict me." *Chicago Tribune* headline: NO SWEETHEART WORTH KILLING—MRS. GAERTNER.

Right after Belva Gaertner, also in 1924, came the aforementioned Beulah Annan, the model for Roxie Hart—"the prettiest woman ever charged with murder in Chicago," to quote Watkins' cast list again. Annan, too, killed a boy friend who was through with her, but the city was less interested in what she had done than in how she looked. In *The Girls of Murder City*, Douglas Perry tells us that Annan "was described as if she were a work of art: her hair was not simply red but 'Titian,' her coy smile that of a 'Sphinx' withholding a thrilling riddle."

Unlike Belva Gaertner, who shot her sweetheart and then ran off, Beulah Annan shot her sweetheart and then let him bleed out for some three and a half hours while she played the Victrola, just as Watkins has her doing in that fiery *Chicago* prologue. The coroner testified that Annan's victim died relatively shortly before Annan finally called her husband and set into motion the arrival of the cops. That is, had Annan summoned the law promptly, the man she shot might have survived.

However, that wasn't the fun part, as the press saw it. What was wonderful about this crime was the Victrola, playing over and over a number called "Hula Lou." Some reporters even wrote that Annan danced to it with her dying lover's body. Did she kiss him as they swayed to the inveigling melody, to the lyrics saluting "the kind of gal that never could be true?" Ha! A *jazz slayer*!

Composed by Milton Charles and Wayne King to words by Jack Yellen, "Hula Lou" was everything that American Jeremiahs had been warning Americans about in the new sound of popular music. This Hula Lou danced the shimmy "'neath the trees." She was the toast of the sailors' beer hall! The betrayer of men, of course—all the best ones were, in the world of jazz. The published sheet bore the very imprimatur of the devil with "Introduced by Miss Sophie Tucker"—that notoriously independent woman, you know. And some copies even said, "Featured by Mae West"—West, the personification of disruption. Saying out loud what even men dared only whisper!

In truth, one can easily imagine Mae West oozing erotically to "Hula Lou," her lips occasionally emitting her little trademark mmms and ooos. Today, when everybody knows everything about sex, this may sound tame, but in the 1920s the picture of a beauty dancing with her victim to the strains of dirty music was potent stuff. Dangerous. The flapper was merely troublesome to controlling parents; Mae West was the serpent in the garden. "Suckers," she would say, of those who fell for her act; you hear her do so in the movie *I'm No Angel*, as she saunters offstage after exciting a crowd of infatuated men on the carnival midway. Who needs the vote when you can shimmy? When challenged by the authorities, West later said, "I told them it was a kind of Polish folk dance." *Chicago Tribune* headline: WOMAN PLAYS JAZZ AIR AS VICTIM DIES.

Sophie Tucker and Mae West were self-created talents. They fell into show business as odd-jobbers (Tucker started as a "coon shouter" in blackface), found a unique niche, and developed an "act" that made them Warholian figures, known for who they were more than what they did. Belva Gaertner and Beulah Annan, on the other hand, were product, marketed for the selling of newspapers. No one knew who they were, because they were inventions of the press' "print the legend" recklessness, not unlike Murad's series of Embarrassing Moments.

There's a caustic tone to Maurine Watkins' *Tribune* pieces, as she speaks of Belva Gaertner's "midnight gin escapades," of Beulah Annan's "Hawaiian fox trots." In another of Watkins' reports, Annan is "quite the ingenue in her girlish checked flannel frock." And then of course there's Annan's story—"But which one?" Watkins asks, as there were three contradictory narratives: one, She acted to save her honor; two, Then how come she shot him in the back?; and three, "We both grabbed for the gun."

Most scornful of all Watkins' notations is this statement quoting Belva Gaertner: "It's too bad for [her victim's] wife, but husbands always cause a woman trouble." And, Watkins adds, "While Mrs. Gaertner *chortled* in jail, plans were completed for [the] young [victim's] funeral today. It will be held from his home and will be private." The italics are mine.

Armed with all this information about the two killings and the character of the killers, Watkins headed back east to re-enter George Pierce Baker's seminar, which had moved to Yale because Harvard had never liked fostering anything as abstract as the education of playwrights and Yale was keen. In an odd side-quest, Watkins had already logged contact with the theatre world in the person of actor Leo Ditrichstein, who gave her a $500 advance on one of her scripts and proposed to collaborate with her on another one. That $500 was as much as a Broadway producer would offer to an established name, so it's a fishy story, even though it appeared in Watkins' bio sketch in Burns Mantle's *Best Plays* annual for 1926–1927. In any case, nothing came of a Watkins-Ditrichstein partnership, and it was back in Baker's classroom that Watkins executed her idea for a play on the outrageous comedy that was Chicago justice, entitled—after a line in the script—*The Brave Little Woman*.

This of course refers to the idealization of Roxie that her defense attorney, Billy Flynn, wants to promote: the helpless miss who somehow pulls off the heroism of self-defense. Oh, call it not murder! Say rather *survival*. Watkins' script united two popular genres, the "crook play" and the courtroom drama. The classic title in the former style was Paul Armstrong's *Alias Jimmy Valentine* (1910), from O. Henry's story *A Retrieved Reformation*, about a safe-cracker freed from prison but tailed by a Javert figure. The criminal has no intention of reforming, yet, redeemed by love, he knowingly gives away his identity in order to save a little girl trapped in a bank vault. But now his Javert is himself "redeemed": when Jimmy Valentine gives himself up, the lawman says, "Don't believe I recognize you" and strolls out of his life.

The classic courtroom drama, Bayard Veiller's *The Trial of Mary Dugan* (1927), was once celebrated for MGM's version (1929), Norma Shearer's sound debut. Veiller's tale, too, has more narrative than any motivating idea, as various eccentrics take the stand to inculpate Shearer, a showgirl guilty of playing around but not of the murder she is accused of.

And there's a twist as well, for Shearer's lawyer brother, impatient with the aged clunkabunk sleepwalking through her defense, takes over, young though he be. At the climax, he suddenly whirls to throw a set of keys at the lawyer—in fact, the show's villain—when he's on the witness stand, posing as a righty because the murderer was a lefty. And he catches the keys . . . *in his left hand*. Excitement in the house!

The good old stuff. And that was the tradition that Maurine Watkins was working in with her crook play-*cum*-courtroom drama. But she reinvents genre in *Chicago*. Her predecessors were devoted to plot-driven entertainment; Watkins intended to start a dialogue with the audience about the nature of power in the American republic. Who has it? Who has it more? *Chicago* contained no rogue with a heart, like *Alias Jimmy Valentine*, and no innocent on trial, like *Mary Dugan*. And Watkins offered no twist surprise. Her play moves in a straightforward and deliberate way, and there is no genuine suspense in whether or not Roxie Hart will be acquitted. Watkins simply wants us to see how it happens.

Her structure is basic:

PROLOGUE: The crime.

ACT I: The cops and the press at the murder scene.

ACT II: The jail.

ACT III: The trial.[2]

---

2. This is the layout as given in the 1926 New York playbill. The script, published by Alfred A. Knopf in 1927, combines the Prologue and Act I above into a longer Prologue and breaks Act II above into Act I and Act II, both set in the jail. Act III remains the same.

Or, to fill it out a bit:

PROLOGUE: Roxie kills her boy friend in a sudden rage.

ACT I: The potential consequences of her act begin to scare her.

ACT II: Among other killers, each with her own quirky personality, Roxie gets a feeling about how to present herself publicly.

ACT III: In scene one, in the prisoner's waiting room, Roxie
and her attorney run through their act, with special attention to the pregnancy she has invented to attract sympathy.
Scene two moves to the courtroom itself, where the prosecutor—and justice—cannot prevail. Acquitted, Roxie basks
in fame till, almost immediately, shots ring out offstage, and
here we go again.

Interestingly, Watkins purposely left out an element thought absolutely essential in the 1920s in virtually every kind of play: a romance.
It was especially unusual in that Roxie is a young and attractive
woman: an ingenue. And ingenues are supposed to have boy friends.
At first, in Act One, three and a half hours after the Prologue (the
time, we may recall, during which the real-life murder victim, here
called Fred Casely, slowly bled to death), we believe Watkins has in
fact supplied one. This rather fetching hunk is Jake Callahan, a cynical
reporter who, while interviewing the cops and Roxie for his story, advises her on the dos and don'ts of surviving prosecution. Audiences of
1926 would naturally assume that something will develop between
Jake and Roxie, so Watkins uninstalls that impression right away:

JAKE: When I kneel down by my little bed I'll ask God to put a
hemp rope around your nice white neck! (Roxie shrinks back
and he goes on in rapture) O *baby*, that would mean headlines six inches high—the story of the year!

Jake appears in Act II as well, but by then Billy Flynn (again, Roxie's
defense attorney) has appeared, and he takes over as Roxie's vis-à-
vis, like Jake strictly on business terms. Amusingly, Watkins doubles

down on a theatrical cliché of the day—that all lawyers were either Irish or Jewish. Watkins describes Flynn as "a little man, like Napoleon, and he carries himself with the Corporal's air." And now comes the cliché bundle: "The nose starts out to be Semitic, but ends with an Irish tilt."

As a personality, Flynn is all ham, directing Roxie in how to act before judge and jury like Belasco with a diva and then a Barrymore himself when pleading the case. As Watkins notes in her stage directions during Flynn's closing argument, "He's fighting, gentlemen, fighting, with every drop of his blood, for the life of that brave little woman. The Jury [is] hypnotized, enthralled.... The Press watch benignly; they know his whole bag of tricks."

Watkins is working within a tight scenario, for, adding in Roxie's feckless husband, Amos ("an awkward creature [with] a weak chin") and Mary Sunshine, an "I'll believe anything" stooge reporting from The Woman's Viewpoint, these five characters are the only drivers of the plot. Even the prosecuting attorney has no more to do than try and fail, and everyone else is decoration.

Take, for instance, the prison Matron, one Mrs. Morton, with no first name. She functions as an interlocutor and explainer; not till the *Chicago* musical was she to take part in genuine plot action. And the "chorus" of murderesses, mostly though not entirely modeled on people Watkins met while on her beat, mainly gives the two prison scenes splashes of color. This is especially true of Velma, with, again, no last name. She's a piquant character, but you could cut her out of the script and all you'd be missing is playing time. Still, Velma's calm demeanor and social pretensions give the jail sequence a lot of oxygen. Velma is suave, sophisticated, fashionable: everything that Roxie isn't. When the latter, reading one of her many press cuttings, sees that she is said to have "cast coquettish glances from pansy eyes half hid by her purple turban," she rages that she has *never* worn a turban. I mean, Jeez, a *turban*?:

ROXIE (to Velma): Why, I'd look as old as you!
VELMA (affably): Yes; you gotta have chick [she means: you
    need to be glamorous and chic] for a turban.

Not till the play's final scene—the trial itself—did Watkins crowd her stage, making use of the era's fondness for big casts. (There were twenty-six billed roles, along with a horde of extras in the courtroom, from jurymen to reporters to newsreel cameramen.) "The trials I covered," says Ben Hecht in *Gaily, Gaily*, of just such a trial as *Chicago*'s, in the Cook County Criminal Court, "were redolent with frame-ups, police fixings, witness buying, jury bribing, perjuries," and the like. However, Watkins shows us not corruption but rather justice overwhelmed by the art of the performance: one, of Flynn's portrayal of Roxie as helpless when she is in fact an aggressive sociopath; and two, of Roxie's playing to the jurymen (remember, women didn't serve on juries at this time). And, again, Roxie has faked a pregnancy; who is more sympathetic than a young mother in trouble?

So Roxie gets off (*Chicago Tribune* headline: JURY FINDS BEULAH ANNAN IS "NOT GUILTY"), and then, as we know, the next headliner bangs into play with gunfire outside the courtroom. This new killer, "Machine-Gun Rosie," has slain her boy friend and his wife, so it's twice as big a story as Roxie's.

"Gee," says Jake, "ain't God good to the papers!" as the photographers ready their shots. But Rosie declines to take part in this circus. Jake, however, knows how to bring her into the system, into America in the 1920s:

JAKE: Come on, sistuh, yuh gotta play ball: this is Chicago!

And "Flash, bang," says Watkins, in the highly personalized stage directions she favors, "curtain!"[3]

This much is the script; now for the staging. Watkins was lucky, for Sam H. Harris, one of Broadway's top producers and the co-owner (with Irving Berlin) of one of the most audience-friendly theatres in

---

3. In a late but not final draft of the script, that last spoken line was given to Roxie, not Jake, probably to show how well schooled she has become in the etiquette of twenties salesmanship. Watkins may have then changed her mind and reassigned the line to Jake because he really is the one who knows and observes the rules by which "Chicago" (meaning American commerce) is governed. Jake is, in effect, the "intellectual" of the system, while Roxie is all instinct, acting impetuously and lacking perspective.

New York, the Music Box, picked up Watkins' play, to be directed by George Abbott. Harris was not only Big Broadway: he was a nice guy. In 1904, aged thirty-two, Harris partnered up with George M. Cohan just as the Yankee Doodle Boy was about to break big; Cohan & Harris became one of the most successful outfits on Broadway for fifteen very busy years. The 1919 Actors Equity strike broke them apart, as Cohan was fanatically anti-union while Harris was eager to settle on sympathetic terms. As a solo, Harris went on to present some of the outstanding shows of the day, from Marx Brothers musicals and the comedies of George S. Kaufman and Moss Hart to Cohan's spectacular turn as Franklin Roosevelt in *I'd Rather Be Right* and Gertrude Lawrence's standing-room-only run in the straight-play-with-musical-dreams *Lady in the Dark*, in 1941, the year Harris died.

So Watkins didn't merely make it to Broadway. She fell into step with, arguably, Broadway's smartest producer, one famous for high-budget stagings and personal integrity. George Abbott, on the other hand, was just arriving as a writer and director after some twelve years as an actor, and he, too, had been in George Pierce Baker's playwrighting workshop: a sound choice if not a famous one. (At that, Broadway's producers, such as Florenz Ziegfeld, Charles Dillingham, the Messrs. Shubert, the Theatre Guild, and of course Sam Harris, were far better known than any director. Formerly the exclusive prerogative of the actor-manager, the playwright, and the producer, directing by itself was a new profession, not yet well known even among devoted theatregoers.)

However much Harris may have admired Watkins' script, he must have been impelled to take it on because he had the perfect Roxie under contract: Jeanne Eagels. She had dazzled The Street in 1922 in Harris' production of *Rain*—and *Rain*'s heroine, Sadie Thompson, was comparable to Roxie in an interesting if vague way, as both are outlaws. Sadie is a good-time girl (as they used to be called), bound to irritate churchly hypocrites and the bane of British colonial authorities anywhere she travels in the Far East. However, Sadie does no harm. Further, Sadie is a dramatic role and Roxie a comic role, and the acting profession marked a sharp distinction between the two at the time.

Still, Eagels might have made a fascinating Roxie; she was fascinating, period. But hadn't *Rain*'s spectacular success turned Eagels into a diva? She was unstable, too—a drug addict, apparently—and thought nothing of showing up late for rehearsals or missing them altogether. "She was taut and wary," Abbott recalled in his memoirs, entitled *"Mister Abbott"* because that's what almost everyone in the theatre called him. "I felt as though I were dealing with [a] wild animal."

There are always directors who are willing to work with difficult prima donnas; the talent is supposed to be worth the trouble. But Abbott wasn't one of those directors. He was a gentleman, but a commanding one, totally in charge, and he expected everyone, from the playwrights he edited (which included Watkins) to the actors he coached, to cooperate with him. When Abbott didn't care for a title, such as *The Brave Little Woman*, he changed it—to *Chicago*, obviously. And when Abbott told an actor never to be late again, that actor showed up on time for every single appointment for the rest of his or her life.

Eagels didn't, so Abbott had her fired. Now Sam Harris had to find a new Roxie, though the 1926–27 season was well under way. All the best actresses were already signed. And then Noël Coward's *This Was a Man* opened.

As Coward himself noted, in a letter to his mother back in England, quoted in Cole Lesley's *The Life of Noël Coward*, the cast "played it so slowly that there was time to go round the corner and have an ice cream soda between every line." Clearly, the actors would be free very soon, and one of them, Francine Larrimore, would be a perfect Roxie—"small and red haired and very sexy," Coward goes on, "and as far as I can gather [she] has already made plans about every man in the cast."

Well, that does sound like Roxie, so a week after *This Was a Man* closed, Larrimore opened in *Chicago*, presumably having rehearsed the show on her matinée-free days. At the time, she was something between an ingenue on the rise and a youngish, already arrived lead of the second rank. She worked constantly, but had enjoyed few genuine hits, though she did claim that Harris had offered *Rain* to her before he signed Eagels; prior commitments forced Larrimore to turn it down.

She had an interesting backstory, with a French father—Larrimore was born in Verdun—and a mother related to the famous Adler acting dynasty. Young Francine was on the New York stage at twelve, had one great hit in *Scandal* (1919), and was for a time married to the songwriter Con Conrad, composer of the music to the first Best Song Oscar, "The Continental." Larrimore even appeared in a piece by Rudolf Friml, *Sometime* (1918)—yes, in a singing role, though it was her only musical. Completely forgotten today, she was nevertheless big enough at the mid-century mark to be included among the one hundred fifty profiles in Daniel Blum's picture book *Great Stars of the American Stage*. Filling out Blum's questionnaire, Larrimore gave among her likes "Yorkshire terriers, sapphires, melons" and, as her pet peeve, "under-rehearsing."

It's hard to imagine that Larrimore was anything *but* under-rehearsed for *Chicago*, given how quickly she moved into it from *This Was a Man*. Perhaps that was why she always claimed to have hated *Chicago*. Her favorite role, ironically enough, was in *Shooting Star* (1933), in which she appeared as an actress unmistakably modeled on Jeanne Eagels. In effect, Larrimore got to play *Rain* after all.

One of Watkins' aims in *Chicago* was to give the audience a full view of prison life, using a few of Roxie's fellow murderesses to interact with one another as samples of this women's underworld. The oddest of them is Liz, who killed her boy friend for laughing when she asked him to marry her. Oddly, Watkins made Liz a cautionary figure of religious fanaticism, giving way to shrieks and taunts and a metaphorical Bible pounding—a renegade version of Watkins' own spiritual identity. After the murder:

LIZ: I knelt beside him and prayed . . .
MATRON: Look out for them that's allus readin' the Bible and
    prayin'. Somethin's wrong *some* place.

The original Liz, Dorothy Stickney, was just then on only her second Broadway role in a very long career (and life: she reached one hundred two years). Stickney got more famous as she got older, playing Mother in *Life With Father* (1939), still the longest-running narrative straight play in Broadway history, and *Life With Mother* (1948), paired in both with her playwright husband, Howard Lindsay. Stickney also replaced Irene Ryan in *Pippin* (1972), helping to make a one-song cameo into a star part. It did, however, cement Stickney's profile as a Sweet Old Lady, where she had first become prominent for a number of vibrant performances as half-crazed young women.

None of the other *Chicago* principals is of minor note to even the most avid aficionado, except for the Jake, Charles A. (for Ambrose) Bickford. Some readers may place him as the movie producer to whom Judy Garland pours out her contradictory feelings about James Mason in *A Star Is Born*. But that was the senior Charles Bickford (who dropped the middle initial shortly before going Hollywood), aged sixty-three. In his youth, Bickford was quite studly in a rough-diamond way.

So Bickford was no sheik. Let Buddy Rogers be the boy girls could bring home to meet mother: Bickford would be the tough guy who fascinates Society ladies. Leaving the stage for the screen in the first year of regular sound production, Bickford was a coal miner in *Dynamite* (1929) and a chauffeur in *Passion Flower* (1930)—and Daddy disinherits Bickford's wife for marrying out of her class. Kay Johnson was the wife in both films, looking like a skinny Mary Pickford, and she very ably shows us the fascination a "real" man has for a high-born woman used to pantywaists and tools. In *Dynamite*, Bickford tries to educate Johnson about where everything comes from, and it isn't Daddy's money but hard labor. "Even those diamonds sparkling on your wrist there are coal!" he cries. But it's a hopeless lesson. "You don't know what I'm talking about!" he almost shouts, a big rock candy mountain with a snarl behind his smile. Yet through it all, Johnson's dazzled. by him. He has no appreciation for the finer things, but when your ship goes down, you want this guy in your lifeboat.

Jake is actually the most important character in the *Chicago* play after Roxie herself. Billy Flynn does more, and he dominates the final act. But Jake is Watkins' spokesman, the person who tells us how Chicago works. So it is helpful to visualize what Bickford was like in trying to get close to just what the team of Harris and Abbott put on the stage in 1926. And it should be noted that Bickford's alpha-male personality weight is but half of his presence. The other half is Bickford the rebel, under contract to MGM but refusing to submit to dictatorial control. In his autobiography, *Bulls Balls Bicycles & Actors*, Bickford remembers calling MGM's tyrannical studio chief, L. B. Mayer, "a venomous little junk peddler" (a reference to Mayer's youth in the family scrap-metal business) and a "posturing little ignoramus," right to his face. On his way out of Mayer's office, Bickford added, "Fuck you, Mayer," whereupon MGM had him blacklisted in movies, though Bickford continued to work in indie productions and even at major studios when no one else of the Rough Trade type was available.

This refusal to kowtow before power (a very twenties attitude) was Bickford's salient quality, and it comes through in all his performances. Thus, we see that *Chicago*'s reporter is not of the Lee Tracy kind, so giggly and insubstantial, a con man doing a fan dance. Jake is a natural force disguised as a cynic, related to the Clark Gable kind of reporter, especially his rogue of a good-guy newsman opposite runaway heiress Claudette Colbert in *It Happened One Night* (1934). And given that Francine Larrimore would play Roxie in her hoyden style but with plenty of contemptuous putdowns, she and Bickford would have made an alluringly discordant couple, just as Gable and Colbert did a bit later. In fact, such mésalliances would become standard Hollywood plot-starters.

So, again, we wonder if George Abbott tried to get Maurine Watkins to set up a romance between Roxie and Jake when Abbott assumed script leadership. After all, whatever else it conveyed, show biz was about romance—and Roxie is the kind of woman who defines herself by the quality of her male companionship; a man is security, status, entertainment. Or so said the writers of the American show-biz text.

Besides, Abbott was very traditional in his approach to play production. The Abbott style was marked by speed, clarity of action, and what we might call "freshness of cliché." That is, he made actors pick up their cues quickly, he brooked no ambiguity in line delivery, and he could make the corniest gags work through timing and inflection.

He had some imagination, however. The second-act opening of *Wonderful Town* (1953), a comic look at the devotion of a squad of cops to a pretty girl behind bars, wasn't going well till Abbott suggested that the girl play it like a duchess commanding her servants. In *Damn Yankees* (1954), to bring on the devil, Abbott had the other actor in the scene look intensely into the stage-left wings as if seeing something worrisome while the orchestra played eerie music. The audience would look, too—letting the devil slip onstage, undetected, from stage right, as if materializing. But Abbott would spare no time for discussions about a character's inner life or the subtextual thrust of a scene. To Abbott, what mattered was how the show played, not what it meant.

As we'll see, this is going to drive Gwen Verdon crazy when she and Abbott rehearse *New Girl in Town* (1957). Still, whatever his faults, Abbott knew how to address an audience. A simple piece of business (the old term for "shtick"), such as Watkins' directing the jury's attention to bounce from Flynn to Roxie and back to Flynn during his closing, would have given Abbott the kind of treat he loved to throw to the audience. Thus, Flynn describes Roxie's pitiable state of mind after the fatal shot—"The soul's Gethsemane," he intones. "Alone!"—and the jury is intent on Flynn. Wait—now they look at Roxie, and now Flynn again, who has caught their concentration by raising his voice. "He grinds it out like a minister" is Watkins' description, as so often using religion as her guide.

Now, this is Abbott's plate of choice, as he virtually cooks up the laughter. He'll tell the actors on the jury to gaze Roxie-ward slowly, each head moving at a different time and a different angle. Then they turn back to Flynn, all at *exactly the same time*. There was a rhythm to Abbott's handling of crowds when he was working them in jest, almost a choreography. It wasn't realism, but then Abbott specialized in musicals and comedies. *Chicago*, said the *New York Times*' Brooks Atkinson in his first-night review, "is played with a knowing smirk...lest the audience believe the players duped by their lines." Here was "a raucous lampoon," Atkinson thought, "not...a firm, compact satire, deadly in its import."

Well, but as we read Watkins today, her script most certainly is deadly in import. Perhaps Abbott's direction misled Atkinson, for *Chicago* is a Swiftian diatribe—not only satire, but a "sinner in the hands of an angry God" sermon on what happens when the freedom to create one's life bumps up against other people's rights. It's worth noting, too, that after Watkins had gathered material for her play, she abandoned newspaper work forever. To her way of thinking, journalism was a loose cannon of data as often dramatized or just plain dishonest as not. Yet a free press is the bedrock of democracy; its rights, one might say, overwhelm all other rights. As Thomas Jefferson famously said, "Were it left for me to decide whether we should have a government without newspapers or newspapers without a government, I should not hesitate a moment to prefer the latter."

So the press, as democracy's law-enforcement department, must strive to maintain absolute honesty. Yet it has failed to. In his *Flat Earth News*, Nick Davies, a much-honored reporter for *The Guardian*, coined the term "churnalism" to describe the state of news-reporting today. Churnalism is the work of "journalists who are no longer out gathering news but who are reduced instead to passive processors of whatever material comes their way, churning out stories, whether real event or PR artifice, important or trivial, true or false." Then Davies quotes Nigel Hawkes, an editor at the *London Times*, who says, "Almost everything is recycled from another source....The work has been deskilled."

Thus, a lying narrative can be created through a combination of laziness and subterfuge. "News" outlets become—not in effect, but literally—propaganda shops. And once the free flow of genuinely honest information is clogged with this debris, democracy evaporates and liberty is over. This will come up again when we reach the *Chicago* musical itself.

Opening on December 30, 1926, at the Music Box, Watkins' play was an immediate hit, scoring 172 performances, a good run for the day, not least in the second-busiest season in Broadway history, with 263 productions. (The following season, that of 1927–28, was the all-time busiest, with 264 titles.) Larrimore and company toured the show—yes, to Chicago itself—enjoying a certain frisson as members of a Zeitgeist club. *Chicago* was the *twenties* show, the play about *now*, and such success tends to attract a jackass or two. *Chicago*'s was one John G. Archer of the Yale Divinity School, who called the piece "vile" and asked why the "stench" of "that sort of life" in our midwestern capital was allowed to offend "the nostrils of our Eastern public."

Watkins' blurb was ready: "I wonder whether, in his sermons, Professor Archer pretends that the world is a rose garden." Did God Himself, on His visit, never speak of evildoers, thus to unmask their wrongs? Wasn't it bad enough that Brooks Atkinson failed to catch Watkins' excoriating tone simply because George Abbott made her piece so sheerly entertaining? Satire isn't a lecture in dark robes. It's a fiesta of fun. Your laughter shocks you: so you'll think twice.

Watkins' next play, *Revelry* (1927), based on Samuel Hopkins Adams' eponymous novel using the characters of Warren G. Harding's Teapot Dome gang, was a failure. We note that neither Sam Harris nor George Abbott was involved; nor was the *Revelry* cast arresting in any way. Watkins wrote other plays, but some were not optioned, and those that were were not staged, except for one that closed during its tryout.

Occasionally one reads on the title cards of old movies that a script has been pulled from something by Watkins, presumably un-produced, as with *The Strange Love of Molly Louvain* (1932), with Lee Tracy as yet another wisenheimer reporter: "Based on the play *Tinsel Girl* by Maurine Watkins." By this time, Watkins was writing screen-plays herself—*No Man of Her Own* (1932), for instance, famous as the only time Clark Gable co-starred with his later wife Carole Lombard, or *Libeled Lady* (1936), which does take a jaundiced look at the press in a gentle version of the *Chicago* manner.

However, Hollywood's habit of stacking writers on top of each other till no one knows who wrote what apparently discouraged Watkins, and she moved to Florida to be close to her parents. And while a few in the theatre community remembered *Chicago* well, it faded from memory. The 1920s was filled with classics, from *Anna*

Christie to *The Royal Family*, but *Chicago* never seemed to get mentioned anymore, even by devotees of nostalgia.

And Watkins was glad. Somehow, it hadn't worked out right. People can be so stupid: did they really think that Watkins *wanted* her murderess to get off? Don't they understand irony?

New York Times Chicago review headline: JAZZ SLAYER ACQUITTED.

4

cᐱↄ

The First Movie

Amos Is the Hero

Naturally, *Chicago* was sold to Hollywood, a ready market for plays even before the talkie was habilitated. In the movies' early days, in the age of the two-reeler, the studios ran on genre, character stereotypes, and condensations of the classics: thwarted young love, a tempted bank teller, *The Three Musketeers*. The theatre and its concerns belonged to a completely different sector of the arts, except when a household name such as Sarah Bernhardt or James O'Neill (father of Eugene) filmed a medley of scenes from his or her stage successes.

The mid-1910s introduced the shortish feature, expanded in the 1920s to some ninety minutes of fully developed narration—and this was when Hollywood realized it needed Broadway as a story source, for plots with meat on their bones and a selection of alluringly wayward personalities. *The Gold Diggers*: flappers on the make for money and even love. *What Price Glory?*: two straight men locked in a love-hate affair on the battlefield of France. And now *Chicago*: the woman who kills. Better, with the strict enforcement of the moralistic Production Code yet to come: the woman who gets away with it.

When Sam Harris unveiled Maurine Watkins' play—again, in 1926—the talkie was still about three years away from regular production, so most of what Watkins wrote would be reduced to visuals. Still, *Chicago* was a story Hollywood had to film, and it beckoned particularly to Cecil B. DeMille, because he liked to amuse his public by mating wicked doings with farce: exactly as *Chicago* did.

DeMille must have moved quickly to secure the rights to the play, for every studio in Hollywood (except Universal, absolutely bonded with once-upon-a-time values of virtue rewarded) would have wanted its own shot at this Zeitgeist exposé. However, DeMille did not share Watkins' didactic fervor, her use of Chicago as a Breughelesque hellscape where, just outside the courtroom windows, the population rages with lawbreaking fever. What DeMille saw in the play was something so latent Watkins herself hadn't used it: the tale of a troubled marriage. Of a decent and loving guy married to a user.

Today, DeMille is remembered as a purveyor of spectacles, vast in both geography and culture—*The Ten Commandments* (1923; remade 1956); *The King of Kings* (1927), adapting the Gospels; a sensational and very DeMillian blend of sex and religion in *The Sign of the Cross* (1932); *The Crusades* (1935), with, as Richard the Lionheart, the English Henry Wilcoxon, who somehow managed to be a dreary actor and a smoldering sex rocket at the same time; *The Plainsman* (1936), starring Gary Cooper and Jean Arthur as Wild Bill Hickock and Calamity Jane; *Samson and Delilah* (1949). However, in his early years in Hollywood (which began in 1913, when just a few small filming operations had opened shop there), DeMille favored marital comedy and melodrama. These often contained somewhat lavish flashback sequences, in which the leads appeared as figures of the ancient world, paralleling the modern-day story. Nevertheless, these were intimate shows, using only a few locales and with no hint of any larger world outside courtroom (or any other) windows.

DeMille's specialty was to address husbands' complaints about wives and wives' complaints about husbands, giving equal weight to both within a single picture. Thus, in *Why Change Your Wife?* (1920), on the separation and reunion of husband Thomas Meighan and wife Gloria Swanson, DeMille starts on Meighan's side, with a title card introducing Swanson as the spouse "who willingly gave up her husband's liberty when she married him." We see Meighan trying to shave while Swanson, hungry for attention, keeps on interrupting him.

A bit later, however, the point of view shifts when Swanson senses Meighan's affections wandering as Bebe Daniels enters the picture. At the dressmaker's, Swanson overhears other women mocking her dowdy ways. Ha! A teaching moment! For now Swanson forswears being "modest and decent." She tells the designer—the usual fluttery queen, all the same breaking ground for such later events as *Midnight Cowboy* and *Brokeback Mountain*—"Make [my new clothes] sleeveless, backless, transparent, indecent." She holds a dress against herself to see how it...no, that one! A feathered headdress! Looks control! Glamor, chic, truth!

Then as now, DeMille was thought vulgar and hokey. For all his comedy, he loved to shock and was obsessed with the lifestyles of the wealthy and the carnal yearnings of the sexually avid. It was a mishmash, the critics cried. It was disparate elements incoherently blended—the lure of sex, some high finance, a little seltzer down your pants. For DeMille was, above all, popular. He could appeal to the widest audience, which already tells us he was going to have to change Watkins' play considerably, because the mass audience doesn't understand satire. Let's recall George S. Kaufman's famous remark: "Satire is what closes [on the first] Saturday night."

Similarly, when filming James M. Barrie's play *The Admirable Crichton* in 1919, also with Meighan and Swanson, DeMille wanted to alter the title. Wouldn't most people get it wrong? "Admirable" is going to turn into "Admiral," and who's going to know that "Crichton" is pronounced *Kryton*? DeMille suggested calling the movie *Male and Female*, but Barrie was one of the most prestigious playwrights of the day; wouldn't he balk at this populist approach? In his autobiography, DeMille tells us that when he applied to Barrie for permission, the Scotsman replied, "Capital! I wish I'd thought of that myself!"

So once more we note how different this first filming of *Chicago* is bound to be, for it, too, will become a *Male and Female*, a Marriage on the Rocks—and not just because of the five-year trembles, when a spouse's quirks, once so endearing, start to get on your nerves. No, this marriage, of Amos and Roxie Hart, is the kind DeMille didn't use very often: a doomed union in which one partner simply isn't worthy.

Also unusual for DeMille is the social aspect, for the Harts present a lower-middle-class union in a two-room flat, and Amos has a little tobacco shop. The more typical DeMille marital tale focuses on the well-to-do, so he can show his public something it isn't used to: sheer guiltless, wasteful luxury. Commentators make much of the DeMille bathroom, stocked with all the fluff and artifice that the socially important can't live without.

But it was more than just bathrooms—the dinner parties, for instance. In DeMille's *Forbidden Fruit* (1921), we watch a grande dame making the seating arrangements for her coming evening using a little scale model table and paper cuttings bearing the name and likeness of each guest, the miniatures to be inserted and taken out and moved around until Madame is satisfied with the symmetry of her congregation.

Another staple of the DeMille production was that touch of larceny, though for context we should note that the popular arts made constant use of petty thievery at this time. Many musicals couldn't get through their second act unless someone Stole the Jewels; it was a handy way to thicken the usual thin plot. It may seem bizarre to add a non-violent crime to a work as filled with murder as *Chicago*, but DeMille liked his films to bulge with plot, and the *Chicago* that Maurine Watkins wrote had very little actual story once Roxie shot her lover—no events, secrets, reverses. She goes on trial and is acquitted, period.

DeMille needed more—not just the Amos-Roxie marriage as a thing in itself but some romantic interest by which the long-suffering Amos can replace Roxie. Billy Flynn needed story expansion, too—what if Amos burgles Flynn's house to raise the money for the lawyer's five-thousand-dollar fee? That's a tremendous amount for a guy like Amos. In Watkins, he labored in a place called Phillips' Garage: overalls and grease. DeMille of course dressed him up, in suit and tie. Still, where does a guy who sells cigarettes and cigars over the counter get five thousand dollars?

DeMille thinks. Let's see—he raises half of it . . . yes . . . wait . . . *Right!* He *steals* the money back from Flynn to pay the other half! But he leaves a clue behind . . . yes . . . and the suspicious Flynn spends the rest of the film not only pleading Roxie's case but trying to nail Amos for the robbery! Now, *that's* a plot!

So far, so good. Yet, despite his unprecedented longevity as a top producer-director from the earliest days of the feature right into the Cinemascope era, in the late 1920s DeMille was in trouble. He had virtually founded Paramount—his partners, Jesse Lasky, Samuel Goldwyn, and Adolph Zukor, were business guys, in the front offices in New York. It was DeMille who made the pictures. Yea, DeMille made Paramount. But Zukor forced him out, irritated at DeMille's headstrong style, working with his hand-picked staff in a self-contained atelier within the studio, spending big and refusing to let New York rein him in. "You are *not one of us!*" is how Zukor explained it, in words that haunted DeMille till his death. Various DeMillian commentators analyze the line differently, but I see it as: You think the pictures matter, and you're wrong. What matters is the cost and the net. And your costs are too high, because they eat up the net!

So the director perforce became his own mogul, at Cecil B. DeMille Pictures Corp., directing a few titles each year but closely supervising all the others. This lasted from 1925 to 1928, the final days of silent film; had *Chicago* begun shooting just a bit later, it would have been a talkie.

Ultimately, DeMille couldn't survive this way; he was an artist, not a businessman. He had foolishly started up a full-service studio, and the overhead was killing him. So he closed up shop and went over to MGM for what turned out to be only three titles (including the aforementioned *Dynamite*, with Maurine Watkins' Jake the reporter, Charles Bickford). MGM proved no more hospitable than Paramount, but at length Zukor and DeMille made an uneasy peace and Paramount took back its prodigal son. They never parted after that.

Now. The direction of this first *Chicago* movie is credited to Frank Urson. DeMillians see that as a cover, for several possible reasons, which we'll get to in due course. However, a few of them may be cited at once: as so often in DeMille's pictures, there are few twenties stereotypes in his *Chicago*—no flapper, no Lee Tracy–style newsman. More important, Amos, a hapless stooge in every other version of Watkins' tale, is here a romantic leading man, handsome and fit but also noble and resourceful. He not only burgles the lawyer's place but defeats the lawyer's fiercely territorial houseman and escapes with the loot.

In truth, this is a DeMille production in every particular. The shooting script was the work of Lenore J. Coffee and the title cards were verbalized by (an unbilled) John Krafft, both DeMille regulars. Then, too, the atmosphere comports totally with DeMille's brand of comic melodrama—fast-paced, crowded with incident, and decorated with bizarre incidentals. There's a trio of girls following the trial with such concentration that their gum-chewing is co-ordinated: they chew, stop, then chew again, all three in unison. Further, one of the jurymen is heavily bandaged on the left side of his face. Why? It's one of those DeMillian things. This director never does crowds; he does gatherings of individuals.

Or let DeMille tell us himself. Katherine Orrison's *Written in Stone*, about the making of DeMille's *Ten Commandments* remake, records the director's interview with a potential extra for his circus picture, *The Greatest Show on Earth*. This aspiring extra is a woman with actual experience as an elephant rider—but "There are no extras in my movies," DeMille tells her. "I only have actors."

He was clearly impressed with this one, because she knew elephants and their world. "What elephant is this?" DeMille asked her, holding up a photo. It was a challenge, of course: DeMille's relationships with everyone were challenges.

"That's Big Ruth," the actress replied. "She's the specialty elephant...the best one to use when doing publicity photos."

She got the job there and then, because she had what DeMille looked for in scenes thronged with people. "I tell everybody the story we're making," he said. "The who, what, and why of their character." It was up to them to add to the narration creatively—another reason that the silent *Chicago* is almost certainly the work of DeMille, not Frank Urson.

Now let's examine the continuity of DeMille's *Chicago* to see how much story detail he added to Watkins' original. Here's the blueprint:

Sequence 1: Morning at the Harts' apartment as Amos caters to the unappreciative Roxie. We meet the building's housekeeper, a charming young woman who idolizes Amos.

Sequence 2: With Amos at work, Roxie's boy friend drops by. She murders him, as in Watkins, because he's leaving her.

Sequence 3: Roxie summons Amos for help. The law arrives.

Sequence 4: The jail. Roxie gets into a physical battle with The Perfect Lady [Velma]. THE MATRON: "This is a decent jail—you can't act here the way you do at home!"

Sequence 5: Having to raise $5,000 for legal representation—ROXIE: "Shouldn't blondes [like me] be cheaper?"—Amos raises half and steals the rest from a locker inside Flynn's desk. Amos fights off Flynn's houseman and gets away. But he has left his watch behind! Flynn suspects Amos, but he needs proof.

Sequence 6: Backstage at the courthouse, prepping for the trial. This is the only scene strongly corresponding to one in the play.

Sequence 7: The trial.

Sequence 8: The play ends right after the trial, but DeMille has more to say. First, Amos throws Roxie out of the apartment and his life. Then DeMille brings Amos and the housekeeper together with a wonderful touch: she cleverly provides a (false) alibi to free Amos from suspicion about the watch he left at Flynn's place. Then we see Roxie outside in the rain, as a newspaper with her headline and an artist's rendering of her likeness—her, as we now say, fifteen minutes—is trampled and muddied and finally swept into a gutter drain. Bye-bye, Roxie, who through silent-film symbolism is thus swept away herself. For the fadeout, DeMille returns to Amos and the housekeeper. We expect a kiss, rainbows, cherubs. But Amos is so distraught he scarcely notices the housekeeper bustling about behind him. If this weren't a silent, she'd be humming *Lohengrin*.

THE END

Note that DeMille has no interest in Watkins' view of a city, a society, a nation trapped in a tumult of media input, nor in an essentially libertarian population pushing back against authoritarian control. Even in his grand spectacles, DeMille's storytelling centers on individuals exercising free will in life and love. *Cleopatra*, for instance, isn't about the tectonic intersection of the plates of Western and Eastern civilizations; it's about what happens when Claudette Colbert isn't wearing a heck of a lot when Julius Caesar and Marc Antony happen by. Further,

DeMille's intimate stories—and his *Chicago* shows us just a few people up until the courtroom sequence—are the same only more so.

Of course, everything in *Chicago* turns on Roxie, and DeMille cast Phyllis Haver in the role, probably because she specialized in conniving vamp parts. Blond and sassy—and with such splendid diction that one can "read" her lines before the titles come up—Haver had been freelancing among the studios but then signed with DeMille Pictures after it had merged (to DeMille's intense distaste) with Pathé, a studio known for cranking out product made of hackneyed situations and used-up characters. True, DeMille himself loved the good old stuff. But he did everything with a fillip of surprise. The movies were there to show you what you didn't already know.

DeMille and Pathé shared Haver about equally, throwing her into picture after picture; in 1927, the year she filmed *Chicago*, Haver appeared in ten features. But then, she was a very useful talent, not least because this was an age of vamps. The woman whose day job is homewrecking was a fixture of early Hollywood storytelling, because she suited the Victorian morality favored by most early directors. Woman as saint or sinner, a hoary religious concept (think of the Gospels' two "opposite" Marys) was so intrinsic to how the movies viewed the world that even F. W. Murnau's *Sunrise* (1927), which many call the greatest American movie, even the greatest movie ever made, balances its premise on the two Marys.

Well, we know which one Phyllis Haver was. In *Fig Leaves* (1926), a modern-day story intercut with a caveman-era parallel in which the modern married couple turns up as Adam and Eve (he commutes to work in a wooden "bus" pulled by a triceratops), Haver plays the snake. And of course the vamp has all the best lines. In *The Battle of the Sexes* (1928), directed by no less than D. W. Griffith, Haver's character is introduced by a title card saying she "wasn't as hard as most gold diggers—she was harder." Later, she tells a prospective mark, "You're handsomer than the front of a bank."

Given Haver's abilities, it seems odd that *Chicago* was her only major title. She did at least take part in Paramount's *The Way of All Flesh* (1927), a lost film (unrelated to the Samuel Butler novel) directed by Victor Fleming and starring Emil Jannings, who won the Best Actor Oscar that year. Billed only as The Temptress, Haver is instrumental in destroying Jannings, a happily married, honest man who happens to be carrying a security bond when Haver crosses his path.

Haver wants that bond. Haver steals that bond. And when Jannings tries to get it back, Haver's confederate drags Jannings to the train tracks, silent Hollywood's favorite method of taking plot action to the tipping point. In a fight, Jannings sends Haver's partner-in-crime to his death, and the corpse, ripped apart by the train, is assumed to be Jannings'. Now he can't return to work and family without inculpating himself and must survive alone. Twenty years later, as a hobo, Jannings accidentally meets his beloved son, now a young man, who gives him a dollar without recognizing him. Jannings, crushed, moves off in his lonely exile without having told the boy who he is.

And that is so DeMille in every aspect—the sex, the temptation, the good and the bad, the unhealed wound, the startling coincidence, the cruelty of life—that it's amazing that DeMille didn't direct *The Way of All Flesh* himself. After all, Paramount was *his* studio—yes, even during his years of exile, for it was DeMille who had set the tone of its pictures, its visual content. It was the dressy studio: because DeMille's films were dressy. And DeMille would surely have been aware of *The Way of All Flesh*, aware that The Temptress who causes all that havoc *is* Roxie Hart. So DeMille signed Phyllis Haver as Roxie for a fall shoot later in 1927.

Now: who should play Amos Hart? In Watkins he's a stooge, but in DeMille he's the one supplying the "heart interest" (in the old phrase), as a counterweight to the loveless Roxie. The director gave Amos to one of his dependable romantic leads, Victor Varconi, who gets side-by-side billing with Phyllis Haver, though both names are below rather than above the movie's title on the main card. Varconi was a valid hunk, but he was also Hungarian, so his heavy accent instantly demoted him to character roles when sound came in. (For her part, Haver made a few talkies and then took her gold-digger stereotype seriously enough to marry a millionaire and abandon acting forever.)

As the only Amos in the various versions of *Chicago* who gets to create a full-blooded character, Varconi is very believable in a role a bit short on contours. In the opening sequence, he is the loving husband, getting up long before work to prepare Milady's breakfast. Then we see him charming his customers at his tobacco shop. However, once Roxie summons him back to their apartment after the murder, Varconi has nothing to present save a disillusioned sweetheart, finally aware of how worthless his marriage is yet helplessly needing Roxie at the same time. His expression of stalwart disappointment almost never changes.

In this, Varconi is very unlike the more typical DeMille husband of Thomas Meighan, who, rather than stumble around crestfallen, remasters his partnership by forcing his wife to return to bridal obedience. In the *Male and Female* flashback, Meighan becomes a Babylonian king, cowing Swanson in a lion's pit—filmed, incredibly, with a real lion, who lay on top of the supine Swanson for a shot that, DeMille's public knew, couldn't have been faked. That touch of alarm amid the fun is another element of DeMille—and at least, after getting the shot and calling, "Print!," he did offer Swanson her choice from a tray of trinkets. "I picked out a gold-mesh evening purse with an emerald clasp," she wrote in her memoirs, "and immediately felt much better."

As a married couple, Roxie and Amos are no flapper and sheik—these figures were single as a rule—but DeMille does offer us a babbitt, in Roxie's murder victim, Fred Casely. Maurine Watkins gave him scarcely any presence at all—obviously, as he's shot just after the curtain goes up. Though Watkins' stage directions describe other characters with relish (Velma gets fully eight lines of delineation, culminating with her "topaz earrings that match a certain tawny gleam in her smouldering eyes"), Fred Casely is simply "a man perhaps of thirty." And after the murder prologue, even his corpse is out of view—"Coroner's just gone with the body," reporter Jake tells his paper's rewrite man, on the telephone.

From the 1975 musical on, Casely is invariably cast with a sexy boy, but DeMille gave the part to Eugene Pallette, a portly older guy without the slightest romantic appeal. Famed later on in talkies for his acutely grating voice, Pallette is not Sinclair Lewis' babbitt, fearful of letting his individuality show in a repressive society. Rather,

Pallette gives us the more popular view of the babbitt, as simply a businessman lacking class and culture—maybe two notches above a boor, but well-heeled and suited up.

DeMille expanded the role with a lot of screen time, first in a chat with Amos at the tobacco shop, then with Roxie. In a typical DeMille effect, the murder is twisty rather than straightforward: where the play's Casely is shot after—apparently, as, again, we see the murder the second the curtain goes up—a verbal disagreement, the movie gives us a real fight, as Pallette shoves Roxie with a hand on her mouth, hurling her to the floor and spilling out the contents of a drawer full of household items. You know—papers, gewgaws…a pistol. As Roxie lies there, stunned and furious, Pallette pauses at the door to fix his tie in a diamond-shaped mirror flanked by coat-and-hat pegs set into the door itself. He leaves as calmly as when he came in. *Oh, you're through, are you?*

"You bet your sweet life you're through!" cries Roxie's title card (a bowdlerization of Watkins' version of the line, which I used as the subtitle of Chapter 3), as she grabs the gun off the floor and takes a shot, the bullet cracking right through the center of the mirror and the wood behind it, we presume.

Then nothing happens.

Roxie freezes, still holding the gun. Pallette's hand, all we can see of him as it clutches the door, does not move. But then the door swings open and Pallette's body sags to the floor. He's dead. And on the front of the open door we take note of black mourning crepe; Roxie had tied one of her stockings up to put off a debt collector. All this is movie stuff, designed for the camera to pick up, unavailable to the procedures of the stage. And we note that, while Watkins accompanied the murder with jazz on the Victrola—just as had obtained in Beulah Annan's real-life killing—DeMille substitutes a player piano, keyboarding merrily away as we glimpse such sheet-music titles as "She's Just What the Doctor Ordered" and "Sad 'N' Blue," a recent hit for bandleader Ben Bernie.

We recall that the music Beulah Annan played when she killed Casely was "Hula Lou," and that was the kind of thing Watkins wanted—"heavy, rhythmic jazz," she requests in her stage directions, "with the sinful insistence of the tom-tom and the saxophone's wailing plea." It's a very twenties concept: the outlaw music provokes outlaw behavior. Every preacher said so.

But DeMille wants irony, so the tune must be gaudy, a happy trip across the dance floor. At least, that's what it *looks* like. Meanwhile, Roxie is stunned by what she has done. "Get up!" she shouts at Pallette, so vividly the screen skips titling it. Now for a last bit of suspense: DeMille shoots a man's feet coming down the building's stairway. Roxie, *close the door*! Oh no—Pallette's body is in the way! As Roxie struggles with it, the movie has slyly put us on her side. There is no such thing as an "objective" camera.

Of course, the movie features that definitive twenties figure, the salesman. Here it's Billy Flynn (Robert Edeson), the defense attorney, who "sells" to the jury Roxie's "innocence." The movie is weak here, for not till Adolphe Menjou's hammy Flynn in the talkie remake would this character really come alive. Edeson is an old walrus by comparison (and the musical completely reinvented Flynn—physically, that is—as a sort of matinée idol).

DeMille did at least cast a lively soubrette, Virginia Bradford, as Amos' new love interest. True, her job as the housekeeper of the Harts' apartment building keeps her out of the continuity except at the beginning and the end. But Bradford catches our interest. She literally kicks Eugene Pallette away when he sees her in the hallway and takes a liberty, and, again, Bradford's quick thinking tricks suspicious police detectives into exculpating Victor Varconi of the Flynn burglary. Note, though, that in this movie Amos—just like Roxie—gets away with a crime. That is, both avoid a *legal* penalty, even if Roxie is thrown out onto the street with no apparent means of survival.

On its release, this *Chicago* did quite well commercially, grossing nearly $200,000 over its production cost of about $300,000. The *New York Times*' first-string movie critic, Mordaunt Hall, said *Chicago* "dashes along with considerable wit and occasional splashes of tragedy and pathos"—and he did understand that DeMille's version of Watkins' satire was only "quasisatirical." In other words, DeMille cut the play's cynicism with the "human interest" without which virtually no Hollywood picture could be made at this time.

And while not given to hyperbole, Hall called Haver's performance "astoundingly fine."

In truth, Haver does hold the film together, as her co-star Varconi is almost tiresomely noble and everyone else save Virginia Bradford is no more than sedately competent. Again, as so often in art, the killer has all the scenes, especially when we watch Haver planning her next move as her features narrow around her darting eyes. Maurine Watkins' Roxie is not unlike a rag doll in the way she lets everyone position her in "attitudes"; her one self-motivated act is the murder. But Haver's Roxie is more active, even aggressive, and she caps it all with a spectacular fainting bit at the climax of Flynn's closing argument.

Further, DeMille's inspection of the Harts' marriage gives Haver more to play than Francine Larrimore did on stage. The silent Roxie is one of those people who never listen to anyone but themselves, so she doesn't know the most basic element in her husband's world-view: his acute sense of morality. In Roxie's jail cell, as the two await the lawyer's grand entrance, Amos suffers a moment of revulsion at Roxie's utter disregard for her actions:

AMOS: Don't you realize that you just killed a man? Aren't you even *sorry*?

As always in a silent, the actors convey more "dialogue" than the title cards, and here Roxie shows us just how sorry she isn't, shooting a look of sheer malice at Amos for daring to chastise her. You can keep your "sorry" crap, she seems to be "saying," as Amos struggles manfully between his love for her and his ethical perspective; alone among the *Chicago* authors and presenters, DeMille wants us to like *somebody* in this shocking tale. But Roxie doesn't get it. She thinks everyone's like her:

ROXIE: You're just jealous 'cause I'm getting all the publicity!

Even thus enlarged, however, Haver's Roxie is very much Watkins' Roxie, the one important element linking the film to the play with absolute fidelity. Everything else is dropped, shifted, or simply invented. Of Watkins' two lead reporters, Mary Sunshine simply isn't in the film, and Jake has been demoted to an "under five."[1] Of the many additions to the play, perhaps the oddest—to modern eyes—is Flynn's houseman: a Japanese, as all housemen were among the gentry. It was a talking point in the 1920s; three years earlier, Edna Ferber's novel *So Big* used her young hero's hiring of a Japanese butler as a sign of his alienation from important personal matters in a wish to acquire social prestige. Again, DeMille loved to regale moviegoers with signifiers of upper-class chic: if only you had money and taste, you, too, would employ a Japanese houseman.

One thing we do lose in DeMille's adaptation is the wisecrack cynicism of Watkins' wording—in her exuberant, sarcastic stage directions, obviously, but also in her dialogue. "Another murder!" Mary Sunshine cries ("avidly," Watkins directs) when we hear Machine-Gun Rosie paying her respects to her boy friend, who's been cheating on her...with his wife. Rosie kills the wife, too. The movie loses the line's touch of zany Guignol, but it does at least give Jake (who is so demoted in the film that he's called simply The Reporter) a Watkinsesque remark of his own when Roxie is perplexed at how suddenly everyone has dropped her for—note the new sobriquet—Two-Gun Rosie. Says Jake, "Listen, sister, you're yesterdays news and that's deader than last year's hat!"

Even so, DeMille knows that every movie that isn't a Christian retelling is more or less about romance. "You couldn't trust even the man who loves you," Victor Varconi solemnly tells Phyllis Haver, and in DeMille's world this is true condemnation. Murder isn't nice, no—but to fail to cherish your life's partner really crosses a line. Finally, after the trial, Varconi opens up drastically, with "I'll see my soul burn in hellfire before I'd touch you again!"

With so much added into the story, something had to vanish, and that is the myth of Chicago as the ultimate American city, all the

---

1. This is modern parlance for a movie player a bit above an extra, with a small handful of spoken lines. Of course, in the silent *Chicago*, this Jake can't "speak." Still, his tiny allotment of title cards suits the definition.

resonance that the word "Chicago" had for Americans at the time. Given the technical limitations of set design and set changes in twenties theatre, Maurine Watkins couldn't take her characters to many different places. Indeed, most straight plays used a single set for the entire evening. Only musicals, using cumbersome little vignettes or musical numbers "in one" (that is, way downstage before a curtain while the stagehands shifted the scenery behind it), could map around with any freedom. Movies, however, can go anywhere at any time, and we expect the *Chicago* film to show us this city of a hundred meanings, from anarchy to industrial might.

DeMille, however, has a story to tell, not an epic to unfurl, and while Watkins' *Chicago* is filled with comments on how the town's personality drives the action, DeMille wants to show us nothing more than a bad marriage and a crazy trial. He goes outdoors seldom, as when Eugene Pallette, on his way to his fatal date with Roxie, stops off at Amos' tobacco stand. In effect, DeMille leaves Chicago out of his *Chicago*.

The film's shooting schedule, in late 1927, is supposed to have lasted into November or even December of that year, which would have made it impossible to release till well into 1928. The notes enclosed with the picture's DVD release give the film's premiere as March 4, 1928, contradicting all other sources, which give very late 1927 instead. The later date makes sense, as it takes time to develop prints and launch the PR campaign, quite aside from the orderly calendar of releases that even an indie studio like DeMille Pictures would have set up in advance.

On the other hand, Mordaunt Hall's *New York Times* review is dated December 24, 1927, and he specifically states that *Chicago* opened "last night at the Gaiety Theatre." Just as definitive is the movie's title card, giving a copyright year of 1927. Some of the confusion may be traced to *Chicago*'s apparent disappearance: it was thought, till relatively recently, to be lost. Not till a complete print was discovered in DeMille's own collection were we of today able to fill in this chapter of the *Chicago* saga.

Now let us consider the question of the film's authorship—Frank Urson or Cecil B. DeMille? Even Mordaunt Hall, who would have known only what other informed outsiders could know, mentions in his review that DeMille was responsible for at least some of the direction. As Hall phrases it, "it is understood" that Urson's work "was supervised by" DeMille.

But it goes yet deeper. Urson was a cameraman and assistant director, just then being graduated to full leadership capacity, and *Chicago*'s direction is frankly too assured and imaginative to be the work of a recent assistant. (We can't compare *Chicago* to Urson's later work, as he was credited with one very obscure film before dying in a drowning accident, in 1928.) To give just one more example of DeMillian expertise, shots of the reporters' table during the trial show us only men's hands rapidly taking notes, tapping telegraph keys, and moving papers, creating an impersonal chorus of newsmen, losing their humanity in the hunt for sexy headlines.

Besides, the movie's aforementioned claustrophobic atmosphere, its lack of a larger geographical context, is very much in DeMille's style. His spectacles roamed widely, but again, his domestic stories were indoors-only affairs. And, finally, that *Chicago* print in DeMille's private collection points to a more than "supervisory" involvement, for DeMille kept personal copies of pictures he directed, but not those he merely produced.

But why did he assign the director's credit to Frank Urson? DeMillians have the answer: *The King of Kings*—on the essential Christian narrative, remember—was still playing when *Chicago* was released, and it would have been unseemly for DeMille to have signed so scabrous a piece as *Chicago* just when his name was attached to something as transcendant as the Agony of Christ.

It's worth noting that DeMille's *Chicago* was released when the nation's disgust with the hypocrisy and violence of Prohibition was starting to reach critical mass. The more its failure became a public scandal, the more resolute—or do I mean vindictive?—its devotees became. In 1926, the year of the play *Chicago*'s premiere, H. L. Mencken wrote of the drys, "What moves them is the psychological aberration called sadism. They lust to [do harm to] everyone who is free from their barbarous superstitions, and is having a better time in the world than they are."

This view, already extremely widespread among the educated of the day, is about more than Prohibition. It points up the reckless governmental overlordism that antagonizes a free people, or at least the portion of it that wants to remain free. Also in 1927, four months before the *Chicago* film premiered, Wayne B. Wheeler, the maximum leader of the Anti-Saloon League and the undisputed force behind the invention and enforcement of prohibition, died of a chronic heart condition. It was a terrible death, because, a week earlier, his wife had died of burns suffered in an accident. All the same, Wheeler's passing heartened the law's foes to come together to work toward liberation—toward a release from an insane, destructive attempt to regulate the human appetite by the application of self-righteous, pietistic dogma. A release from a pile-on of regulations. Or, as everyone in the nation phrased it at the time:

Repeal.

It was as though, until Franklin Delano Roosevelt's election, in 1932, and the subsequent removal of Prohibition from the calendar of laws, Americans were living as Russians did under the Soviets: as people divorced from their own government. Because it wasn't theirs. The government belonged to itself, not to the voters, and this is what replaces community with anarchy.

So when a musical, in this same 1927, first addressed the question of which folks are really in charge and what they and their minions want from the rest of us, an atmosphere of cynicism entered the sensory model of a form—carefree, zany musical comedy—that had once been essentially optimistic. Because, after all, those doing no harm have no enemies. Right?

5

⌒∿⌒

The Invention of the Satiric Musical

How Can You Tell an American?

The very first musical told of rival criminal gangs, of the joys of the thief and the killer, of whores, of corruption so comprehensive that there is not a single decent character in the entire show. It was a sensation: *The Beggar's Opera*, first performed in London in 1728, as I've already noted, and still vital today.

John Gay wrote the book and lyrics (to use modern parlance), and there was no composer: Gay applied new lyrics to pre-existing tunes. Historians emphasize its spoof of Italian opera, then most popular among the rank and fashion of the town. As well, Gay meant to assail the administration of the country's unofficial ruler, Robert Walpole, the very model of the one per center made of graft and secret sweetheart deals for his cronies.

Even so, *The Beggar's Opera* must have delighted Londoners mainly because it really was their first musical, with a script punctuated by situation and character songs in the popular style. Better, those first audiences must have been tickled to hear innocent melodies wedded to sarcastic and even licentious lyrics, as when this jolly trifle:

> Oh, London is a fine town,
> And a gallant city,
> 'Tis governed by the Scarlet Gown,
> Come listen to my ditty...

turned up in the Gay version as this parents' lament:

> Our Polly is a sad slut!
> Nor heeds what we have taught her.
> I wonder any man alive
> Will ever rear a daughter!

The dialogue, too, was deliciously shocking, now scathing in irony, as in this bit from a fence and informer:

PEACHUM: Like great statesman, we encourage those who betray their friends...

and now brutally philosophical on the ins and outs of the social contract:

PEACHUM: The [financially] comfortable estate of widowhood, is the only hope that keeps up a wife's spirits.

In short, the English-speaking musical has been critical of the establishment and its protocols right from the start, not least in its protection of minorities. Women were given great latitude as performers, though it was popularly supposed that all actresses of less than Shakespearean prominence were prostitutes—thus the so-called wicked stage. And Ned Harrigan and Tony Hart's depictions of the Irish in the 1880s followed hard upon New York leaders' destruction of Manhattan's "Boss" William M. Tweed—possibly, some historians now believe, because he was letting the Irish share power in a city till then run exclusively by WASP bankers and the socially consequential Knickerbocker caste. Comparably, Florenz Ziegfeld challenged an unwritten racial-segregation law by hiring black Bert Williams for the white *Follies* throughout the 1910s—and this was not stunt casting, though Ziegfeld was notorious for pulling off PR didoes. What attracted him to Williams was the latter's versatility in both sketch comedy and song, with a gift for dry underplaying cut with pathos and wonder.

We tend to forget how nonconformist the American musical really is, because for its first century (starting roughly in the 1860s) its songs were the national melody—"After the Ball," "Night and Day," "My Heart Stood Still." Storytelling songs, dance numbers, love ballads: the accompaniment of life. How could something so popular be subversive?

Besides, the American musical show's most apparent ancestor was the Gilbert and Sullivan titles, so Victorian in tone, with their switched-babies plots, their grand dame of a contralto bossing everyone around, their whoopsiedoodle comedian with the funny hopping dance. These are lovable, not revolutionary, works. Yet they quite openly pass remarks about the incompetence or shady dealings of the elites—the pack of idiots making up *Iolanthe*'s House of Lords or the pompous official in *The Mikado* rationalizing his etiquette in the taking of bribes. He even gave his character's name to a type, the self-important grandee, a term still in use today: a Pooh-Bah. "I can't help it," says Pooh-Bah. "I was born sneering."

Granted, there was always a fear of state censorship in those days. *The Beggar's Opera* so offended Robert Walpole that its sequel, *Polly*, was, though published, banned from stage production, and Gilbert and Sullivan, despite a phenomenal popularity, were inclined to self-censorship rather than irritate the authorities *too* much. In their penultimate piece, *Utopia (Limited)* (1893), on the Anglicization of a South Pacific island, Gilbert poked fun at all sorts of aspects of English life. Yet when the local princess, an alumna of Girton College, Cambridge, merrily recommends that her homeland adopt the political party system, Gilbert was crossing a line:

> PRINCESS ZARA: No political measures will endure, because one Party will assuredly undo all that the other Party has done.... Inexperienced civilians will govern your Army and your Navy; no social reforms will be attempted because out of vice, squalor and drunkenness no political capital is to be made....

Gilbert and Sullivan expert Leslie Baily tells us that one newspaper called this "the bitterest speech" of Gilbert's career, and in the end Gilbert cut the second half (after my first ellipsis) of the lines quoted above, not only in the stage performances but in the published text as well.

Clearly, some saw a danger in an unfettered music theatre. Yet when we cross the ocean to the United States, we find the enemies of the musical stage concerned entirely with sexual immodesty—ballet girls in tights, women characters expressing unmaidenly interests, or the insinuating maxixe danced (in a Ziegfeld show) by a young lady and her beau, the latter also a woman, dressed as a man. Ministers thundered from their pulpits at these sexy capers, but because the musical was thought to be empty-headed frolic, its *politics* did not truly register.[1]

All the same, a progressive worldview kept peeking out from behind the sheer gaiety of musicals. Jerome Kern and P. G. Wodehouse's "We're Crooks," in *Miss 1917*, troubles to tell us just where a self-respecting felon establishes his limits:

> Our crimes at times are things to shudder at,
> But we've never been in Congress, for we draw the line at that.

Or, in the title song of Kurt Weill and Ogden Nash's *One Touch of Venus* (1943), we hear "The world belongs to men and women"—true enough—"but the banks belong to men," a surprise topper that reminds us who has all the power. And it's the babbitts, not the sheiks. For, as a lyric in *The Golden Apple* (1953) explains, when war talk is in the air, "Old men always do the shouting" while "Young men have to do the shooting."

So there is a thread of pungent social observation sewn into the tapestry of the musical's history. Not till the 1920s, however, did anyone attempt a full-scale narrative musical satire, and on a risky subject, willful militarism. This show was *Strike Up the Band* (1927),

---

1. Similarly, Margaret Sanger, who pioneered the birth-control movement, was hounded by the authorities, even though her issue was preventing unwanted pregnancies, not aborting them. At the very same time, spokesmen for systems of government antagonistic to our own were generally left alone. Sanger was arrested numerous times, but the Communist Party took part in presidential elections from 1924. In 1932, its candidate, William Z. Foster (nominated at a convention in, not surprisingly, Chicago) polled 102,785 votes.

with a book by George S. Kaufman and a score by George and Ira Gershwin. An ensemble piece, *Strike Up the Band* gives us the sheik, flapper, babbitt, and salesman figures. It was the ultimate twenties musical—and it founded a line of musical-comedy satires that leads straight to *Chicago*.

The sheik is Jim, a reporter, but true-blue and moral. A hero. The flapper is headstrong Joan, who loves but incessantly bickers with Jim. Joan's father, Horace Fletcher, an industrialist in the cheese business, is the babbitt, and he drives the plot. It seems that America's protective tariff has locked Switzerland's cheese out of our market, so *this means war!* All the male leads get involved, including a certain Col. Holmes. He's the salesman figure, and what he sells is conflagration:

> HOLMES: Costs a lot of money, war does. What do you think we ought to have, a little war or a big one?

Fletcher suggests they get investors to back the war as if it were a theatrical production:

> HOLMES: I could see the steel people, Y.M.C.A., all those folks.... Gives them a lot of advertising.

This look at elites viewing death and destruction as a source of profit was very bold for the era; men were imprisoned during the previous wartime for saying as much, including the socialist leader Eugene V. Debs, who ran for president while locked up in a federal penitentiary, in 1920. He polled 919,799 votes, not that much less than William Z. Foster.

But that's the real world. In *Strike Up the Band*, Jim, resourceful as all sheiks were, devises the strategy for a decisive battle and peace breaks out. Then, just before the final curtain, Russia protests the caviar tariff, and *this means war!*

As I've said, such debunking was the favorite indoor sport of the 1920s; satire was its ideal playing field. What makes *Strike Up the Band* special (and bonds it with *Chicago*) is the way the score supported

the lampoon. This wasn't a satire with songs: it was a fully musical-
ized satire, a hurdy-gurdy Jeremiad monitored by a zany chorus to
echo, converse with, and sometimes defy the principals in spoof-
operetta musical scenes. And Ira's lyrics match Kaufman's irony: in
the title number, war is called a "patriotic pastime," and if "We don't
know what we're fighting for," that's fine because "We didn't know
the last time."

Alas, problems bedeviled the show early on, partly because producer Edgar Selwyn didn't assemble a first-rate cast. All the non-
sweetheart roles needed comics of particular kinds, not always easy
to find. Thus, Kaufman saw Fletcher as the evening's straight man,
a dim bulb—but he has too many silly lines to be played straight.
And the rest of Selwyn's crew were unfunny or miscast. Here's one
example: the Col. Holmes, a behind-the-scenes fixer of deadly authority wearing a folksy mask, was Lew Hearn, neither deadly nor
folksy, and known mainly for his outré vocalism suggesting a mad
goat singing "Nessun Dorma." Holmes disappears in a crowd; Lew
Hearn stood out in one.

Then, too, George S. Kaufman tended to plot chaotically (which is
why he almost always wrote his scripts with collaborators). He *was*
funny, though. Here's Fletcher and an underling considering National
Cheese Week:

UNDERLING: There was a very large celebration in Des
    Moines, Iowa.
FLETCHER: A very big cheese town.
UNDERLING: The parade was led by a naked girl symbolizing
    law and order and was followed by the entire male population.
FLETCHER: That shows how popular cheese is.

Still, by the Philadelphia tryout, some of the leads were quitting,
because the show was playing so badly. Was it the scathing commentary? Was it because much of the cast couldn't sing well enough to
justify the music? There's a tale, retold in various versions, in which
Kaufman and Ira Gershwin are standing outside the theatre when
two distinguished older gentlemen disembark from a taxicab and

head into the house. "That's Gilbert and Sullivan," Ira tells Kaufman, "coming to fix the second act."

To which Kaufman replies, "Why don't you write jokes like that in your lyrics?"

Selwyn closed the production, but he persevered. He had Morrie Ryskind rework the book, now to build the action around an emerging star-comic duo, Bobby Clark and Paul McCullough. Friends since childhood, the pair maintained an unusual partnership, as McCullough was less a straight man than a participant in the jesting, romping around in outlandish outfits, especially a collegiate raccoon coat. Clark was known for his cigar, cane, painted-on eyeglasses, and extremely fancy duds, and his lines were dotted with allusions to the latest shows and movies, names in the news, and so on.

So the team was easy to write for, as when Fletcher's receptionist bars Clark's way. "Sweet Adeline!" Clark cries, adding, in a reference to Rudy Vallee's newest song hit, "Believe it or not, I'm the vagabond lover." Later, Jim says he has some bad news, and Clark replies, "Don't tell me my tailor died." As so often with this generation of drolls, from Bert Lahr to Eddie Cantor, the laughs inhered in not the lines but the delivery.

But did Ryskind bowdlerize Kaufman's sociopolitics? The new script reconfigured the war adventure as a dream: Fletcher suffers a mild heart attack, is sedated, and falls asleep at his desk as the violins shimmer over a belligerent theme for horns and violas and the woodwinds gush overhead. (Gershwin liked the effect so much he had it included in the show's overture.) Further, Ryskind changed Fletcher's product from cheese to chocolate.

However, does all this really sweeten anything? Because, contrary to legend, Ryskind did not soothe Kaufman's satire. Just for example, the scene I just quoted between Fletcher and Col. Holmes in which they conspire to "stage" a war—easily the most dangerous passage in Kaufman's original book—was tweaked a tiny bit but survived as Kaufman intended it in Ryskind's final script, dated November 8, 1929, a few weeks before rehearsals began. In short, what put this new *Strike Up the Band* (1930) over was a vastly better staging: the two star jesters, more accomplished singers, and a re-vised score with two hit titles, "Soon" and "I've Got a Crush on You [sweetie pie]."

So here was a satire that didn't close Saturday night. Thus heart-ened, Kaufman, Ryskind, and the Gershwins wrote two more politi-cal spoofs, *Of Thee I Sing* (1931) and a sequel called *Let 'Em Eat Cake* (1933), respectively on a presidential campaign and ensuing failed impeachment and then on a revolutionary uprising. *Of Thee I Sing*'s working title was *Tweedledee*, on the notion that all presidential can-didates are as alike as Lewis Carroll's Tweedledum and Tweedledee.

True, some do strive to appear unnuanced, to appeal to the broad-est possible electorate. "Talk less," Lin-Manuel Miranda's Aaron Burr advises the young Alexander Hamilton. "Smile more." Such is the way upward: "Don't let them know what you're against or what you're for." Yet we still entertain such personable candidates as Theodore Roosevelt and John Fitzgerald Kennedy. They talk more.

Interestingly, so do virtually all the principals in the American musical. More often than not quixotic and flamboyant, they can't wait to tell us of their moods, to sing about their plans, to let us know not only what they're for or against but also how wonderful it feels to be in a musical. Ethel Merman shares joy in "Riding High" or "I'm Throwing a Ball Tonight." Pal Joey and his soigné protectrice duet in a lightly bragging gavotte on their "den of iniquity." Puccini's Rodolpho and Mimi, transported from *La Bohème* to New York's East Village in *Rent*, re-enact the opera's dainty meeting scene in more worldly terms that just as eloquently plead the cause of love.

These are rich characters, and it's worth noting that, once *Oklahoma!* and *Carousel* boasted extremely arresting individuals after decades of standard-make sheiks and flappers, Rodgers and Hammerstein's third show, *Allegro*, failed to please in part because its people, especially its gentle doctor protagonist, were bafflingly earthbound. Even music didn't lift them.

True, it is less the people in *Of Thee I Sing* than the very funny script that keeps the story popping, as when the French Ambassador marches in with a plot twist and the authors playfully nudge the French war debt:

AMBASSADOR: I have received another note from my country.

PRESIDENT: . . . We've got a lot of notes from your country, and
some of them were due ten years ago.

AMBASSADOR: But this is not a promise to pay—this is serious.

It is the astonishing score, though, that gives the show its tang, for,
even more than in *Strike Up the Band*, the music takes part in the
satire, as in a spoofy Viennese waltz at an extremely dramatic
moment, or in a torchlight parade stippled with worldless vocal bits
of familiar old melodies. The Gershwins are doing what Kaufman
and Ryskind are doing, something that before them only Offenbach
and Sullivan did well and often: creating music that laughs.

Among his innovations, Gershwin cast aside the overture model
as a medley of the principal tunes. Jerome Kern seems to have been
the first to revolutionize the overture, most notably in *Show Boat*
(1927), which presents a kind of tone poem on racial tension. For *Of
Thee I Sing*, Gershwin does quote his two prime melodies, the title
song and "Who Cares?," but this five-minute *sinfonia* is really an
étude on one excited dotted-eighth-note theme from "Because,
Because," a number for reporters covering an Atlantic City beauty
pageant and reprised by the show's villain, Diana Devereaux. The
song's A strain consists of two adjacent pitches relentlessly teeter-
ing back and forth; speeded up, they provide a nervous bonding element for the entire overture. It mirrors the restless energy of the
show as a whole, as the contest winner becomes the First Lady while
the luscious Ms. Devereaux keeps horning in like Katisha in *The
Mikado*.[2] Gershwin seems fascinated by this scatterbrained little riff,
using it to irritate "Who Cares?" and then varying it propulsively as
if preparing another of the classical pieces like the *Rhapsody in Blue*
with which he was changing the history of American concert music.
To repeat—and, again, to prepare the way for how *Chicago* makes its
points—the truly facetious musical needs a facetious score.

2. Leonard Bernstein made this comparison before me, on television (on *Omnibus*),
as principals and chorus illustrated the relationship between the two shows' first-act
finales. His point was the same one I'm making in this book—that the "popular" nature
of the music in musicals is only deceptively simple: it can in fact draw on a sophisticated musical intelligence to make its effects.

Let's get our bearings on this important matter by interrupting the chronology to consider a truly fulfilled satiric score that will likely be familiar to my readers, that to Frank Loesser's *How To Succeed in Business Without Really Trying* (1961). A sell-out hit running three and a half years, *How To Succeed* tilted all its elements toward the goofy idea of a rascal plotting his way to the top of a big industrial firm. The sets, for example, were colored-in line drawings; the workers were screwballs, while the boss, Rudy Vallee, underplayed in a kind of oblivious monotone; the protagonist, Robert Morse, was lovable despite his treacherous persona; and a recorded voice, detailing the title's do-it-yourself lessons in self-advancement, was Carl Princi, the very model of the suave radio announcer who brings dignity and omniscience to everything, a Stepford voice hovering benignly over the drastic tizzies of real life. (Revivals have used Walter Cronkite and Anderson Cooper.)

So the staging was excellent—but the main point is that *How To Succeed*'s score reflected this mocking craziness, from the musical suggestion of the addict's withdrawal when the coffee maker fritzes out, in "Coffee Break," to the parody of a revivalist rave-up in "Brotherhood of Man." We even get a dopey touch of the classical in a love song, "Rosemary," when the three title notes provoke an orchestral tutti echo worthy of Puccini, followed by the opening measures of Grieg's Piano Concerto. Some of the numbers are simple take-offs—"Grand Old Ivy" of the college fight song and "Love From a Heart of Gold" of the Gilded Age ballad. But "I Believe in You" turns the traditional Boy Loves Girl hymn into Boy Loves Self. Morse sang it in the executive men's wash room, as a group of his fellow suits used their electric shavers to smooth the cheek for an afternoon conference, the shaving scored for kazoos.

In all, a salty intelligence guides *How To Succeed*'s score just as it does the book and the original design: all the departments of the production were harmonized. However, this is not always the case in musical satires, as witness Irving Berlin and Moss Hart's *Face the Music* (1932), which arrived concurrently with the three Gershwin political shows.

Face the Music, too, was political, a reaction to the corruption in the administration of New York's Mayor James J. Walker, and Hart is mordant but Berlin is his usual amiable self. He lacks the fantasy of Gershwin's busybody choruses or Loesser's Heckle and Jeckle cutups. "(Castle in Spain) On a Roof in Manhattan" graced *Face the Music* with a Latin number danced in a mirrored setting, the design and choreography by outstanding specialists of the time, respectively Albert R. Johnson and Albertina Rasch. This is beautiful art, romantic art: it doesn't belong in a satire. Yes, *some* of *Face the Music's* numbers second Hart's spoof, as in "Lunching at the Automat," picturing the leadership class, from "the Rock'fellers" to "Missus [August] Belmont," enjoying fast food. Still, the score in general is what Berlin might have written for any musical comedy.

So the very genre of the musical satire was newborn and tender at the time—and that may be why there was no musical version of *Chicago* then. Or was it because of all that "Chicago as the ultimate American city" baggage, the unbridled capitalism on one hand and anarchy on the other? Because while twenties musical comedy seemed almost improvisationally chaotic in its plotting, it worshipped the authoritarian idylls of love and marriage as givens in every American life. Only villains remained bachelors.

And what about *Chicago's* murder factor? There had been killings in *Rose-Marie* (1924), by an adulteress no less, but only to save her lover from her enraged husband; in *Deep River* (1926), in a duel; in *Rainbow* (1928), in self-defense. But these were serious musicals; *Deep River* hasn't a single laugh in any of its three acts. *Chicago*, after all, is a *comedy* with a killing.

Nor was Maurine Watkins' assault on that other authoritarian idyll, the American way of justice, suitable for adaptation. When twenties musicals used plays as source material, they were invariably skylarking farces about mistaken identity or the like. Besides, was any musical-comedy star capable of actuating a character as rough and selfish as Roxie Hart?

There was one: Marilyn Miller. An elfin blond dancer and the particular pet of Florenz Ziegfeld in both book shows and revues, Miller had been Broadway's official Cinderella ever since the aforementioned *Sally*, playing a waitress who crashes the *Follies*. Singing in the Victorian heroine's head-voice soprano and adept in both hoofing and ballet (that is, in populist and elite strains of dance) Miller personified the melting maid of the happy stage with infusions of flapper—the bobbed hair, the ambition. We remember her establishing number in *Sally*, "[I wish I could be like] Joan of Arc": determined yet wistful, a lovely wonder.

But that was the public Miller. Offstage, she was intensely self-oriented and sensually appetitive: a Roxie Hart. And Miller had Roxie's temper. When Ziegfeld brought his little girl, Patricia, to a matinee of *Sally* and father and daughter paid a visit to Miller's dressing room, Patty found the magical star in a highly unmagical mood, and when the Ziegfelds beat a hasty retreat, a jar of cold cream flew crashing against the closed door.

Though only five, Patty caught the contradiction between art and life. "It's different back here, isn't it?" she observed: for she had seen Roxie Hart for fair. So wouldn't Miller have been a sensation in a musical *Chicago*, turning the musical-comedy damsel icon inside out? Or was Broadway ready to see Public Sweetheart Number One turn killer? Would Ziegfeld or Charles Dillingham, Miller's contracted producers throughout the 1920s, have allowed Dolly Dearest onstage in such a predatory role?

The musical simply wasn't that rich a form then. But the narrative satires as such kept coming, two presenting the public with replicas of Franklin Delano Roosevelt, a very easy way to dress one's show with an extraordinary character. The first of the two, *I'd Rather Be Right* (1937), was the Absolutely Guaranteed Smash, not because of the second-rate Rodgers and Hart score, but because of a very amusing Kaufman and Hart script and the outstanding star turn of the decade, by George M. Cohan, in a role—everybody suddenly realized—he was born to play. In rimless spectacles and a morning coat over striped dark trousers, Cohan was Roosevelt's double. (The show didn't put the actor in Roosevelt's wheelchair, but then few of the public knew how crippled the President really was.)

Billed as "a musical revue," *I'd Rather Be Right* was more of an episodic book show: to enable two kids to afford to get married, the President tries to balance the budget, each new attempt creating a new comic or musical "act." They all fail, but the kids decide to marry anyway. Besides, most of what happens turns out to have been a dream, with FDR strolling through New York's Central Park without a security detail, his actual cabinet materializing in song befitting a Gilbert and Sullivan touring company, the nine Supreme Court judges (all in Chief Justice Charles Evans Hughes' beard) popping out from behind bits of the scenery crying, "No, you don't!" when the President tries to pass a law, and captains of industry getting in on one of Roosevelt's welfare-for-work programs by manning picks and shovels to transfer a little twig from one spot to another.

The zaniest bit was the cabinet's radio show, the *White House Jamboree*, with "Franklin D. Roosevelt's Hillbilly Swing Orchestra," Postmaster General James Farley as emcee, Secretary of State Cordell Hull telling a "Pat and Mike" Irish joke, Secretary of Labor Frances Perkins sharing insider D. C. dish while someone tapped a telegraph key in the style of Walter Winchell's radio spots ("Fashion note: Senator William E. Borah [FDR's worst enemy in Congress] sleeps in just his pajama tops"), and Secretary of the Treasury Henry Morgenthau Jr. flavoring "A Baby Bond For Baby" with the vapid honey of the airwave crooner. Clearly, *I'd Rather Be Right* is an unusual work, yet it is as if the score submits to the book rather than matches it.

The librettist-lyricist of the other musical about FDR, Maxwell Anderson, was not a Rooseveltian. On the contrary, Anderson saw the President as a war-mongering fascist, which led the audience to assume Anderson had in mind not Roosevelt but Adolf Hitler. This show was *Knickerbocker Holiday* (1938), with émigré composer Kurt Weill, and the setting was old Nieuw Amsterdam. Anderson's Roosevelt was Pieter Stuyvesant, played by Walter Huston in the first great musical turn by a star not associated with musicals. Reveling in his trick pegleg costume, copping the show's main ballad, "September Song," joining a line of cuties in a "Dutch Dance" of mixed meter, $\frac{2}{4}$ varied by $\frac{3}{8}$, to suggest the clomping wooden leg, and slyly euphemizing to tart up his tyranny (controlling the economy to favor the oligarchy is "a slight financial sophistication"), Huston had a ball. And he knew who his nemesis was almost from the moment he stepped on stage: the show's First Couple boy, Brom Broek. He's what happened to the sheik when he got political; his idea of team sports is revolution.

So this is the beginning of the musical's series of rough diamonds, attractive and powerful men who, in one way or another, refuse to fit into the prevailing social landscape—*Carousel*'s Billy Bigelow, *Brigadoon*'s Tommy Albright, *The Pajama Game*'s Sid Sorokin, *1776*'s John Adams, *Sunday in the Park With George*'s Seurat. Brom is a conscientious objector, born to exasperate fascists:

STUYVESANT: Democracy? What's a democracy?
BROM: It's—where you're governed by amateurs. It's—a free country.
STUYVESANT: Ridiculous.... Arrest him!

And there will be no trial:

STUYVESANT: Trial, hell! When a man's guilty what the hell good's a trial!

Knickerbocker Holiday is a funny but secretly bitter piece, for Anderson really did think that power attracted the worst people as a rule. As he explained in his preface to the show's published text, "Government...must be drastically limited in its scope, because it...will automatically become a monopoly in crime and devour the civilization over which it presides." As if adducing proof of Anderson's observation, in 2016 the President of Germany, Joachim Gauck, said in a television interview, "Die Eliten sind gar nicht das Problem—die Bevölkerungen sind das Problem." (The elites are not at all the problem—the people are the problem.)

Heretofore, musicals were written to give the public a break from the struggles of life; Maxwell Anderson wrote *Knickerbocker Holiday* to force the public to confront the struggles of life. This gave the show a distinctive tang next to its contemporaries *The Boys from Syracuse*, *Du Barry Was a Lady*, and *Hellzapoppin*. Further, Kurt Weill was the ideal musician to give Anderson's lyrics music with spice and bite, in that unique Weillian orchestration suggesting the dance band engaged for Sadie Hawkins Night in Mother Courage's bordello. And while "September Song" was the hit, the show's key number was "How Can You Tell an American?," as it aligns with Anderson's belief that we as a people instinctively refuse to obey: because obedience is in itself anti-democratic.

It's the *Chicago* thing, the Prohibition thing: America is anarchy at its best. The libertarian Anderson thought even the Social Security Act (just three years old at the time) "bureaucratic absolutism"— but "How Can You Tell an American?" doesn't go that far. Rather, it says—no, proclaims—that we insist on living "without the supervision of a governmental plan, and that's an American!" Weill gave the lyrics a swinging tune with a healthy undertone of willfulness in it, so the music *sounds* like the words.

And there it is: a musical with politics. The aim of this chapter is to monitor the development of the kind of show that will lead us to *Chicago*: the commentative musical, individualized in not just story and characters but its music as well, singing in its own unique idiom. Up to this point, in the 1930s, virtually every American musical employs the popular song style of the day. Richard Rodgers was different from Cole Porter, yes. Still, even at their most imaginative, such writers use the available forms, which gives the musical in general a shallow texture. We want to hear outlandish music to match the outlandish dramaturgy.

So now we come to a pair from the late-middle 1930s that marked the satiric musical's first absolute deviations from popular-music norms, Kurt Weill and Paul Green's *Johnny Johnson* (1936) and Marc Blitzstein's *The Cradle Will Rock* (1937). These two very different pieces seem like partners, as both are political and use exaggeration and mannerism. Neither show is entirely a satire, and they certainly cannot be seen as forerunners of the *Chicago* musical per se. Its template is show biz, glamorous and slick. Instead, *Johnny Johnson* and *The Cradle Will Rock* adhere to the line of socially progressive drama that disdained the allure and kicks of the Broadway show shops.

Thus, at one point during *Johnny Johnson*'s rehearsals, when a member of the company made a suggestion to the director about how to pep up the climax of a number that wasn't going over well, the director shut him up with "Don't come around here with your vaudeville tricks!"

Johnny Johnson—and *Cradle* as well—were conceived to adopt performing styles alien to what the public expected of musicals. It was the Group Theatre—progenitor of the American version of Stanislafsky known as "The Method"—that produced *Johnny Johnson*, so its cast would be not entertainers but human beings, startling in their honesty. The very word *musical* meant Ethel Merman, Bert Lahr, and a chorus of cute kids who were Very Happy All the Time. *Johnny Johnson*, however, follows the adventures of a shy and naive—really, an unformed—young man who enlists in World War I and, shell-shocked, tries to pacify the Allied generals with laughing gas. It's a grim but poignant work, a kind of screwball tragedy, for Paul Green—like Kurt Weill's next collaborator, Maxwell Anderson—was a playwright rather than a musical-comedy guy. Not knowing the form's rules, Green breaks them all, creating a musical unlike any other.

For his part, Weill was more or less fresh off the boat from Europe at this point, and, far more than in the succeeding *Knickerbocker Holiday*, *Johnny Johnson* luxuriated in the *Symphonie-mit-Jazz* sound-scape expected of an enfant terrible in Weimar Germany. This is deliciously creepy music; the prelude's first notes suggest an ethnic-cleansing roundup of innocents, and the score as a whole is so drastically imaginative that, watching the show unfold, one has no idea what the next number will be about—a mother confiding fey autobiographical arcana as she works at her sewing machine; an army captain singing a tango about a burglar and his entranced woman victim; the history of psychiatry outlined by a mad psychiatrist. Such surprises never occurred in other musicals, because standard libretto writing called for genre numbers, from love ballads to the New Dance Sensation, and the cues were blatant, as when college co-ed Flo sets up *Good News!*'s title tune:

FLO: I've had a dozen omens of good luck, so Good News *must*
    be on his way.

Johnny Johnson isn't a "title tune" kind of show, but it does have "Song of the Guns," as the muzzles of three huge cannons appear in the darkness of no-man's land, pushing forward over the heads of sleeping soldiers with a lullaby of death. The entire evening is like that: a musical about a nonconformist that must therefore be non-conformist itself.

Unfortunately, the Group, brilliant actors though they were, did not field the necessary vocal talent. Remember *Johnny Johnson*'s director a bit ago, snarking about "vaudeville tricks"? That was Lee Strasberg, a guru of acting naturalism but musically ignorant and professionally stubborn. Worse, the actress struggling with the song in question was his wife, Paula, and he was giving her no help whatsoever.

And that was *Johnny Johnson*: the most miscast musical in history. Are the intriguing musical satires bound to be this primitive, wary of Big Broadway's ritzy dexterity, its Dream Ballets (for art) and its chorus lines (for beauty)? Yet *Chicago*, arguably our most potent satire, will be the utmost in Big Broadway expertise, as the utmost Bob Fosse musical, exposing the fraud of razzle dazzle even as it revels in razzle dazzle. Because Fosse was Mr. Show Biz; but Fosse had edge.

The edgiest of all the commentative shows is *Johnny Johnson*'s evil twin, *The Cradle Will Rock*, also a product of the independent theatre community, though backed by the state, under one of President Roosevelt's safety nets for the arts, the Federal Theatre. *Johnny Johnson* is a piteous *Bildungsroman* mixed of the comic and the mournful, but *The Cradle Will Rock* is a *carmagnole*: Unionization or Revolution! And *Cradle*'s cast was another gang that didn't really sing, partly because the Federal Theatre's casting pool took in the lowest echelons of the professional acting ranks and a lot of hopeful amateurs as well. Though this is seldom mentioned today, the established Broadway community intensely resented this subsidy for rival productions while seasoned Broadway pros continued to suffer in a Depression economy.

That might be why Actors Equity forbade the *Cradle* cast from playing on a substitute stage when the production lost its theatre, because of *Cradle's* incendiary look at a Chicago-style confrontation of management versus labor in the fictional Steeltown, U.S.A. In a colorful switcheroo, the company found an empty playhouse and the actors defied Equity passive-aggressively by performing from seats in the auditorium in perhaps the most famous first night of all time.

Thus, *Cradle* flourishes in revival (as *Johnny Johnson* does not), as a historical tourist stop rather than as a beloved classic. It's a purposely off-kilter piece, for author Blitzstein uses stick figures, off-accents in the lyrics, and comic-book character names[3] in a stark scenario with irony rather than drollery and no dance numbers. Further, as the more or less original-cast 78s reveal, Orson Welles, the show's director, coached the decent characters to seem "normal" but Mr. Mister and his minions to overplay in caricature, giving the show a fantastical air even within its true and timeless look at how the rich buy their allies and enslave and murder everyone else. Oddly, Blitzstein, a lifelong Communist, saw this only in America, though in *Cradle's* 1937 this was exactly how Stalin was running Russia.

Actually, there is an entire Mister family, though Junior and Sister Mister are goons and Mrs. Mister is the sort of ditsy grande dame that *Face the Music's* Mary Boland played in Big Broadway outings and the movies. Blitzstein's dame's chauffeur-driven Pierce-Arrow plays a slight variation on the second theme of Beethoven's *Egmont* Overture (the strings' A flat major figure, at bar 82), and she collects creative talent. "Who says I haven't brought about a union of the arts?" she brags, meeting violinist Yasha and painter Dauber in *Cradle's* most comic scene. A medley of dialogue and songs, it starts with the two mens' duet "The Rich," revealing the sad paradox of arts philanthropists: they're "so damn low" and "far-fetched," but utterly necessary. Yasha and Dauber need even each other, because who else understands them? Blitzstein seethes under

3. Mr. Mister and Mrs. Mister run Steeltown through the intimidation of money power; their stooges among the opinion-makers take in Reverend Salvation, Editor Daily, and Dr. Specialist. The good guys bear more naturalistic names—Moll, Gus and Sadie Polock, Steve, and the union-organizer hero, Larry Foreman.

the jesting, however. When Mrs. Mister asks the pair to join her husband's euphemistically named Liberty Committee—"You will, won't you?" she asks, meaning "You'd better"—they're enthusiastic:

> MRS. MISTER: But don't you want to know what it's all about?
> YASHA: Politics?
> DAUBER: Cora, we're *artists*!

For perspective, consider Yasha and Dauber's counterparts in Richard Strauss' opera *Capriccio* (1942), the composer Flamand and the poet Olivier. They, too, are rivals for the attention of a powerful sponsor, the Countess, but, as the two men themselves put it, they are "loving enemies," "friendly opponents." *Capriccio* asks which opera values more, the music or the words, and while it never answers the question, it sees Flamand and Olivier bonded in a synergistic energy: the two arts are inseparable. Thus, composer and poet are bonded by the intelligence of music, the lyricism of poetry.

Yasha and Dauber, by comparison, aren't artists: they're money-grubbers exploiting music and painting. But of course *Capriccio* is "sacred" in tone and *Cradle* "profane." Opera treats nobility, beauty, passion. The satiric musical treats hypocrisy, egomania, greed. *Capriccio* longs for the harmony of art, while *Cradle* wants to teach its audience to recognize the damage a professional ruling class does to the ideal of a republic.

We have reached the early 1940s, which brings us to the next chapter in the *Chicago* epic, that of the Hollywood remake with Ginger Rogers. But let us first see how the newish form of "musical play," building on the breakaway worldviews of Green and Blitzstein, proceeds to the next step, in questioning some of the most deeply held beliefs of its public.

These include especially, one, love guarantees a good marriage, and, two, hard work guarantees a happy life. But Ian Marshall Fisher, who runs the Lost Musicals series in London, noticed that three American shows he revived, all from the late 1940s, seemed to be the first musicals to challenge these beliefs—to deflate, quite deliberately, middle-class ideals. Each of the three titles was an extremely creative endeavor, well out of the traditional formats, and each ran for a while but proved commercially disappointing and is seldom seen even today, in our age of rediscovery: Lerner and Loewe's *The Day Before Spring* (1945), Rodgers and Hammerstein's *Allegro* (1947), and Weill and Lerner's *Love Life* (1948).

All three are romantic-satiric pieces, one reason why they baffled some of their audience. *The Day Before Spring* tells women, You may have married the wrong man. *Allegro* tells men, You're going to be tricked into making choices that will wreck your happiness. *Love Life* tells both men and women, Modern Society will drive you crazy.

What do wives want from their husbands? The hot man? In *Spring*, he was played by Bill (later William) Johnson, a seductive baritone and so two-fisted that, years later, in a tour of *Kismet* with Zero Mostel as the Wazir, Johnson got so fed up with Mostel's comic ad libbing that he hauled off and decked him, right on stage. *Spring*'s heroine feared this guy's adventurism. Yes, he's exciting. But is he safe? Indeed, she had married a safe man, played by John Archer, a B-film Hollywood actor and the essence of humdrum. Now a college reunion brings her face to face with the hot man, and they run off together. The safe man overtakes them, and, in the ensuing argument, Archer hits on his own defense-of-marriage act by crying out that he needs his wife. He *needs* her.

What woman can resist that? But would she have been happier with the hot man? You never *do* know, because hot men need only themselves—and the musical has thus finally caught up with real life. *Johnny Johnson* and *The Cradle Will Rock* were fables. But these three forties musicals tell naturalistic stories containing psychological puzzles. Further, they were all artistically imaginative—*Spring* boasted choreography by ballet's Anthony Tudor and a bizarre interlude in which the heroine got advice from Plato, Voltaire, and Freud (with a Jewish accent). The Lerner and Loewe score was typical forties Broadway, from the bouncy waltz "This Is My Holiday" to the graceful boogie-woogie "A Jug of Wine, a Loaf of Bread, and Thou [baby]." Nevertheless, the narrative was unique, asking the eventually eight-times married Alan Jay Lerner's favorite question: how do we know whom to love?

The artistic choreography of the era enlivened also *Allegro*, in Agnes de Mille's stylizations of children's games, a college mixer (with a startling pas de deux by Annabelle Lyon, in toe shoes, and Harrison Muller, in taps), young wives roughing it on a tight household budget, and the neurotic helter-skelter of contemporary life. *Allegro* is famously the first Big Broadway musical without scenery, but there was actually a lot to look at—furniture pieces, two black traveler curtains (transparent and opaque, depending on the lighting), and back projections. The unique staging gives today's writers so much to describe they tend to miss how much *Allegro* devastates middle-class hopes. Here's a fine fellow, handsome and ethical and the son of a doctor, imbued with the doctor's wondrous healing mission. Yet somehow he ends up with a manipulative and unfaithful wife, nursing rich hypochondriacs.

Further risking the audience's discomfort, *Allegro*'s first act was romantic and its second act satiric. Romantic: the young doctor courts his bride-to-be in "You Are Never Away [from your home in my heart]" as the show's omniscient chorus sings along in an elaborate vocal arrangement and the girl herself dances. But she does not sing. Is *he* the only one who loves?

Satiric: as social leaders in our favorite location, Chicago, the couple gives At Homes, staged by de Mille with the ensemble crowded together in the center of the stage, singing, "Yatata, yatata" and mouthing eulogies of their empty activities.

Love Life, too, concerned a vexed marriage, here because of external pressures from an ever-changing environment that tests the bond of Sam (Ray Middleton) and Susan (Nanette Fabray) Cooper. It's money troubles, feminism, business, politics. By the second act, Sam and Susan, separated, were so confused about why their marriage failed that Weill and Lerner seemed confused themselves, because the story didn't end: the Coopers were last seen trying to reach each other from opposite ends of a tightrope. As we wonder if they will, the curtain falls and the show is over. Okay, but what happened?

Some of my readers may be reminded of Stephen Sondheim's *Company* (1970), and, indeed, this chapter is concerned with where satire fits into our complex modern musicals that psychoanalyze their characters while opening up a cultural perspective. They may even dare to quiz the evasions and pretensions of the audience— *Follies, Nine, Dreamgirls, A Doll's Life, Sunday in the Park With George, Marie Christine, Parade, Hamilton*. These mostly dark shows are not satires, no. On the contrary, even when they deal in part with comic irony and exaggeration, they are romantic, drawing us into a dream of reality.

Satire is the opposite: self-aware, didactic, Brechtian. It's heartless, and the closer we get to the musical *Chicago*, the more we will notice how its first two movie versions emotionalized Maurine Watkins, while the musical celebrates her caustic tone. What does Roxie utter as an exit line after she shoots Fred Casely (three times, no less)? "Good gracious, what have I done"? Or "I must call for an ambulance"? No:

ROXIE: I gotta pee.

Or think of this merry little snippet, between prison inmate June and the matron:

JUNE: If my husband, Wilbur, comes here . . . you tell him I do
   not want to see him.
MATRON: June, your husband is dead, you killed him.
JUNE: Oh well, forget it, then.

Or even this spoken bit in the "Cell Block Tango," as Liz recalls being exasperated at Bernie's habit of popping his chewing gum. She cautions him not to pop it again, he does, and she grabs the family shotgun to fire two warning shots:

LIZ: Into his head.[4]

4 The globally popular 1996 revival has given us many different performers as the killers, with many different ways of putting over their spoken solos in the "Cell Block Tango," but we often hear this line banged out defiantly. For the original production, however, Fosse had Cheryl Clark deliver it deadpan, apparently to show how nonchalant she *still* is about what she has done. In fact, *Chicago*'s guilty women never show the slightest sense of remorse or even ambivalence. He had it coming; now it's good.

Strange as it may sound, while the dark, commentative modern musical is as evolved as it could be from the musical's earliest days, the musical satire—and *Chicago* in particular—marks a return to proto-musical comedy. Remember, *The Beggar's Opera*, that mother of the musical, was a satire. Later, Jacques Offenbach, CEO of the French school, *opéra bouffe* (basically "joke opera"), was very influential in America with his "genre primitif et gai": silly, loony, irreverent, and sexy, as guiltless as a child and all but lawlessly free. Offenbach's musicals were fantastical, and satire, too, is fantastical—a war over cheese, an army private merrily anesthetizing warlords, a Pierce-Arrow playing Beethoven. Most of our classic titles are not fantastical—*Show Boat*, *Oklahoma!*, *My Fair Lady*, *A Chorus Line*. But *Chicago* is: silly, loony, irreverent, and sexy, in the Offenbach manner.

And *Chicago* is political as well, at least subtextually (as we'll see in due course). *Chicago* says the System is corrupt. And that would be because the Establishment is corrupt, and we can secure our freedom only by voting politicians out of office every generation. As Maxwell Anderson says, "Government must never be trusted."

But then Mark Twain responds with "If voting made any difference, they wouldn't let us do it." And Joseph Stalin tops Twain with "The people who cast the votes decide nothing. The people who count the votes decide everything."

6

cosmo

The Second Movie

*"I'm Going To Make a Character Man of You
If You Don't Behave Yourself"*

Darryl Zanuck, the head of Twentieth Century-Fox, had a recipe for the lighter A pictures, musicals and romantic comedies: a blond heroine and a tall, dark hero, with bright lighting and lots of festive screwballs in support. A Fox teaming was Alice Faye and Tyrone Power, or Betty Grable and John Payne, with assistance from sarcastic Patsy Kelly or Joan Davis; bumbling Andy Devine; the young Nicholas Brothers, arguably the best black dancers in Hollywood; lavish, high-kicking Charlotte Greenwood; and ineffable, even inexplicable Madame Sul-Te-Wan.

Maurine Watkins' play, with its large complement of press and law enforcement folk, would justify the format beautifully (especially once a romance could be established), and Alice Faye was to be the next Roxie Hart. Zanuck even planned to call the movie by her name, instantly losing the resonance of that laden word "Chicago." But then, Zanuck didn't want anything sociopolitical to complicate this project. It wasn't planned to be satire or—as with DeMille—a melodrama. It was going to be a romantic comedy.

However, Faye suddenly became pregnant and bowed out of film production for a time. So Zanuck turned to Ginger Rogers, freelancing after having spent the 1930s at RKO, most notably of course with Fred Astaire in a line of musicals by the best of Broadway—Vincent Youmans, Jerome Kern, Irving Berlin, the Gershwins—because the series' producer, Pandro S. Berman, had a thing for show tunes. Zanuck, too, liked musicals, because once you figured out how they work (exotic setting, bickering sweethearts, more of those eccentric shtick figures) they basically wrote themselves.

But *Roxie Hart* (1942) would not be a musical. That suited Rogers: she had embarked on an emphatically post-Astaire career as a serious actress. Unfortunately, *Roxie Hart*'s director, William A. Wellman, was good at coaching only men and self-starting women like Barbara Stanwyck and Ida Lupino. With women who were personality stars rather than actresses, Wellman was uncomfortable and insecure. In the World War I buddy film *Wings* (1927), Wellman gets great performances out of Richard Arlen and Buddy Rogers (billed under his Christian name as Charles). Arlen's death scene, as Rogers frantically clutches him, running his fingers through Arlen's hair and totally losing himself in his sorrow—for it was he who caused his friend's death—is shockingly good. Clara Bow, as Rogers' would-be girl friend, is also fine; she was another self-starter. But Jobyna Ralston, courted by both Arlen and Rogers, makes no impression, because Wellman didn't know what to do with her.

This is not to say that Wellman wasn't good at his job. On the contrary, I place him in the top echelon of Hollywood directors, above all in his command of the way striking visuals define the characters. But Wellman is largely unappreciated, mainly because movie critic Andrew Sarris was an idiot.

Let me explain. Sarris was the movie critic who popularized the European auteur theory in America, and Sarris got the theory completely wrong. *Bref*, it holds that the director is the author of a film because, in Europe but not in America, the director conceived, often co-wrote, and participated in the editing of a picture. He was its maker the way a sculptor makes a statue.

However, American movies in the studio age were manufactured on an assembly line, and directors frequently had nothing to do with conceiving a film, were very often (though not invariably) forbidden by the producer to collaborate on the script, and were cut off from the editing process.

Sarris never understood this, so he simply looked for "trademarks" of a director's style. "To be counted as an artist," said Sarris, "the director must exhibit certain recurrent characteristics of style." But this has nothing to do with the auteur theory, and, in any case, Sarris' idea of recurrent characteristics was reduced to noting that John Ford's westerns kept going on location to Monument Valley, Utah, because the rock formations are so picturesque, or that Raoul Walsh repeated in *High Sierra* a scene he had already shot in *Every Night At Eight*.

In other words, Sarris thought that the director who keeps doing the same thing over and over is an artist for that reason alone. A director like William Wellman, who regarded each next film assignment as a new experience, an adventure, baffled Sarris. In *The American Cinema*, Sarris rated directors in categories from "The Pantheon" down to "Miscellany." He placed Wellman under "Less Than Meets the Eye"—which, by the way, takes in also Elia Kazan, David Lean, Rouben Mamoulian, and Billy Wilder.

Sarris' book was unfortunately influential, especially because it came out in 1968, when the auteur theory was little known here; he misled a lot of readers. But let us take our own fresh look at Wellman's style, especially as it is very different from that of DeMille. First, Wellman is much pacier, and he vastly prefers snappy dialogue to the at times Biblical resonance with which DeMille was wont to narrate. Above all, Wellman is an artist of the kinetic, to the point of self-conscious arrangements, studies in motion, the artful physics of letting the camera *show* us the story.

For instance, at the start of *Wings*, Wellman catches Richard Arlen and Jobyna Ralston soaring through the air in a lawn swing: reckless, carefree youth. But now Buddy Rogers drives up in his hot rod, and Wellman shoots him rushing up between them, from the distance over the lawn and right up at one with them, literally coming between them—just as he does in the story itself.

Wings has many such touches, as in a famous tracking shot in a French nightclub, the camera roving over tables to take in, among other couples, two lesbians getting tender and a quarreling man and woman who throws her drink into his face. *Wings'* aerial photography of dog fights is still among the best of its kind, for Wellman had served in both the French and American Air Corps during the war. But Wellman does far more with his camera than recreate his battle memories. In *Wild Boys of the Road* (1933), he arranged a shot of Depression hobo kids leaping off a moving train that astonishes for its unity of the picturesque and the realistic as dozens of boys hurl themselves to earth in a shot so deep it seems to take in the entire train, or maybe the entire blasted American economy.

They called him "Wild Bill"—a nickname, his son William Jr. explained (in a Wellman documentary), that dated back to daredevil flying sorties when Wellman Sr. was in the Lafayette Escadrille. But Sr. was wild in Hollywood as well. When Ronald Colman (who habitually memorized the entire script of each film he made) kept mysteriously blowing his lines and ruining takes during Ida Lupino's big scene in *The Light That Failed* (1939), Wellman called a break and walked Colman out of others' hearing. In an interview conducted by Richard Schickel for *The Men Who Made the Movies*, Wellman recalled telling Colman, "Listen, you son of a bitch, I know what you're doing. . . . You've got a lovely face [but] I'm going to make a character man out of you if you don't behave yourself."

Colman knew he meant it, too; Wellman had actually taken on Darryl Zanuck in a fistfight. *Twice.* Putting together the man and his work, we sense a guy who is a strange combination of ballsy and poetic. Like Sinclair Lewis' Babbitt, he hides his soft side—and this personality guides his directing of movies. Wellman's pictures are masculine in tone, tough and determined. Yet they bear a wistful, wondering quality as well; it steals up on them.

Now, in filming Watkins' play, will Wellman adapt to the *Chicago* material or will *Chicago* have to adapt to Wellman? Is *Chicago* a woman's story or a man's story? The silent made it, almost, Amos' story: he owns all the feelings, and the action starts and ends with him. Yet Zanuck saw the property as a woman-star vehicle, so there might be a bit of tension between what Wellman will want to do and what Zanuck will expect him to do.

First, let's have a look at the blueprint, for Roxie Hart is very different from the *Chicagos* of Maurine Watkins and Cecil B. DeMille. For one thing, this third version obeys the First Rule of the Hollywood Diva in a Courtroom Drama: Be accused of murder, but innocent. (Yes, Bette Davis was guilty in *The Letter*. But Davis' middle name was Trouble.) For another, the entire film is told in flashback, and by one of those reporters again, though this one is idealistic, one Homer Howard:

> The present-day, 1942, narrative frame starts on a rainy night in a bar, where Homer recalls the wonder time of the 1920s. HOMER: "Everything was big. Big money, big crooks, big murders, big stories." He invokes the buzz terms of the decade, from Coolidge to Capone. And the Roxie Hart case was "all of them rolled into one." This bar-narrative will be renewed at intervals throughout the film.
>
> Sequence 1: In the Hart apartment, after the murder. Roxie says she's innocent, but Jake smells a story and persuades her to *seem* guilty to gain the notoriety that will launch her show-biz career.
>
> Sequence 2: In jail, Roxie has the same old fight (to a patronizing soundtrack of snarling cats) with Velma, in Society black with pearls and a grand-dame cigarette holder. The Matron calmly imposes peace by knocking their heads together.
>
> Sequence 3: Billy Flynn's office. Amos phones Roxie's parents out in the sticks, telling them she might be hanged. They don't care. ROXIE'S MOTHER (To Roxie's father, as she sews): "What did I tell you?"
>
> Sequence 4: A musical number: Roxie executes the "Black Bottom" (to the De Sylva, Brown, and Henderson music from *George White's Scandals of 1926*) dance for the reporters in the prison common room, and all join in, some of the pressmen in absurd variations. It's a Wellman touch: some communities are optimistic or venal or drab. This one—the press— is just nuts, because no one believes in anything. Homer, now youthful and thrilling in his vested suit, is the one exception. He gets close to Roxie in a Charleston.
>
> Sequence 5: "Two-Gun Gertie," a real tough, distracts the reporters, so Roxie fakes a pregnancy to regain fame control.
>
> Sequence 6: Flynn coaches Roxie in an anteroom of the courthouse, followed by the big set piece of the trial. As the jury is about to render its verdict, Wellman takes us outside, where a newspaper delivery truck

waits with bales of papers ready for sale, half headlined "ROXIE GUILTY" and half "ROXIE FREED." (This bit will be re-used in Rob Marshall's *Chicago* movie.) A bale is tossed to a newsboy: it's a "FREED" set, while, back in the courtroom, Roxie's victory lap is interrupted by gunshots. The cops are chasing Amos, who now confesses to the murder of Fred Casely.

The flashback frame ends as Homer, once more in his "aging" makeup, courtesy of the Acme Powder Company, leaves the bar to join his wife. It's Roxie! Also present are their five noisy kids, a real crowd in their tiny automobile. For the fadeout, a tender message from Roxie: "We're going to have to have a bigger car next year."

FADEOUT

Obviously, the *Roxie Hart* script, by Nunnally Johnson (amended by an uncredited Ben Hecht, whom we remember as a veteran of the Chicago press corps), is much closer to the *Chicago* play than DeMille's version was. Johnson even uses many of Watkins' original lines. He also brings back Mary Sunshine, though he transforms Jake Callahan from Watkins' young cynic into a middle-aged nihilist. Something of a low-key Lee Tracy, this Jake is an old pro of the oldest profession. He even sounds like a Tracy character, reducing everything to a cliché of itself. "Joe the jerk defends the little nest," he reports in a phone call to his paper about the murder, "while his flapper wife is out mooning over [movie star] John Gilbert."

But then, as the blueprint above reveals, this edition of the *Chicago* material introduces a new reporter figure, to supply a romance with the heroine, for now that Roxie is going to be innocent of murder, she has the movie star's right to a sweetheart. Further, by naming him Homer Howard, the studio clearly sees him as sedate and corny, a foil to Roxie's avid theatricalizing, her volatility, her habit of physically head-butting anyone who thwarts her will. The 1920s are over and the nation is at war; women aren't supposed to be wild anymore, as Roxie was when Maurine Watkins thought the character up. Wild is for the battlefield, not the home front, and *Roxie Hart* is very much a film of its era. Throughout the continuity, we have the feeling that once Roxie and Homer unite, he is going to convert her to homemaking and other bourgeois pieties.

This is a deviation from how the various *Chicagos* look at Roxie's character, because here, for the first and only time, she is not a sociopath. True, she's still brusque and insolent, and especially contemptuous of Amos. But she isn't a walking con job. Previously, Roxies wanted to get off even though they were guilty. This Roxie wants to get off because she's innocent—she has agreed to let the press and the law paint her as a murderess only to become notorious and thus break into show business.

And therein lies *Roxie Hart*'s most significant deviation, the first linking of crime and show biz that will prove so potent in the *Chicago* musical. Even *Roxie Hart*'s murder victim becomes part of this. He's still called Fred Casely, but now he is—was, rather, as he is dead before the narrative starts—half of a talent agency that Roxie has been cozying up to. This brings in another character new to *Chicago*, Casely's partner, one E. Clay Benham, who for unknown reasons is English, rather hifalutin in manner while retaining the residue of a Cockney accent.

Such a role cried out for Nigel Bruce, a real-life Englishman and a specialist in roles ranging from Dr. Watson to various stuttering lords and vacant colonels. (Coincidentally, Bruce starred in the aforementioned Noël Coward play, *This Was a Man*, whose failure gave Francine Larrimore her springboard into the *Chicago* play, back in 1926.) In Bruce's hands, E. Clay Benham is so flavorsome it weakens the movie that he has only one scene. But the character does set up that all-important view that there is only one kind of fame in America, so it doesn't matter whether one attains it through performing talent, athletic achievement, scandal, or crime.

This was a theme especially prevalent in the early thirties talkies, where (at Warner Bros. in particular) gangsters were often paired with singers and showgirls and where outlaws' sidekicks could be hoofers who would smarten up and return to dancing before the fadeout. When Woody Allen's *Bullets Over Broadway* shows a play going up simply because a bad guy has a girl friend with acting ambitions, Allen is in effect making an hommage—and many were those who believed that, when capitalization money got tight in the Depression, only bootleggers were wealthy enough to back a big musical show. It happened to Ziegfeld: all New York knew that his last new title, *Hot-Cha!* (1932) was financed by the underworld.

Thus it seemed logical that James Cagney and George Raft, though maintaining IDs as hooligans, were also stylish dancers. And in a typical early talkie, *Broadway Thru a Keyhole* (1933), Paul Kelly played a gangster lending his protection to a sweet young dancer but finally giving her up to the singer she loves—a plot lifted from the headlines about, respectively, Larry Fay, Ruby Keeler, and Al Jolson. Crime and show business: even stranger yet, in his real life Kelly beat to death the husband of the woman he was adulterously involved with. (He got off lightly, doing two years for manslaughter; the woman in the case did time as well.)

It was as though *Roxie Hart* saw crime and entertainment as equals right from the moment Darryl Zanuck put the story into rotation as an Alice Faye vehicle, for Faye was always playing performers. *Roxie Hart* isn't a musical, but it does contain two samples of the heroine's dancing prowess, first that jailhouse "Black Bottom" and then an unaccompanied tap rhythm solo Roxie playfully executes for Homer alone.

Bob Fosse liked the notion of a performing Roxie, and of course he was building the character for Broadway's greatest dancer anyway. However, Fosse's Roxie was not going to be accomplished. He envisioned a finale for her and Velma that would be the apocalypse of terrible. But Hollywood plays by different rules; movies need to fulfill fans' expectations, and Rogers, despite a new pivot in her career toward dramatic roles, had ingratiated herself in musicals. After all, she danced with Astaire. Technically, she hadn't been his greatest partner, but they were radiant together, so now that Roxie was to be reinvented as stagestruck, she had to be given her, so to say, Ginger Rogers moments.

So Roxie, in her third incarnation, is suddenly new to us. She's still rather tawdry as a human being, but at least she isn't a killer. When Nigel Bruce talks up her incipient career, he speaks of "cabarets," "personal appearances," "radio." Not theatre or the movies, we notice. They would be too glamorous.

Otherwise, Zanuck gave Rogers the Queen of the Lot treatment, mainly in her costumes, which were all too stylish for the taste and budget of someone like Roxie. Her first outfit, a stunning black-and-white playsuit with a fluffy blouse over suspendered short trousers and kiss-me-quick net stockings and black heels, shows off Rogers' ample bosom. Still, it's too obviously a Hollywood creation, the kind of thing that looks great in the PR stills but throws the characterization off. The one constant in the *Chicago* saga is that its heroine—whether in her guilty or innocent version—is a dumb jerk. But wartime Hollywood wasn't eager to celebrate dumb jerks. And while Zanuck had no reason to build Rogers (as, again, she was freelancing among the studios), dressing the woman lead in your movie supplies tone.

One egregious problem is Rogers' wig, a kinky monster probably designed to underline Roxie's low idea of chic. But it's distracting, like Barbra Streisand's afro in her Jon Peters phase. Even worse is Rogers' relentless gun-chewing and touching her hand to her hair, something Roxie must have seen in a movie. One wonders if the incessant gum-play was William Wellman's plan to stabilize the portrayal of an actress who was not independent enough to work out her own arc.

It's not that Rogers was wrong for the role. On the contrary, she was very natural as a kind of classless proletarian, not of the bourgeoisie yet not exactly of the masses, either. Further, Rogers could alter her social class at will (within certain limits; she wouldn't have made a plausible aristocrat). Still, one wonders what *Roxie Hart* would have been like with Barbara Stanwyck, as Wellman loved working with her, and Stanwyck would have guided the spectator through Roxie's thought processes as well as anyone, from Carole Lombard to Bette Trouble Davis.

But Stanwyck would have radiated intelligence, while Roxie must seem no more than peasant-shrewd. Some actors cannot bunt away their innate intelligence—Rosalind Russell and Angela Lansbury, for instance. Some others know how to assume a lack of awareness, letting the camera rather than their line delivery define them. That's why Rogers was so useful as a movie star. She's not an actress. She doesn't try to persuade you, inform you. She lets you watch her.

Thus, the "Black Bottom" dance scene isn't her ploy to ingratiate herself with the press. It is they who lure her into it, Jake bringing it up and the others urging Roxie on:

ROGERS: (fake hesitant, as she reckons the percentage: something meek and prim, or all-the-way Salome?) You don't think it might be what you call...(a dismissive gesture)... out of place?

Oh, pooh. She and they know it's going to happen, and, in the event, Hermes Pan's choreography is just coarse and repetitive enough for Roxie to think it a stunner.

And it is, in a way, because this is the only time in the whole film when Roxie shows us what she *thinks* she is: not a killer but a dancer. She has no talent, but that's the point. This isn't a Ziegfeld tale in which Sally starts with a Joan of Arc Wanting Song and ends starring in the *Follies*. Rather, this is the story of a nobody with nothing to offer except her looks.

Wellman bases his best fadeout on this idea, when the newsmen first photograph her at the murder scene, with her husband, surveying the corpse on the floor. (It's Jake, filling in.) Lift your hemline, Roxie, and show your knees. That's how they'll know you. Rogers eagerly strikes a pose, extending her necklace of dime-store beads and putting on a hot-tamale smile. She's ready for fame but wrong for it; all that the newshounds care about is how much skin she shows. They cry out as one, "*The knees, Roxie! The knees!*" Forget the meaning of anything: sex is the meaning, which is why Bob Fosse was so eager to get the rights to Maurine Watkins' play. He, too, thought sex is the meaning. Isn't that what show biz has always been about?

The rest of *Roxie Hart*'s cast is much better than the support in DeMille's silent. A classic towering male pin-up in the Zanuck mode, George Montgomery never threatens to seize camera control from the star (as Fox's Tyrone Power or John Payne might have done). He has his charms, though, and it's fun to watch him Acting in the many flashback-frame vignettes. Like Rogers, he lets the visuals do most of the work.

Notably, he is the only character in all the versions of *Chicago* to play a Boy Meets Girl with Roxie—the silent's Victor Varconi, of course, is already married to her when the movie begins. It's understandable that Zanuck wanted an old-fashioned courtship romance, particularly in the conservative wartime 1940s. Still, it domesticates Roxie, a figure destined to become one of the musical's great protagonists, like Madam Rose or Harold Hill—the extraordinary character that a great musical dotes on.

As for the lawyer, William Wellman would quite naturally have concentrated his coaching on Adolphe Menjou's Billy Flynn, because this director always responded to the characters who drive the action. And this particular Billy Flynn is much more overtly a plot shaper than his silent predecessor, almost athletically so. It's the perfect Menjou role, too—it would have to be, as he never played anything else: a man of the world, suave yet also blustery and impatient, eager to cut through blather and make the point.

His most typical moment cuts in at one of Watkins' best aperçus about how Chicago criminal law works, a passage so essential that every *Chicago* uses it except the silent (and only because title cards don't run long enough to accommodate all the words). It occurs when Amos has to fork over Flynn's fee of five thousand dollars. Amos doesn't have that kind of money, so he offers to raise dribs and drabs here and there—but Flynn cuts him off. Here's the original version in Watkins' words:

> FLYNN: When you came to me yesterday I didn't say, "Is she innocent, is she guilty?"...No. I said: "Have you got five thousand dollars?"

Of course, every defendant must have legal representation. However, Flynn isn't invoking a sacred absolute of jurisprudence. He's a twenties salesman eager to hawk ware without commitment to the quality of the product.

And Menjou really has this guy's number. His Flynn isn't pompous (as Robert Edeson is in the silent). Nor is he a slippery shyster. This is no ten-dollar whore. This is a five-thousand-dollar whore, smart, resourceful, imaginative. Menjou's comic timing is hurried and volatile, to match Wellman's farcical tempo, as when Ginger Rogers, in her bouquet-crammed jail cell, tells Menjou that she's innocent:

MENJOU: (mildly stunned) You didn't do it? (but moving right along:) Oh, well, then I'm not sure that I'm the man for the job.

Uh oh. A *Follies* girl losing her Ziegfeld, Roxie quickly withdraws the statement:

MENJOU: That's all right, I'll keep it in mind in case of emergency.

But let's get our stories straight. Roxie and the late Mr. Casely both "grabbed for the gun," and:

ROXIE: Everything went purple.
MENJOU: (*What*?) Purple?
ROXIE: (Maybe she went too far) Black? White? Red?
MENJOU: (No, he likes it) Purple's good—it's new.

Wellman's vigorous Flynn makes Menjou almost Rogers' co-star. The Amos, however, played by George Chandler, returns us to Watkins' original conception of a powerless stooge. True, he does pull off one self-defining stunt: it is he who has killed Fred Casely.

Chandler was a Wellman regular, so much so that the two of them worked out a conspiratorial field expedient: whenever Wellman was stumped on the set and needed thinking time, he would subtly signal Chandler, who would then goof up in some way and provoke a feigned tantrum from Wellman and a furious "Take five!" to clear the set. By the time cast and crew returned, Wellman had figured out how to shoot the scene.

Some other cast members were dependable "type" players— Spring Byington as Mary Sunshine, Lynne Overman as Jake, Sara Allgood (born for great things in the Irish theatre, but willing to go Hollywood in starchy-spinster parts) as the Matron. Phil Silvers, a Fox stalwart in musicals and comedies and well ahead of his Broadway stardom, is very much the transplanted burlesque comic as Babe, the press photographer, a holdover role from the play.

But the very little known Helene Reynolds, as Velma (here surnamed Wall; the "Kelly" was invented for the musical), is somewhat unexpected, not just another prison inmate but very much Watkins' Society grandee. Reynolds generally played la-di-das because she actually was one, the offspring of a distinguished family and at one time the wife of a Reynolds Tobacco heir, and she has the look and the voice down cold.

Oddly, the most recognizable of the supporting people—really, one of the most famous faces in show-biz history—has relatively little to do. He's O'Malley, the proprietor of the bar in the flashback frame. (Actually, the sign out front reads "Cafe," and Wellman does glance at a side room of empty tables. Still, the atmosphere is that of a strictly stag hangout of smoke and drink.) Although George Montgomery seems eager to tell his colleagues (one of whom, playing Montgomery's buddy, is a very young and unbilled Hugh Downs) all about Roxie, it is the barkeep who constantly prods Montgomery to go on, to expand, to explain. And as O'Malley does so, he reveals that he is strangely familiar with the story. Indeed, he then turns up in the trial as a prominent member of the jury.

The actor playing O'Malley is William Frawley, immortally known as Fred Mertz of *I Love Lucy*. Frawley was notoriously disagreeable to work with, yet, onscreen, he was always a pleasantly bemusing presence as a babbitt with a Mona Lisa smile and bizarrely unengaged line readings. He's almost mysterious; one has the notion that it was he who arranged for the rainstorm that waylays Montgomery and his fellow reporters, thus enabling the flashback in the first place.

As for William Wellman's contribution, *Roxie Hart* is the better for it, but it is not one of his great pictures. To be fair, that list takes in not only *Wings* but the 1937 *A Star Is Born*, *Nothing Sacred*, and *The Ox-Bow Incident*. What Wellman brings to *Roxie Hart* above all is his characteristic sense of tempo—the running time is only seventy-four minutes, yet there's enough plot material for a two-hour special. There is the Ginger Rogers problem, admittedly, for whenever a woman star hit the set with her entourage of hair, makeup, and costume technicians in grand fuss, Wellman's inspiration would turn into exasperation. He was an "It's not your looks but what you do with them" artist, while Rogers, again, was an "It's your looks" artist.

Luckily, the supporting players were all self-starters, so Wellman could concentrate on angling the shots and guiding Adolphe Menjou in supplying the story energy that keeps the movie *moving*. Wellman loves tumults; his best scenes here are, one, all the press people mooching around while Phil Silvers takes the photographs at the murder scene; two, the "Black Bottom," which comes off as a kind of amateur-hour production number; and, three, the trial.

The last is Wellman's big set piece, the entire event unfolding as a performance—not a trial with stagey elements but a theatrical production in every detail, with entrances, memorized dialogue, "business" (again, the old term for "shtick"), and tons of photographers as if at a picture call for a show. The judge even gets star applause when he enters the courtroom. (He also, amusingly, rises with a photogenically judicial air to get in on every picture taken of witnesses on the stand.) Then, too, we see Menjou mouthing Roxie's words when she speaks—it's script—and then accusing Amos and the prosecutor together of preparing a "performance":

PROSECUTOR: I resent that implication—
MENJOU: Well, if the witness needs more rehearsal...

To top all this, Menjou picks a fight with the prosecutor and throws off his coat as if to do battle even as he murmurs, to a cop behind him, "C'mon, Mike," meaning "Hold me back!"

One thing Wellman's version doesn't have is the Chicago thing. Though Jake at one point praises his town in pure Watkinsese as "the city of opportunity," and though we hear Fred Fisher's song "Chicago (That Toddlin' Town)" on the soundtrack, the picture could be taking place in almost any big American city. Thus, the Chicago narrative in general has by this time traveled quite some distance from the 1926 play. First, the silent all but expunged Maurine Watkins' use of Chicago in synecdoche as a symbol of American culture, populated by babbitts and run by salesmen. Then the talkie dropped even the selling of a murderess as an innocent except as a kind of technicality: because she *was* innocent.

Now comes the turn of the musical, which will swing the action back to what Watkins had in mind. This is partly because the Sondheim-era show could handle irony with ease and partly because, as I've said, Fosse had edge. He had as well access to the ideal Roxie Hart. And he understood that Watkins was saying that everything in American life conduces to show business. This harmonized with Fosse's own view of things, because everything in Bob Fosse's life conduced to show business.

One might call Fosse's *Chicago* a consummation of the musical satire, a work that, quite simply, could not possibly have appeared earlier than it did. *Allegro* and *Love Life* had to invent the concept musical first. *Cabaret* had to perfect it. *Company* had to habilitate the notion of a free and open acting space, to allow for a cinematic flow of images. By the mid-1970s, at last, Broadway was ready for *Chicago*.

But then, Bob Fosse always did have perfect timing.

7

❧

Fosse & Verdon and Kander & Ebb

"You Have To Act Your Dancing"

Bob Fosse (a Chicago native, as it happens) hit Broadway at just the right moment. A chorus dancer in the late 1940s and a Hollywood featured player in the early-middle 1950s, he burst through as a choreographer back in New York for *The Pajama Game* (1954), *Damn Yankees* (1955), and *Bells Are Ringing* (1956). The musical was just then in its utter prime after various revolutions had refined it. *Show Boat*: powerful story content. *Porgy and Bess*: emotional intensity. *Pal Joey*: bluntly sexual concerns. *Oklahoma!*: unique character conflict.

And *Allegro* again: the director-choreographer, in Agnes de Mille, the niece of our own Cecil B. DeMille (and the bearer of the more orthodox spelling of the family name). There had been director-choreographers around 1900, but the dancing was a series of pat routines and the direction mere traffic management. Not till the Rodgers and Hammerstein era, starting in the 1940s, were both dance and narrative content advanced enough in the musical generally to need the high-maestro artistry of one person's unifying vision.

There is this as well: with conflicted heroes and heroines to deal with and thematic throughlines to maintain, it was artistically clumsy for the director to stage a book scene and the choreographer then to step in and stage the ensuing musical number. The scene generated the number; the number completed the scene. The two were no longer separate, so choreographers had begun to stage the scene as well as the number, so that dialogue and music cohere.

Thus, the choreographer already *was* the director—especially because he or she, more than the director, was at one with the music. A show's book tells us what the characters are doing, but its score tells us how they feel, and the feelings are more essential: they guide the audience into the heart of a piece. This is most obvious in the musical play, as when, in *The King and I*, a captivating delivery of "Hello, Young Lovers" prepares us for the climactic confrontation between Anna and the King over Tuptim, a young lover whose crime is to care for the "wrong" man.

However, this construct is important also in the more frivolous form of musical comedy, as when director-choreographer Michael Kidd developed a way of moving *Li'l Abner's* hillbillies that blended its book scenes, musical scenes, and dances till a conventional (if delightfully picturesque) show came off as a dynamic treatise on a sub-culture of American life. A satire on post-war America, from The Corporation to bodybuilding, *Li'l Abner* based its individuality on not an unusual score but unusual kinetics: a kind of roughhouse ballet that filled the theatre with idiot joy, looking at modern America from the standpoint of folks living on its margins. And of course, everything they see, from national politics to eugenics, looks screwy to them. Thus, the supervision of the director-choreographer contributed to the development of the commentative musical.

Amid a pride of imaginative choreographers taking charge of shows all but obsessed with dance, Fosse stood out for his style, a reproportioning of the body into a grimly grinning puppet figure with all its joints broken, accessorized with a derby and those ever inveigling finger snaps. A generation earlier, Fosse would have been hounded from the business for the overt eroticism that oozed out of his dances. He was the musical in its post-innocence phase: shows such as *Lady, Be Good!* and *Good News!* were the Garden of Eden, and Fosse was the snake (a role he actually played, in the film of *The Little Prince*).

By the 1950s, the musical was ready for his sexual gamesmanship, especially after he worked his way in with very characteristic yet all the same audience-friendly dance, in the "Steam Heat" trio in *The Pajama Game* and the "Shoeless Joe from Hannibal, Mo." baseball players' number in *Damn Yankees*. "Steam Heat" is all about those derbies of his, and the dancers moving across the floor on their knees, and—in lieu of finger snaps—tongue clicks. The song itself sounds like a novelty pop hit rather than Broadway, and Fosse gave it a jazzy buzz, a moment when the show's narrative is set aside for some guiltless pleasure. And "Shoeless Joe" catches the athlete's braggy strut, with his chewing gum and the showy placement of his mitt for an inside catch. It was all rather wholesome and spoofy.

But the next show with Fosse choreography, *New Girl in Town* (1957), wasn't. Based on Eugene O'Neill's *Anna Christie*, it told of a prostitute pursuing a new and free life while fighting off yet more possessive men—her father and her rough seaman sweetheart. Over it all loomed "Dat ole davil, sea!," as the father constantly phrases it, in the O'Neillian repetition that serves as a kind of closing line of a poetic strophe.

George Abbott was to adapt and direct the script, using a great deal of the 1921 play (while dropping O'Neill's verbal tics). The plan was to create a serious musical play rather than Abbott's home format, slambang musical comedy. So Anna would be a strong singing actress.

Verdon wanted a shot at the part, even if her smoky (yet endearing) baritone and lack of genuine acting experience made her unsuitable. But the show's producers, the firm of Brisson, Griffith, and (Harold S., our favorite Sondheim collaborator, Hal) Prince had a strong record that included *Damn Yankees*, which featured Fosse and Verdon at their best. So they knew how well a Fosse-led Verdon addressed the public and what a draw she would be.

Still, Abbott thought of Verdon as a "dancer"—meaning, in his case, a decorative empty-head, and, with his vast track record in the making of musicals, he knew that a Verdon musical would of necessity end up as a dance musical, to avoid disappointing the public. Abbott did let her audition, for which she prepped with acting lessons from Sanford Meisner; obviously, she saw *New Girl in Town* as her breakaway.

But it was Abbott's as well, for he had had only one try at a partly dark musical, inconclusively at that, in *A Tree Grows in Brooklyn* (1951). The *Anna Christie* project was supposed to be a dramatic slab of song theatre, to be billed as "a new musical," in a fifties usage designed to herald a show with powerful story content. "A musical comedy," Abbott told the *Herald Tribune*, "implies a kind of [*Ziegfeld*] *Follies* atmosphere," whereas some shows were "serious." Missing his own point, Abbott offered as examples *Pal Joey* and *Carousel*. The latter is serious, of course. But *Pal Joey* is pure musical comedy, for all its adult content. It's worldly and realistic, but it's also a leggs-and-laffs piece from start to finish. At most, it's a fun show with an obnoxious hero.

And *New Girl in Town* was a gloomy show with a troubled heroine. Bob Merrill's rather upbeat score did not venture all that deeply into O'Neill's problem play, but the real drawback was Abbott. His book followed the doings of too many nonentities, and O'Neill's pungent waterfront atmosphere got watered down to silly filler lines like this one:

ALDERMAN (to a sailor): And you can become a member of the
   Young People's Democratic Club.

In fact, Abbott—so adept in comedy, as with the 1926 *Chicago*—was boxing above his weight in the challenge of a serious musical. He ruined *New Girl in Town* just as he had ruined *A Tree Grows in Brooklyn*, splicing too much musical-comedy wiring into a musical play. Nor could he direct O'Neill's psychological character interplay. As Verdon recalled in Dennis McGovern and Deborah Grace Winer's interviews-with-actors book *Sing Out, Louise!*, Abbott didn't discuss character analysis with actors: "He could never find a way to make me understand what I was doing. . . . He'd tell you where to go [on stage] like he was a traffic cop."

But Verdon knew there was more to storytelling than blocking and the timing of the laugh lines. And it wasn't just the book scenes that needed sensitive coaching. In 1975, during the *Chicago* run, on *The Mike Douglas Show* (of all places), Verdon said, "You have to act your dancing." Characterization coursed through a show, in the dialogue, the songs, the choreography.

But Abbott thought of characters as types, their self-expression pre-fabricated, as if the musical were still working the flapper, the sheik, the raucous comic. However, O'Neill's Anna, like all his great inventions, was typeless, richer than what the Abbott formula could handle. One of the most famous Abbott tales finds him telling an actor to cross left after his line. The actor asks what his motivation for moving is. "Your paycheck," Abbott replies.[1]

Abbott did know enough to retain almost intact O'Neill's best lines, as when Anna meets up with her father's old wreck of a girl friend, Marthy (played by Thelma Ritter), a scene immortalized in MGM's early talkie, with Greta Garbo and Marie Dressler:

MARTHY: I got your number the minute you set foot in that door.

ANNA: I got yours, too. You're me forty years from now.

Garbo puts it over with a light touch, but Verdon made it bitter, and I still remember, as a child, how nervously the audience reacted. It's a bit of a laugh cue, really, yet Verdon was laying down the exposition of her portrayal: as an abused young woman whose bluntness betrays a lack of interest in pleasing anyone anymore. Still dressed in the streetwalker's flamboyant style (her entrance was a shock; the public gasped), Verdon presented Anna in the limbo between hell and more hell. As she gradually accustomed herself to her new life, always dreading that her boy friend would find out about her past, Verdon created something special, naturalized yet captivatingly special. Strong actors are common in the musical today; they weren't in the 1950s. Especially not when they are thought to be one of those decorative empty-heads.

Exasperated by Abbott's superficial direction, Fosse and Verdon sought ways to choreograph Anna's "between two worlds" existence:

---

1. Abbott denied saying it, but in *Sing Out, Louise!* Verdon remembers hearing him utter those words to Stephen Douglass, on *Damn Yankees.*

her sunny yet anxious new life and her terrible old one. The first was easy: a production number at the neighborhood ball, closing with the company in a kick line way downstage, Anna in bliss as the belle of New York: a stupendous "last shot" as the curtain came down on Act One. When it rose after the intermission, everyone was exactly where he or she had been when last seen, still in the kick line, in one of those rabbit-out-of-the-hat touches that rivaled even Jerome Robbins, by near-unanimous acclaim the greatest of the director-choreographers.

But then Fosse styled that other Anna, the one with the sordid past, in a louche dance set in a bawdyhouse, needling and deliberately offensive. It marked a wholly new Fosse style, one that theatregoers were not ready for. Verdon, too, was reinventing herself. Her Eve in Can-Can's "Garden of Eden Ballet" four years earlier had been erotic but playful. Suddenly, Fosse and Verdon were treating the underside of sex in a way the musical had never done before, looking into how much of Anna's prostitution was hateful and how much helplessly accommodating. This was something even George Abbott couldn't take away from her: using dance to prove she could act.

Spurned by her sweetheart when Marthy tells him of Anna's background, Anna sang a lament, "If That Was Love [it hurts an awful lot]," and the stage cleared save for a few chairs and a huge staircase in one of the last of the Dream Ballets, a Broadway fixture since The Band Wagon, in the early 1930s. As Anna saw it, a Masher (dancer John Aristides) from an earlier book scene now became Anna's customer; the published text says only that the dance climaxed as he carried Anna up the stairs "to the derisive laughter" of the other bordello girls.

Fosse biographer Sam Wasson did some interviewing to reconstruct this central artifact of Fosse-Verdon style, noting first of all that it supplied what was missing from Abbott's New Girl in Town script: a physical delineation of the revulsion dominating Anna's interactions with men. On the 46th Street Theatre's great open stage—"in sharp contrast," says Wasson, to the "colorful Victorian" look of the rest of the production—Fosse gave a show with too little personality its definitive moment. The prostitutes perched on their chairs spared the public nothing in the depiction of eros for sale, though there was some comedy, too. Young Harvey Evans played a guy on what appeared to be his first "date," so turned on by Verdon that his entire body went hard, from his foot up his leg, shaking as it rose. Later, Verdon's "backward dive off the top of the stairs into [Aristides'] arms," Wasson reports, led to "a sexy pas de deux," after which came the aforementioned visual coup as Aristides slung Verdon over his back and carried her up to their passion suite while the music wailed and thundered to its conclusion.

Too soon. It was simply too soon in the musical's history to expect the public to accept something so honest, and the reception, once tryouts began, in New Haven, was icy. Abbott, who had okayed the ballet in rehearsal, now wanted it cut. However, to Fosse and Verdon the ballet *was* their *New Girl in Town*. Without it, the show was a mediocrity in which all sorts of uninteresting people kept singing about odds and ends—"Roll Yer Socks Up," "Flings," "Chess and Checkers," numbers that had nothing to do with the story.

The score, Bob Merrill's first for Broadway, was certainly tuneful, and he did justify the four lead characters, especially in a startlingly rabid autobiographical number for Anna, "On the Farm," so outspoken that the final line had to be euphemized for the cast album, from "vicious sons of bitches" to "lecherous, treacherous cousins." It must have greatly irritated Fosse and Verdon that Abbott, so magisterial in his direction yet so inept at getting at the heart of the story, was now demanding that they delete the ballet—the one piece of the show with an intensity to match that of O'Neill, albeit in highly different language. Fosse and Verdon, said Abbott in his memoirs, "fought for it like tigers," and while Abbott allowed Fosse to retain it in a revision, the director felt it was still "the same old peep show."

Indeed, after the New York opening, Fosse redrilled the dancers to put the ballet back into its original form. And he never let go of his anger at how Abbott and the three producers—yes, including the later courageously nonconformist Prince—forced him to compromise artistically. It was yet another reason why a choreographer needed to become director as well: to be so powerful that every show would fulfill his conception without interference. Nobody told Jerome Robbins to change a ballet; Robbins could override even Leonard Bernstein. And when David Merrick would show up out of town to tyrannize Gower Champion, the latter simply vanished from the scene till Merrick departed.

Still, *New Girl in Town* cemented the Fosse-Verdon partnership. Compared with other musicals drawn from interesting plays—*Carousel*, say, or *Street Scene*—*New Girl* was a misfire. Yet it was a commercial hit, because of Fosse and Verdon (and Thelma Ritter), and it showed them how they could revolutionize the musical with an honesty about the rough edges of life that the musical didn't know it could have. This was a personal matter as well: "Gwen and Fosse were so, so in love," Hal Prince told Sam Wasson, "it was almost dangerous." Because they could fight as lavishly as they loved, digging away at each other's weaknesses even as they affirmed each other's ambitions—a seemingly random provocation might sour their affair for a week. This may be why they put off marrying till 1960, after they had done three shows together.

So Verdon had hit Broadway at just the right moment, too, not only to partner with Bob Fosse (after some years with Jack Cole, at the time the leading exponent of "jazz" dancing in the musical) but because the firm of Fosse and Verdon could build a business revising the musical's oldest element: the heroine.

The key quality here was versatility—acting, singing, dancing. Establishing the three talents as, in effect, a single gift meant writers could create shows enlarging the leading woman's presence, and it couldn't have happened before Verdon. Marilyn Miller was versatile as the 1920s understood the term, but there was no acting in twenties musicals as we know acting today. Acting was reading lines, not shaping a character arc. Among other major woman stars, Gertrude Lawrence was versatile but mannered, and she was a dance faker, as they were called: able to move well but not proficient. Mary Martin was similarly limited, and Ethel Merman wasn't versatile.

Verdon was not only versatile: her revolution started so early that, for a time, she was more or less irreplaceable. On a small-scale *New Girl in Town* tour with Joan Blondell starred as Marthy, Evelyn

Ward featured as Anna, and some of the Broadway cast, a dance double had to play Anna in the ballet (opposite John Aristides again), as if no one but Verdon could encompass all the facets of a musico-dramatic lead who also dances.

One might say that, from this point on, *Chicago* was Fosse and Verdon's destiny. And they knew it, because they were among those trying to get Maurine Watkins to agree to an adaptation. They knew as well that it was Fosse's lot to showrun all of Verdon's musicals even as he worked on other titles without her, because at least then she wouldn't have to work with George Abbott anymore.

No one knew it at the time, but Abbott's production style was in eclipse. After three decades and an almost unbroken string of smash hits, Abbott hit a slump in the mid-1960s: his last three new musicals were bombs, because the form is protean while Abbott was conservative, focused on technique at the expense of content. Fosse may not have been a great actor's director; there was a lot of variation in how he coached his people, depending on everything from how he liked you to how good the sex had been the night before. But he understood and sympathized with Verdon's ambitions—and a lot lies in that understanding. People who really "get" us are so rare that we meet only two or three of them in our lives. Yet without them we feel isolated. Thus, an artist who gets another artist—in a love match, at that—becomes a very compelling presence in his or her life.

So even though the next Fosse-Verdon shows, the twee *Redhead* (1959) and the earthy *Sweet Charity* (1966), were not acting challenges, Verdon approached their respective narratives with an honesty beyond their apparent worth. She could have coasted on her charm, her husky once-in-a-century voice, and above all her dancing, but Verdon wanted to *realize* the characters she played, to fill the empty head of the musical-comedy decoration. She was a Mrs. Anna talent in Reno Sweeney looks. George Abbott himself, in his memoirs, called her a "magnificent actress."

This made Verdon extremely influential, because a newly elaborated acting style was beginning to inhere in the musical as never before. Merman's Madam Rose and Alfred Drake's Kean (in the eponymous musical about the early-nineteenth-century English actor), coming shortly after *New Girl in Town*, helped habilitate this new thespian depth, especially as both Merman and Drake had theretofore been known for colorful yet thin portrayals, she hurling her lines at the public without relating to anyone else on stage, an orchestra of me; and he a soigné ham speaking the speech trippingly on the tongue. Once Verdon proved that rich character delineation had a place in even frivolous shows, the rest of the community stopped posing and indicating and began to explore character reality.

Then, too, the rise of the concept musical made such acting naturalism all but obligatory, because its multi-level psychologizing of a show's characters gave actors greater living space to occupy. Ironically, the concept musical was not a performer's but a director-choreographer's medium, because it is the musical's most imaginative format and, saving exceptionally inspired directors such as Rouben Mamoulian and Hal Prince, the choreographer is often the most imaginative of the staging personnel. Then, too, the concept musical's meta-theatre exchanges the old backdrop-and-wing-pieces scenery (in use through much of the twentieth century) for a more open space—a dancers' space—to create a playing area hosting multiple locations simultaneously.

Thus, characters can address other characters who are elsewhere in the action yet physically present (as in *Allegro, Company, Nine*), songs comment on the story from outside it (in *Love Life, Cabaret, Company*), narratives take on a fable-like transcendence (in *Allegro, Celebration*), and characters mention that they know they're on stage in a musical (in *1600 Pennsylvania Avenue*).

It's about analyzing a show's themes, yes—but it's also about how a show looks and moves: the choreographer's domain. In short, the concept musical swept away the George Abbott style, with its cartoon acting, realistic scenery, and clear-cut division between the book scenes and the musical scenes. In the concept show, everything is going off at once. The old musical was lantern slides; the concept musical is a kaleidoscope.

So there were several revolutions occurring at the same time just when composer John Kander and lyricist Fred Ebb partnered up, at the instigation of music publisher Tommy Valando. Each of the pair had been working with other partners; Ebb nearly got a show on (with Bob Fosse directing), and Kander actually had one, *A Family Affair* (1962). As partners, they clicked at once, though each was personally very different, Ebb a born performer keen to engage all the trappings of show-biz success while Kander was uninterested in the swank parties at which legends collide. It could be the difference between Manhattan and the Midwest, for Ebb embodied the racy mischief of the urban fast-tracker while Kander, from Missouri, played his cards more discreetly.

So they enjoyed the creative disturbance that conflicting personalities tend to spark, from Gilbert and Sullivan to Rodgers and Hammerstein. It takes two, one tending *this* way and the other tending *that*, for ideas to flower in a burst of challenge and encouragement.

They had this in common: a love of razzamatazz, one of the key elements of the Golden Age musical. A stageful of dancers banging out a routine to "Anything Goes" as the orchestra celebrates the melody. Ethel Merman ripping into Happy Hunting's "[Gee, but] It's Good To Be Here" with a backup of male choristers to take the A strain as Merman holds her Big Long Note over them and then, instead of giving up for breath, slides up to a higher note. *Hello, Dolly!*'s title number, with its staircase entrance and parade along the runway.

The Kander and Ebb catalogue is filled with such spots, perhaps most notably in *Cabaret* (1966), a serious show that plays as a musical comedy. "When I go," the heroine promises us, in the title number, "I'm going like Elsie," and while she's really (and unknowingly) talking about letting fascism take over your life because it's so much easier than fighting, she *sounds* as if she were about to break into a cakewalk.

So the Kander and Ebb style is a rich mix. Confronting the musical comedies are musical plays—*The Rink* (1984) or *Kiss of the Spider Woman* (1993). Balancing all these is their generically free adaptation of Thornton Wilder's *The Skin of Our Teeth*, performed under different titles and now unfortunately withdrawn because of a rights problem, as it is one of the best of the Kander and Ebb scores, clever and pointed but also emotional despite the coldly intellectual nature of its source.

Versed in the classics as he was, Wilder set forth Goethe's *ewig-weibliche* in Sabina, parlormaid and voluptuary, the woman every wife fears: delicious and available. In "You Owe It To Yourself," Sabina sings of her value to Wilder's eternal husband, George Antrobus. It's a commercial, really, Sabina's ad copy. Yet the whole thing is musically oriented, each A strain launched with a suavely confident "La, la, la-la, la," propelled of course by the strongly rhythmic John Kander vamp, a construction unique to this team. As Sabina cajoles Antrobus, the "la la"s take on a mystique of their own, universalizing the situation: the Goddess of Love and the Tempted Husband. The "la la"s even start to create imagery: Sabina offers to let Antrobus "la la," and later, she says, they can "la la" together. And, as we watch this outrageously amusing seduction reach its closing, all we hear is the vamp . . . again . . . again . . . and then, suddenly . . . "*La!*"

The Kander vamp is another example of how this team operates within an upbeat show-biz milieu. The vamp (a rhythmic underpinning heard before the vocal that defines a song's tone) is ancient, but it came into its own in the 1930s, as in the Latin throbbing that initiates Cole Porter's "Begin the Beguine," and was still capturing the ear in, say, the oddly glowering intro to *A Chorus Line*'s "One," which Marvin Hamlisch built on the always nonconformist sound of the major seventh.

Stephen Sondheim very often uses vamps, but his are jagged and demanding, warning us that we must above all ponder the number's intellectual content. Wait—can't we simply enjoy the song as music? Maybe later. But the Kander vamp tells us we can enjoy it now. Indeed, his vamps take on an ID of their own, even though Kander doesn't initiate the composition of a song with a vamp: rather, he pulls the vamp out of the rhythmic pulsing that drives the music he has composed.

Of all the Kander vamps, the one that launches the "Theme from New York, New York" is the most famous, but they generally run through all the Kander and Ebb shows, marking and "describing" them. Thus, *Cabaret*'s "Willkommen" vamp—the very first thing we hear in the show, after a drum roll—is alluring yet reserved, a kind of worrisome treat. It says, Yes, we'll have fun tonight . . . *but.*

Is there a spirit of musical comedy? A uniting and guiding feeling inherent in a form that started as populist and, over time, reinvented itself as (partly) elitist? Kander and Ebb embody that evolution, in the sheer exuberance of their dance tunes set next to the poetry of a searching ballad such as *Steel Pier*'s "First You Dream," a love song couched in the terms of an aircraft flight. Or next to the masterly arrangement of three melodies heard separately then simultaneously in the military number from the unproduced *Tango Mogador* (and later used in the *Skin of Our Teeth* adaptation). The trick, of course, is to create musical periods that can dovetail without crowding one another, even as the lyrics goof on the "advantages" of the warrior's life, creating a mouthful of a number that nevertheless remains crisp and pointed.

Fred Ebb is seldom if ever compared to the clever lyricists of the old days, from Porter to Harburg, because they are showy while he aims for a conversational atmosphere. *Chicago* originally had an extra principal, a talent agent named Henry Glassman,[2] who began his establishing number, "Ten Percent," by addressing the audience as if confiding in an old acquaintance. As he arrived in the prison, someone called out, "Hey, Velma, the worm is here," and, to a daintily strutting, minor-key Kander vamp, Glassman asked us, "Did you hear that?" Repeating the insult, he sang, "Well, maybe it's a figure of speech," as if Ebb wants him to steal his way into our sympathy. Who hasn't overheard something unhappy about ourselves and needed to put a neutral face on it?

This is nothing like Cole Porter's insinuating facetiae or E. Y. Harburg's flopsy-mopsy whimsy, whereby, for instance, "manishish or mouseish" rhymes with "Eisenhowsish." On the contrary, Ebb's "Ten Percent" is candid and even shameless, a hymn to greed, for Henry is not only an agent but a slimy one.

Chicago is filled with slimy types, of course. And *Cabaret* is decadent; *The Rink* (1984) includes a rape of one of the leads; and *The*

---

2. This character is sometimes cited with the first name Harry, but historian Ken Mandelbaum points out that it was Henry in the Philadelphia tryout and New York preview programs, as well as in *Variety*'s out-of-town review. Further, in an audiotape of one of the New York previews, Rivera calls him "Henry."

Visit (2015) is revenge murder. Yet the essential Kander and Ebb quality—at first—was sweetness. The team's Broadway debut, *Flora, the Red Menace* (1965), told of a young artist involved with Communists in the Depression, and while it sounds like something fit for Marc Blitzstein, it was actually a spoofy musical comedy.

In *Flora*'s source, Lester Atwell's novel *Love Is Just Around the Corner*, the artist, one Flora Meszaros, is grumpy and off-putting. But this was a George Abbott show, concerned with the springtime of youth, and the heroine was retempered as Liza Minnelli: avid and needy but above all appealing. So, after an opening to set up the hard times of the 1930s, the music moved to Flora's high-school graduation. Here was early Kander and Ebb at their most character-istic—"Unafraid," for Flora and her fellow students, their shaky sense of self gradually surging into an anthem of self-belief as the theatre rocked with joy.

Came then Flora's wonderful establishing number, "All I Need (Is One Good Break)," as she soars into a classic musical-comedy pose: the independent kid determined to make it. It's Sally, Miss Turn-stiles, Annie Oakley, thoroughly modern Millie, the flapper herself. All she needs is the real-life performer's super-talent to match the character's ambition.

Liza with a Z offered a *pow!* voice in a smashing Broadway debut that created the Minnelli mystique of a young girl of birthright talent (as Judy Garland's daughter) swept up in dire matters she cannot comprehend (cutthroat show business). It was a version of Dorothy in Oz, so winning that Minnelli came to be the Voice of Kander and Ebb in other shows, on television, and on film.

Yet she nearly lost the part of Flora. George Abbott, usually one of the best judges of fresh talent there ever was, somehow didn't appreciate her; he wanted Eydie Gormé. However, in one of those unaccountable events with which the entertainment world is pep-pered, Gormé failed to show up for a dinner date with Abbott. Kander and Ebb, who had passionately backed Minnelli, were thrilled. Because no one blows George Abbott off and then stars in his show.

Anyway, Gormé, a superb singer, could not have caught the raw vulnerability that bonded Minnelli and Flora. "Survival," Kander told Greg Lawrence, "is a theme that runs through our shows." Flora's "Unafraid" propelled *Flora*'s score forward, but it also could be the Kander and Ebb motto. True, Ebb called the survival meme "fortuitous." Yet there it is—that old musical-comedy equation of (energy + likeability = success).

As the first Kander and Ebb score, *Flora* has none of the shrewdly outrageous flair we hear in some of their later works. Yet it has its surprises, as in the way Kander gives harmonic depth to the simple melody of "A Quiet Thing." The song's premise is itself a surprise, on the idea that good news (here about a desperately needed job) doesn't necessarily create fireworks. It's a quiet thing—yet it resonates all the same. From the first note, Kander is in the nonconformist tonic major seventh, and a few seconds later he takes in the submediant seventh, the supertonic minor seventh, and (in the published key of B flat major) the intricate F_6^7, letting the sixth tone slide down to the fifth before hitting not the expected tonic chord but the mediant minor. To put it another way, Kander reinvents "pure" melody with what we might call "pensive" chording, as befits Flora's mindset at that moment.

Flora did not succeed, despite PR about (and a Tony for) Minnelli's exciting debut. Perhaps it was the Communist subject matter, or the ugly poster art of a dumpy little figure claiming to be Flora. Perhaps the production was inconclusive, a show with the right ingredients that somehow doesn't blend them persuasively—as with *Pipe Dream*, *The Grass Harp*, *A Doll's Life*.

But the next Kander and Ebb title became a classic: *Cabaret*, the team's first experience in the concept musical. One of the most conclusive shows of all time, *Cabaret* gave Kander and Ebb a chance to invoke a very particular atmosphere. (*Flora*, despite the thirties setting, sang mostly in a sixties Broadway style.) In *Chicago*, the tinta would recall vintage American show business, with the salesmen of pop notions (from soft-sell crooners to red-hot mamas) and their products (from the torch song to the New Dance Sensation).

For *Cabaret*, however, it was the Weimar Berlin of *The Threepenny Opera* and "Just a Gigolo" (though the latter actually came from Austria). Kander prepares by soaking up the music on old recordings,

then setting them aside to compose in his own way, guided osmoti-
cally, approximately, generally. It's comparable to the African dances
Agnes de Mille laid out for *Kwamina* (1961). What did de Mille know
of African dances? "I have a nose," she explained, when asked.

Of course, the usual wisenheimers claimed to "hear" Kurt Weill in
Kander's *Cabaret* music, not least because Weill's own Voice, Lotte
Lenya, was in the cast. Discussing this with Greg Lawrence, Kander
recalled assuring Lenya that he did not incorporate Weill in his *Cabaret*
music. "It's not Kurt," she agreed. "It's Berlin that I hear when I sing
your songs."

And Kander ends the tale with "If she feels that way, then fuck
everybody else."

Cabaret brought Kander and Ebb out of sweetness into irony.
A paradox: the most tender number in the score is a Nazi anthem,
"Tomorrow Belongs To Me," first heard in an eerily haunting interlude in which a few of the cabaret waiters sing it as if in passing,
joining in on a song they all know. The script describes them as
"handsome, well-scrubbed, idealistic," and only the Emcee's sardonic
grin at the audience (and a reprise in which the tune is banged out
as a raucous march) lets us in on this crazy juxtaposition of lovely
hymn and ugly ideology.

So if *Flora*'s score was a mixture of ballads, character songs, and
situation novelties, *Cabaret* marked an astonishing expansion of
the Kander and Ebb style, in which the genres of musical-comedy
songwriting were given a topsy-turvy makeover. Lotte Lenya's establishing number, "So What?," was the solo we expected, on the
Kander and Ebb "survivor" meme and illuminating one of the outstanding survivors of the twentieth century (flight; obscurity; come-
back; transfiguration as the Voice of the arts world's anti-fascism).
But "If You Could See Her Through My Eyes" was a shock, a lightly
syncopated fox trot for the Emcee and a mute gorilla on the subject
of (but we only learn this in the last line) Jew-hatred.

To put it another way, Kander and Ebb, along with their producer-
director, Hal Prince, and book writer, Joe Masteroff, were writing
something vaguely comparable to *Johnny Johnson* and *The Cradle
Will Rock*—political, opinionated, and theatrically high-strung. Kurt

Weill would eventually Americanize his sound, but in *Johnny Johnson* he was still singing in Weimarisch enfant terrible, and Marc Blitzstein made *Cradle* out of jigsaw cuts of art song. But Kander and Ebb gave *Cabaret* a score as socially aware as these earlier shows entirely within the sound of contemporary Broadway—a revolution, one might say, from within. The team thus created a partly satiric score without having to alter their style. Instead, they discovered the versatility of musical comedy, exploiting its accessibility while enlarging its reach.

Thus, *Cabaret*'s title song, out of context, sounds like a celebration of hedonism. In the show itself, however, it reveals the *danger* of hedonism: of lacking a politics when barbarians make one of their periodic assaults on civilization. The American musical, I repeat, has long been a protean form, ever-changing its physics, and now, in the age of the commentative piece, we see it turning into a form without limits, entertainment that opens a discussion with its public. Thus it becomes somewhat similar to a free press, as a form of communication outside of state control.

From *Flora*'s musical comedy and *Cabaret*'s concept musical, Kander and Ebb next came up against the director-choreographer syndrome, and everything came apart. This show was *The Happy Time* (1968), drawn from Robert Fontaine's tales of a young boy's French-Canadian family in Ottawa. It was a book, then a play, then a film, all called *The Happy Time* and all successful because of the boy's colorful relatives, especially worldly Grandpère and dashing but unreliable Uncle Desmonde. David Merrick owned the rights to musicalize the material, and he approached N. Richard Nash to do the book, as Nash was always writing about families, anyway. However, Nash countered with an entirely different project, though it did feature a family and a dashing but unreliable uncle in it.

Eager to monetize his *Happy Time* option, Merrick persuaded Nash to mash his people into Fontaine's French-Canadians, and when Kander and Ebb joined the concern, they and Nash saw the piece as a smallish domestic drama, a tidy idyll looking in on the boy's relationship with his fascinating uncle. There was no need for a chorus or production numbers. *The Happy Time* would be a musical play about how those we love can hurt us, tender and a bit sad but above all—here it is again—sweet.

So far, so good, and, better, Merrick hired Robert Goulet as the uncle. In the six years since he had played his last *Camelot* Lancelot on Broadway, in October of 1962, Goulet had been going to and fro and up and down in show business, like the Devil in the Book of Job, and he was an expert in how to present himself. On the stiff side as Lancelot, Goulet was now ebullient, ready to command the stage with captivating ease. He had always been a wonderful singer; now he was a *fantastic* singer. He was, even, French-Canadian, and actually raised up north (though born in the United States).

Co-starring above the title was David Wayne as Grandpère, and the third (and final) important principal was young Mike (later Michael) Rupert. These three centered the action in a conflicted way, as Grandpère Wayne was fond of Goulet while intensely disliking his way of showing up out of nowhere to vex the stable family circle, and nephew Rupert admired uncle Goulet as if he alone could save the boy from the baffling tribulations of childhood.

Goulet had a romance, too, but Kander and Ebb concentrated on their three most interesting characters, using the score to discover who these people were, writing and discarding song after song to penetrate to the core of the story. This is typical of the late–Golden Age musical, when narratives had become rich in character content; in the 1920s and 1930s, it wasn't hard to pin down who, for example, *Anything Goes'* principals were, especially because the roles were written on specific actors. (Guy Bolton's pre-script treatment didn't even use character names, citing "Merman," "Gaxton," and so on.)

The title tune was the first one heard, a beguiling waltz for Goulet setting forth the renamed Uncle Jacques' outward charm while deliberately hiding from us, for now, his interior contradictions. Grandpère's special number was "The Life of the Party," launched by the wordless vocal vamp Kander likes to deploy, here a "Boom boom boom *boom*!" to underline Grandpère's braggy two-step. And Bibi, the nephew, had "Please Stay," addressed to Uncle Jacques and framed by a touching aperçu. It seems the boy used to go through life saying, "I love you" to everyone and everything. One day he stopped. It was too vulnerable a habit, perhaps, too honest. Even in youth, Bibi knows the world prefers self-censorship to ... what? Weakness?

All this leads to the "Please Stay" refrain, as he implores his uncle not to go away again, because Bibi senses that his uncle is the only one who—to repeat my paradigm about Fosse and Verdon—"gets" him. The music moves quickly, as if aware that the boy is blurting out too much of himself, and, indeed, he will be rejected. His uncle is a man of the world, not of a small town near Ottawa. Then Bibi, about to turn in for the night, utters the words he gave up years before:

BIBI: Uncle Jacques ...
JACQUES: Yes?
BIBI: I love you.

It's an unbearably sensitive moment, because we know that, before this show is over, everyone we like is going to have his feelings hurt very badly.

So, in all, *The Happy Time* was a little family tale. But Merrick brought in Gower Champion as director-choreographer, and Champion had something big in mind: a cyclorama bearing projections of Jacques' photography work. These varied greatly in size, and could be moved and distorted as well. It was an intriguing idea, but in fact the uncle's camera art was not the stuff of the story but rather its maguffin—a plot driver of no interest to the audience. Worse, the cyclorama left a vast empty stage poorly furnished with a wooden disc, as if ready for the next Bayreuth *Ring* cycle. More: the family in this version was much too big, fully ten people (the movie has only seven), including a badly miscast George S. Irving as the father. Fontaine's father is playful and clever, especially as Charles Boyer limns him in the film; Irving was just grumpy. Further, Goulet's romantic plot never resonated. And Champion had to fill that big open stage somehow, so he hired thirty-seven extra performers, as music-hall chorines and Bibi's fellow students, who simply overwhelmed the family scenes. The staging was at war with the story.

And then Merrick himself goofed up, holding the first-night curtain for forty minutes because the *New York Times*' idiot critic, Clive

Barnes, had irresponsibly scheduled something in Pittsburgh that day and was late getting to the theatre. True, the *Times* review was crucial. But why humiliate all the other critics, waiting in their seats like poor relations? As Broadway's Topsy, Merrick always loved a PR dido; raising the curtain on time and then publicizing Barnes' recklessness would have been a perfect Merrick fiesta. As it was, Barnes meekly gave *The Happy Time* its one (slightly) positive review, and the show ran for 286 performances, a sort of respectable bomb. Despite the busy *Regie* staging, the only things that worked were the three leads, the score, and Don Walker's orchestrations.

However, the rise of Verdon and Fosse, and of Kander and Ebb, reveals how much the musical was transforming itself at this time, how comfortably it moved between musical comedy and the musical play, uncovering ways of aligning them in innovative mutations; how it amalgamated the responsibilities of director and choreographer; and how it made the rise of the naturalistic actor not only possible but necessary. In a way, one could say that a *Chicago* musical was unthinkable till the liberation of Fosse and Verdon and the evolution of Kander and Ebb, out of musical comedy into the commentative show. Like *Show Boat*, *Oklahoma!*, and *West Side Story*, *Chicago* is an exhibition piece in the development of our elite yet populist and idealistic yet subversive national art form, the musical.

8

⌒✺⌒

The Musical

"No Show Is Worth Dying For"

Tony Walton's logo art showed seven scrumptious babes posed on a stage, each wearing *Follies* headgear, bra, *cache-sexe*, and one gartered stocking. At right, in a box overlooking the playing area, sat a group of men, dimly glimpsed but presumably stage-door Midases, each mentally selecting his date for an after-theatre rendezvous: *sex*. Below the girls was a band in which a banjo, clarinet, trumpet, and trombone could be seen: *jazz*.

Not for more than twenty years had a Fosse show so gloried in the values of oldtime leggs-and-laffs musical comedy in its poster art. The last one was *The Pajama Game* (which Fosse only choreographed), presenting a Peter Arno cartoon of a young woman, eyes chastely lowered but clearly naked under a pajama top. To her left, looking her over, were the "tired businessmen" for whom these coyly sensual concoctions were conceived. Even the show's title beckoned to Men of a Certain Attitude About Women in Musicals; yes, it could denote a line of work but suggested also an erotic overnight.[1] Admittedly, the logo art of another Fosse job, the "musical staging" of *How To Succeed*, sported the silhouette of two people

---

1. The show's source, Richard Bissell's novel, was called—demurely, by comparison—*7½ Cents*, though a paperback issue whose cover bore artwork of a couple in a down-and-dirty mood, was called simply, and enticingly in the innocent 1950s, *Pajama*.

ensconced in a chair, presumably an executive and his secretary in an amorous mood. But that was just so much hanky-panky. *The Pajama Game* and *Chicago* used their poster art directly to address the physical appetites: sex and jazz.

These were the key elements of Fosse's art, the carnal act on one hand and, on the other, the indefinable American something that toys with our imaginations and infuriates the authorities. Sex and jazz worked as a set, like crime and show business in the early talkie, as I've said, and in his very faithful adaptation of Maurine Watkins (again, much more so than either of the *Chicago* movies), Fosse brought out all the bawdy chaos that "Chicago" meant in American mythology.

Fosse had Tony Walton reproduce his seven babetastic showgirls for the proscenium curtain at the Forty-Sixth Street Theatre (today the Richard Rodgers); it was what ticketholders saw as they took their seats. After the house lights dimmed, a member of the ensemble appeared in front of the curtain, warning us that the evening's bill would treat the Seven Deadly Sins of modern life, from greed to murder—"all those things we hold near and dear to our hearts."

Today, we chuckle at the jaunty cynicism. But when *Chicago* premiered (on June 3, 1975), this was a cold open of the daring sort, correct in setting up the show's tone yet possibly offensive to those who don't hold crime near and dear to their hearts. I saw the original *Chicago* many times, and though I always heard at least some laughter at this line, it was the nervous kind. Was this really a Kander and Ebb show? You know, the Survival guys and Elsie from Chelsea?

The music began: a lazy trumpet line of nine notes, repeated a half-step up. Suddenly, the conductor, Stanley Lebowsky, called out, "*Five, six, seven, eight!*," and his thirteen players swung into a short prelude as the show curtain rose to reveal a unit set dominated by a gigantic drum on top of which the band was seated. A sign came down, in the same art-deco neon red used in the lettering of the poster: "CHICAGO" and, directly below that, "late 1920's" [*sic*]. As the orchestra built up to a climax, Chita Rivera rose into view on an elevator in silhouette and came through doors built into the drum to launch the opening number, "And All That Jazz."[2] At the second chorus, the ensemble slithered in to assist and, very unexpectedly, Roxie and Fred Casely turned up on a stage right elevator for their date.

We actually got to witness their tryst, as a bed slid out on a winch[3] from inside the drum. Fosse staged the Roxie-Casely date as a comic mating of the most animalistic yet perfunctory kind. In previous *Chicago*s, Roxie's motivation for shooting Casely is his rejection of her. Here, there's a bit more going on: adultery wasted on an ungiving partner—or, in Fosse terms, sex without jazz. The script even calls for Roxie to sit up in the bed while Fred dresses, a bewildered look on her face, "as if to say, 'Is that it?'"

It's a case of the cheater cheated. As Velma and the chorus carried on with the number, the show caught up with Maurine Watkins' stark opening: the murder, followed by Roxie's exit and the stage then ringing with Velma's gleeful cry of "And all . . . that . . . jaay-yuz!," to the echo of:

CHORUS: That *jazz*!

It is as though the authors encapsulated Watkins' worldview in a single song—sardonic, detached, fantastical. This is pure concept-musical thinking: in a playing area without a fixed location, the ensemble were sharing the stage with Roxie and Casely. Those two were in Roxie's bedroom, but Velma and her equivalent of what in twenties operetta would have been Merry Villagers were somewhere "in" Chicago, or in the idea of how Chicagoans view their time and place, or even in an America hopped up on a frontier-town, anything-goes mentality. And some of the audience, in 1975, were

2. The song was published under this title and appears thus in the Samuel French text. However, it is invariably referred to now simply as "All That Jazz," and is so listed in the current New York revival program.

3. A winch is a shaft of spooled cable operated by a hand crank or automatically, used to tow small platforms on and off the stage. By theatrical shorthand, machine and platform together are called a "winch." Stephen Sondheim used the word more precisely in a new song for the movie of *A Little Night Music*, on the highlights of the actor's existence: "Brought on by winches to recite," cries the singer, "what a glamorous life!"

uncomfortable seeing a show laughing as its heroine commits murder. But irony doesn't play well to everyone in the auditorium. As we saw with the original production of Watkins' play, some of the spectators will miss the point.

Then, too, Fosse had a savage idea of fun. Everyone's on his side for the "Rich Man's Frug" in *Sweet Charity*, wherein pretentious trendies move as if on stilts, gazing down on the unforgivably un-fashionable. This, to the general taste, is sound social commentary exposing snobbery. But Fosse presented also a comic murder in the aforementioned *Redhead*, right at the start of the show, as in *Chicago*. True, the killer was a performer unknown to the public, not the show's star and, for that matter, not a woman. But it was murder and it was played for a grisly laugh, as a louche aficionado of snuff-lust came stealing up on a chorus girl at her dressing table. To the uneasy rustling of the tympani, he fondled a purple silk scarf as he advanced, and the act of murder was clear to the view.[4] Thus, Fosse was often ahead of his audience, an innovator within the main-stream. He can be as nonconformist as, say, *The Cradle Will Rock*, but he works entirely in the precincts of Big Broadway.

This gave him national prominence, yet feelings of unworthiness dogged him all his life. Am I inferior to Jerome Robbins? Am I infe-rior, even, to that poky Donald Saddler? Do all those chicks like me for my fuck or because they're Roxie Harts, working an angle? I let everyone down all the time, even Gwen. Maybe especially Gwen, yes, but shouldn't they forgive me because of *what I can do*?

He would never have believed it possible when he was alive, but today the Fosse style remains the most immediately recognizable of his generation of director-choreographers, of de Mille, Kidd, Layton, and even Robbins. To Fosse himself, however, "Fosse" was a fraud and his work a ruse. He had showmanship, yes, but so did Hitler.

---

4. *Redhead* was a murder thriller, obviously, with Verdon as a clairvoyant who "saw" the murderer in a vision and thus was his next target. The catch was that he had dis-guised himself for the crime—as a redhead. There were three in the show: Verdon, the killer in his phony get-up, and another man whom Verdon mistook for the killer but who was actually trying to help her. To maintain audience confusion till the finale, Fosse hired as the bad guy one of the most unknown actors on Broadway, Leonard Stone. He won a Best Featured Tony all the same, in a tie with Russell Nype for *Goldilocks*.

Sam Wasson quotes Dustin Hoffman, who played the title role in Fosse's film *Lenny* (1974): "This guy wanted so desperately to be an artist—and that was his tragedy—because he already was [one]."

"Job without God," Wasson calls him: he was plaguing himself. Fosse even denounced his own work in this very *Chicago*, in "Razzle Dazzle," the accusation we make against the shape shifter who scams us with frivolity so deep we think it has content. It looks meaningful, but it's air. What did they say about him? That he took from Jack Cole, he took from Verdon. He stole the way vaudevillians stole from each other, jokes, dance steps, songs. Is that why *Chicago* was billed as "a musical vaudeville"?

Seldom has an arts chief been as attuned to his material as Fosse was to *Chicago*, which is why the adaptation—book by Fred Ebb and Bob Fosse, music by John Kander, lyrics by Fred Ebb—is so very close to the *Chicago* play. In fact, it was less adapted than resuscitated, with Fosse spaces designed to penetrate and elaborate the original text while emphasizing Watkins' contempt for the entertainment production of murder cases—or, more broadly, her preference for fabulists of Christian faith over fabulists of news.

So there would be no romance for Roxie (though there is in Wellman) or Amos (as in DeMille). Had Fosse and Verdon secured the rights to *Chicago* back around the time of *Redhead*, there surely would have been. After all, the first concept musicals, *Allegro* and *Love Life*, depended on a central couple; *Cabaret*, which finally habilitated the concept musical a generation later, did as well. But *Company*, just a few years after, gave its protagonist minor dalliances and a more or less secret crush on one of his friends but no linear romance. *A Chorus Line*, contemporarily with *Chicago*, allowed a sorta kinda (but inconclusive) thing between the director and one of his auditioners. And, after *Chicago*, *1600 Pennsylvania Avenue* and *Pacific Overtures* were occupied with history, not romance.

Nor did Fosse think it necessary to go all twenties on the show, using an F. Scott Fitzgerald here or a Calvin Coolidge there. *Tenderloin* (1960), an antecedent musical on the war between vice and its killjoys, sought a balance between those who indulge and those who refrain. Fosse would have none of that; why would anyone want to refrain? Anyway, that's not what *Chicago* is about.

Take, for example, the song "Roxie." It is arguably the show's central number, our date with Gwen Verdon, so to speak. Most musicals give the heroine a Wanting Song early on, such as "Waitin' for My Dearie" or, for the Second Couple woman, "Ribbons Down My Back." It's the musical's way of letting us into how she feels about what she wants, a sensitive moment. Even a jokey musical comedy like *Hello, Dolly!* has emotional needs that it wants to share with us. Even *Johnny Johnson* and *The Cradle Will Rock* do.

But Roxie has no emotional character structure. She's an opportunist whose wants are entirely self-oriented, whereas the musical's typical heroine always plans to be a part of something larger than herself. True, *Gypsy*'s Madam Rose has a self-oriented Wanting Song, "Some People." But Rose is not a typical heroine.

Let's test the point with a more conventional show, the 1973 *Irene* revisal, an antique Cinderella piece turned into a cliché-ridden star turn in the George Abbott style (though it was rehearsed by, of all people, John Gielgud and doctored by Gower Champion). The star was Debbie Reynolds, and Wally Harper and Jack Lloyd wrote her a Wanting Song, "The World Must Be Bigger Than an Avenue." It's a purely ego-driven piece, even while envisioning, in passing, "a hero who's got fancy charms." Still, Harper and Lloyd knew that Reynolds' personal magnetism (and perhaps also her past as an MGM sweetheart) would soothe the number's apparent aggressiveness.

Then, too, Reynolds knew how to build a song in a crescendo of above all innocent determination, splitting the difference between "Waitin' for My Dearie" and "Some People": less romantic than the one and more tolerant and friendly than the other. "The World Must Be Bigger Than an Avenue" ends in telling the audience, I will succeed because you like me, because you have excellent taste in heroines.

Two years later, Verdon's Roxie offers a pointedly unlikable heroine. *Chicago* gave her several numbers before her "title" tune, but "Roxie" is where she lets us inside, and there's nothing charming or admirable about how she sees her place in the world. She brags about "ugly guys" taking her out to "show [her] off," capped by "Ugly guys like to do that": the edgy, honest, and almost misanthropic Fosse tone of the man who knows the Goethean delight of sex as ennobling mankind but also the Roy Cohn depth of jazz that sees everyone as either destructive or powerless.

So Verdon went into a long spiel about what she had been up to till this point, moving lightly in time to one of those irresistible John Kander vamps—dah...dah...dah-dah-*dah*-de-dah—as she gloated over a newspaper headline: "ROXIE ROCKS CHICAGO." Then she knelt down and handed her copy of this diploma in fame to someone in the front row of the house. More talk: she went on to Amos and his love for her, compromised, alas, by his lack of erotic command. So, she tells us, she went looking for it:

ROXIE: I started foolin' around. Then I started screwin' around, which is foolin' around without dinner.

And then there's the career in vaudeville, about which she very shockingly joked (before the line was cut during the New York previews) that she wanted it so badly:

ROXIE: I would kill for it. (Two beats) And I did.

At length she foresaw getting acquitted and starting a new life as a diva of the stage, with her own act.

And then we see it for ourselves as she starts the vocal, without a verse. She'll "get a boy to work with." No—two. Wait, Roxie, she says, "Think *big*": a set of boys, and six of them materialize to show us how the "sex and jazz" meme goes all show biz. Given who Roxie is and what she is guilty of, we should hate it, but Fosse and Verdon together were the hot stuff that entertainment always aspires to, no matter the content. Verdon had looks, talent, and confidence, and she glowed with a kind of promise that she'd give the public everything she had.

Most stars cannot help but share a salient quality. Julie Andrews: elegance. Hugh Jackman: friendliness. Broadway dancers all have the same quality, a chiseled energy—but Verdon had more, a fascination. She was as charming as Debbie Reynolds, but X-rated, and she was able to make the hateful Roxie intelligible because Verdon was greater than the character even as she stayed true to the character.

A great Madam Rose is comparable, making a destructive mother enchanting because the artist transcends the limits of the story. Besides, sociopaths have charm; they rehearse it, finesse it. "Who says," Roxie sings, "that murder's not an art?," which is Fred Ebb understanding what Fosse wants from this show. That's why Fosse remains our contemporary: he very presciently saw how blunt and de-euphemized show business was going to become. After all, he more than anyone made it so.

And what of the show's locale, now—the Chicagoness of *Chicago*? As I've said, musicals have largely avoided the place because of its dense associations. Rather, Chicago is used, if at all, as a convenience or a tourist stop. Two black shows, *Carmen Jones* (1943) and *Raisin* (1973), used Chicago because of its racial society on the South Side. John Kander's aforementioned first Broadway musical, *A Family Affair*, following a wedding from "Will you marry me?" to "I do," explored a middle-class suburban Chicago milieu because the authors, all midwesterners, knew its people.

Sugar (1972), from the movie *Some Like It Hot*, is a rare show exploiting gangland Chicago, with its Spats Columbo (a tap-dancing Al Capone) and its "When You Meet a Man in Chicago [you never, never know the business he's in]." And *Show Boat* devoted most of its second act to Chicago places, probably because its producer, Florenz Ziegfeld, a Chicago native, asked Kern and Hammerstein to indulge his nostalgia for the 1893 World's Fair and the nightclub that Ziegfeld and his father opened to entertain the influx of fairgoers.[5]

So we don't see a penetrating *Chicago* musical—unless we count *Pal Joey*, which in its original (1940) and slightly rewritten first revival (1952) versions sought to mate the idea of a corrupt town with the spirit of musical comedy. From opening to finale, *Pal Joey* shows

5. The show's source, Edna Ferber's eponymous novel, uses Chicago as a symbol of the creations of man, as opposed to those of nature, especially the Mississippi River—which, we should recall, was strategic in Chicago's rise as a trade metropolis. Thus, man and nature are linked in an eternal but uncomfortable bond. Little of this is in the musical. Nor are the tone and color of the Chicago that Ferber played with; at one point, her heroine asks her gambler husband, "Why is he called Bath House John?" Like most midwesterners, Ferber liked to remind New Yorkers that there was, after all, a "second city."

us almost nothing but sinners, its plot runs on adultery and black-mail, and the one percent rule the town, even the law.

The show is routinely misunderstood as a breakthrough in the integration of song and story, though its first two versions moved clumsily into many of its situation numbers and though nightclub performing spots make up about half of the score. The breakthrough lay in the adult nature of the plots because John O'Hara wrote the book, based on his *New Yorker* stories, and O'Hara's worldview conceded nothing to the spirit of musical comedy. His lead characters, the egotistic user Joey and the suavely free-living Vera, were types new to the musical—just as Roxie would be, in her very different way. It doesn't lessen the achievement of *Chicago* to say that there's a whiff of *Pal Joey* in its air because Fosse's sex and jazz, and Kander and Ebb's evocations of show-biz iconolatry, stand far beyond what O'Hara and his songwriters, Rodgers and Hart, had in mind, particularly as the decades after *Pal Joey*, from the mid-1940s into the 1970s (roughly, from *Oklahoma!* to *Follies*), marked the most intense artistic development in the musical's history.

So it is not surprising that this ever more experimental era inspired producers to seek the rights to *Chicago*—but Maurine Watkins always said no. As we know, she had moved to Florida to be near her parents, and a legend grew up that she was a recluse whose rare sorties outdoors were ruled by horoscope readings. She was described as a born-again Christian, haunted by the thought that her newspaper work had heroine-ized murderesses and contributed to their acquittals.

Balderdash. As I said before, Watkins had been an active member of the Disciples of Christ all her life, devoted to the sect's love of Bible study in both translation and the original Greek texts. There was no "born again" about it. Nor would she have felt responsible for the whitewashing of culprits in her Chicago days; we have seen how scathing she could be about Beulah Annan (the model for Roxie) and Belva Gaertner (the model for Velma).

In *The Girls of Murder City*, Douglas Perry blames this absurd caricature of Watkins on one Sheldon Abend, who ran the theatrical licensing firm that controlled *Chicago*. Abend was apparently irritated that he had to turn down every offer sent in Watkins' direction, not only from regional and community stages but from those who had the power to transform the original play into a potentially lucrative Broadway musical. *Oklahoma!*, *Carousel*, *My Fair Lady*, *Hello, Dolly!*, and *Mame* had all been plays first. Who knew what money and prestige lay in *Chicago*, forever in limbo because of this…this silly author, this stubborn copyright holder?

Douglas Perry discovered a thread of misinformation about Watkins stemming from Abend and running through "journalists and theater scholars [who] recycled [Abend's] view of Maurine for years." Perry speculates that she "couldn't bear to have anyone else tinkering with her successful play" and, further, resented the way the 1942 William Wellman–Ginger Rogers film transformed a vicious killer "into a misunderstood innocent." Perry learned also of a 1935 staging of the play in London that "received stinging reviews"; one critic said it "produces only boredom and disgust."

There is this as well: the Fosse-Verdon offer to musicalize *Chicago* coincided with the Cuban Missile Crisis of 1962, the famous showdown between President Kennedy and Soviet premier Krushchof over whether or not Russia would establish warheads in Cuba aimed at America. The West seemed on the brink of nuclear war, and Watkins, through Abend, replied that this was not the time to negotiate over theatrical matters. As Verdon recalled for the interview book *Sing Out, Louise!*, Watkins said, "How can we talk about that piece of fluff when I have guns aimed at me?"

Then Watkins died, in 1969. The rights to her play eventually reverted to Abend's firm, and, as it turned out, Watkins, said Verdon, "had it in her will that I had first refusal." So the playwright had had a Fosse-Verdon *Chicago* in mind all the time, for if anyone else had made an offer, Abend was obliged to allow Verdon and Fosse to meet it and snap up the rights at last. Oddly, through what appears to be a quirk of the contract Watkins had made with Abend, her byline now included, for the first time, her middle name. So *Chicago*'s poster, with Tony Walton's seven hotness babes and the audience of watching men, gave the source credit as "based on the play by Maurine Dallas Watkins."

Really, it's more than merely "based on": the musical *Chicago* adheres to the original work's tone and characters with extraordinary fidelity. True, so did the four shows I mentioned just above. But of their sources, only *Carousel*'s dark, disappointed *Liliom* seemed to forbid adaptation (except as an opera). And while *Pygmalion* appeared at first to defy musical transformation, once Lerner and Loewe found the way in—don't adapt Shaw; just set him to music—*My Fair Lady* was a natural.

Chicago, however, was a coarse and cynical twenties piece, absolutely of its time. And look at how Hollywood switched things around—Amos as a sweetheart, Roxie innocent of crime. But the musical *Chicago* is a musical Watkins, albeit with some deviation, especially in the dramatis personae:

1926	1975
ROXIE: Sociopathic dope, caustic in tone.	The same, now with ambitions to get into show biz.
VELMA: Society type, oo-la-la in tone.	New social status: low. As caustic as Roxie. Also keen on a show-biz career. For the first time, as important a principal as Roxie.
BILLY FLYNN: Manipulative and unscrupulous attorney. Oldster without glamor.	The same personality, but young-old, to be played by an attractive leading man.
AMOS: Hapless squish.	The same hapless squish.
MARY SUNSHINE: Simpering professional idiot.	The same, but played as a pseudo-operatic drag queen, because in Chicago (i.e., in American glitter-bomb performance culture), "Things are not always what they appear to be."
THE MATRON: Capable but with a cruel streak. An ordinary figure—exactly what she appears to be.	Like Mary Sunshine a shape-shifter, nominally a state employee but also a show-biz go-between, connected to an outside hierarchy of destiny makers.
MOONSHINE MAGGIE: A heavily accented immigrant convicted of murder (JAKE: "She had a bum lawyer") and sentenced to death. At one point called "the Hunyak" (a derogation for "Hungarian," probably derived as a correspondence for the equally crummy "Polack").	The same, now known only as the Hunyak and speaking entirely in Hungarian, except for "Not guilty." Hanged onstage as if in a deranged trapeze act.

The reporter Jake, so useful in 1926, was dropped in 1975, though some of his duties as Roxie's link to the system were assigned to a brand-new character, the aforementioned Henry Glassman. He served outside the plot action as Chicago's master of ceremonies (though America's vaudeville format used not announcers but cards at the sides of the stage, such as we usually see in *Gypsy*). Within the plot action, Glassman was a theatrical agent, amorally uniting *Chicago*'s world of crime with that of entertainment: another of those twenties salesmen. His was clearly a lively life, and he cut a jaunty figure in his checked jacket and vest over striped white trousers and topped off with a boutonnière, now leaning against the proscenium arch, hands in his pockets and everything hunky-dory, now speaking the intros to the numbers as if he and the audience were in on some occult show-biz joke that was larger than the show itself. ("And now, the six merry murderesses of the Cook County jail...")

True, Glassman did have to take a personal moment now and again to resent the way everyone looked on him as scum. I've already noted his pique, at the start of "Ten Percent," when he comes to see Velma in prison and someone calls out, "The worm is here." But he gets over it quickly enough; the song is really an explanation of The Way It Works. Its refrain is a jiving one-step, the kind of thing that begs for a tap break and a gala exit with a cry of "Thanks for the use of the hall!" as he struts into the wings. Yes, it's all corruption; absolute money corrupts absolutely. And, yes, they call him a "leech." A "parasite." But he earns his commission, doesn't he? He just got an offer of $2,500 a week for Velma in a vaudeville tour. So maybe he *is* a parasite, "But I'll eat lobster thermidor tonight," he crows. And then, sneering at the audience: "And what'll you have?"

The actor playing Glassman was David Rounds, who may have found this role the most congenial of his career. In his *New York Times* obituary, in 1983, he was quoted "in an interview" as saying, "being a song-and-dance man represents everything to me that is show biz and glamorous. The spotlight. The top hat. The cane. It's magic."

Unfortunately, the show needed tightening, and Fosse realized, during the New York previews, that all of Rounds' intros could be shared among the company and his liaison work between the murderesses and the entertainment industry could be reassigned to the Matron. Indeed, it added to her mystique if she could set you up with the William Morris agency simply by "making a phone call" (i.e., accepting your pay-to-play bribe). It was obviously a terrible blow to Rounds. A versatile talent, he had appeared primarily in non-musical roles from Shakespeare to the thriller and won a Best Featured Tony for the 1980 revival of *Morning's At Seven*. Still, as the *Times* obit tells us, Rounds longed for a part like Henry Glassman, with a flashy number like "Ten Percent," and was crushed to have to give it up. This is why the resigned phrase "That's show business" was invented.

Of the rest of the cast, the first-billed Gwen Verdon was the protagonist, the central figure of the storyline (and the reason Fosse was doing the show in the first place). By 1975, however, Verdon was forty-nine and unable to sustain an evening on her own. Today, some lead performers let an alternate handle one or two performances a week or will leave random dates to their understudy. This was unheard of in the theatre that Verdon rose up in and would have been looked on as unprofessional. Shameful. Starting in the late 1940s, when she was the assistant and also primary dancer for choreographer Jack Cole, Verdon worked within a community in which nothing but a serious bout of flu or a hospital emergency forgave a missed performance.

There was an ideal in play: the audience comes to see not just a title but its *staging*—the one that the critics reviewed on opening night. If ticketbuyers wait too long, true, they might see a replacement or two, although certain stars weren't—couldn't be, by the intelligence of the times—replaced. When Eddie Cantor, Al Jolson, and Ray Bolger, for various reasons, left shows that were still doing good business, those shows closed. As for alternates, they were once so rare that when Robert Weede's student Richard Torigi spelled his teacher at matinées of *The Most Happy Fella*, it was regarded as acceptable (because of the role's operatic demands) but all the same startling.

Verdon, despite extremely tiring workouts in her shows (*Redhead* in particular), never scheduled an alternate. True, like all dancers

she was an athlete, capable of the heavy lifting a dance musical demands. Nevertheless, the physics of supporting the singing, dancing, and character concentration drains even a champion's energy.
The Novelty Stars who came from other sectors of show business to
appear in musicals, from Rex Harrison to Tony Randall to Lauren
Bacall, would comment on how exhausted they felt at the end of
each week, even when their dancing chores were at most minimal.

So the art is delightful, but it's hard labor. Verdon did take to
omitting the odd solo in both *Redhead* and *Sweet Charity*, but
Chicago's tight construction left her with no equivalent option.
What she needed was a counterweight co-star, someone to play off
of and share the chores with—but, necessarily, of Verdon's class in
style, commitment, and stamina.

And that would be Chita Rivera as Velma Kelly, a role she was born
to play once the authors expanded and rebooted it from social grandee to mean-streets prison know-it-all. Building up Velma was helpful in another way, turning her rivalry with Roxie into a throughline
to fill out what would otherwise have been a skimpy plot. Watching
Roxie outstrip Velma in publicity tricks lent *Chicago* the excitement
of a diva collision and even premised a few musical numbers.

Rivera's background is not unlike Verdon's. They came into the
musical at about the same time, both as dancers, then revealed that
they could sing and run character, which took them out of the line
and into leads. There was one main difference: Rivera had no Fosse
to glorify her in productions tilted toward her unique gifts. Rivera
did maintain a strong relationship with choreographer Peter
Gennaro. But despite his really quite ecumenical vision, in musicals
set in Paris, the American gypsy community, the more or less wild
west, and from the Charleston to the belly dance to ragtime, Gennaro
never made it into the pantheon of name-checked dance chieftains.

Then, too, while Verdon projected an enchanting vulnerability,
essential for the musical-comedy heroine in almost any role, Rivera's
personality is dauntless. It's this simple: she wins every time. Thus,
they were well balanced as opposites, even if they occasionally
shared roles: Rivera played Charity on tour, and even dropped in on
the London *Chicago* revival (and elsewhere) as Roxie. Still, the classic

Rivera part was *By Bye Birdie*'s Rose, the ultimate heroine—not in a Marilyn Miller Cinderella-flapper way, but in casually modern style. Everyone else in *Birdie* is a fool, a child, or Elvis Presley; Rose is not only the one sensible character but the plot's showrunner. And of course Rivera capped a long career as the protagonist of another Kander and Ebb show, *The Visit*, seen in Chicago, Washington, D.C., and Williamstown, Massachusetts, before trying a run on Broadway, with different leading men but always with Rivera as a ruthlessly loving angel of death (a role she played also in *Kiss of the Spider Woman*).

Further, her Velma was more than a foil to Roxie, something like *Cabaret*'s Emcee, with his out-of-story commentative numbers. So she opens Act One with "All That Jazz," diagnosing, so to say, the illness of twenties "Chicago," later giving it a tiny sarcastic reprise to bring down the first-act curtain after Roxie announces her fake pregnancy. Then, to get the audience back into a *Chicago* mood after the intermission, she calls out a Texas Guinan-like "Hello, suckers!"[6] and goes right into "I Know a Girl," which, paradoxically, is Velma's character piece all about Roxie.

Verdon and Rivera shared the top line in the billing, and just below them was Jerry Orbach. As I've said, this was glamorous casting for Billy Flynn, heretofore viewed as strictly "character," as Orbach had been playing romantic leads since taking over Macheath in the historic off-Broadway *Threepenny Opera*, the Lotte Lenya revival, late in the run in 1958. True, Orbach's heroes always had an edge; in *Carnival* he was lame and bitter, and in *Promises, Promises* he stooged for adulterous executives at his office job, letting them use his apartment for their trysts.

6. The raffish Guinan, known as "The queen of New York night life" as hostess of Prohibition-era clubs favored by the glitterati and informed tourists, greeted each arriving party by addressing its apparent alpha male (who was going to pick up the absurdly inflated check) with "Hello, sucker!" The phrase is often misquoted in the plural (and Velma is obviously speaking to a theatre's worth of people). Still, Guinan used the singular, and a Guinan biography and a musical starring Martha Raye that toured the regions in the late 1960s both bore the phrase as Guinan uttered it. But note the air of hedonistic cynicism, so essential in casting a twenties spell. This is Fosse at his *most*, daring you to resent his defiance of the standard cautions. It's his house; he doesn't have to respect your limits. *Hello, suckers!*.

And it appears that Fosse never intended to cast a character man as Billy Flynn. A Bob Fosse lead can be sex or jazz or both at once, but he's got to have *something*, and the Billy Flynns of the play and the two movies were, let's just say, not *musical* enough. Fosse toyed with the possibilities—one of those called in to audition was Russell Nype, who started as a crewcut preppy in such shows as *Call Me Madam* and who by the mid-1970s looked and sounded exactly like the sort of conservative WASP attorney who is never seen out of his Brooks Brothers suit. Brisk and subtle.

Ultimately, however, Fosse decided to go with a Flynn who oozed opportunism yet gave off an air of mastery as the Fosse of it all. In the theatre world of the very early 1900s, the big behind-the-scenes name was not the director but the producer (then called the "manager"). The biggest such was Charles Frohman, to the point that his last name became a sobriquet for producers generally. So: actor meets actor on Forty-Second Street; they exchange career news; first actor says he has just started rehearsing a new crook play; second actor doesn't place it. "Who's the Frohman?," he asks.

Well, we can do the same with Bob Fosse—he has become that fabulous, a boldface entry in the book of tales, moving people around at his pleasure. And isn't that what Billy Flynn does? In previous *Chicago*s, he was important, but here he is in total command of the action and, unlike everyone else, answerable to no one. Yes, Roxie is the protagonist. It's *her* story. But *he* directs it, and, late in the continuity, it is Flynn who gives us the show's defining number, "Razzle Dazzle." It's as well the Maurine Watkins number, summing up what she thought of news-media accounts of just about anything: politics, false narratives, a confetti of lies. In *Chicago*'s three above-the-title stars, we see Orbach as, really, a producer—the Frohman—and Verdon and Rivera as his contracted stars.

Is anyone not a part of this Great American Show Shop? If we're all on stage, who's in the audience? "Got the dream, yeah," says Madam Rose, "but not the guts." We think of musicals as being about the dream (e.g., "If I Loved You"). But they're really about the guts (the same show's "Soliloquy"), about people we're interested in who make something happen. And it's worth noting that, on the light musical stage elsewhere in the West, we seldom find entertainment used as an evening-long metaphor, while the American musical is fascinated with the link between how we live and what we perform.

Interestingly, the musical always cited as the first great one—*Show Boat*—is a backstager. The musical usually called the great one of the post-*Oklahoma!* era—Madam Rose's *Gypsy*—is about an obsession with show business. The musical often thought of as the great one in the post-*Gypsy* era—*Follies*—sets our show-biz past on the analyst's couch. And the "phenomenon musical" of *Chicago*'s own era—*A Chorus Line*—was about a competition to disappear into a faceless ensemble.

So of course all of *Chicago*'s principals are simultaneously people in a story and stars on a stage. First of the names below the title was the Amos, Barney Martin. He played exactly what Maurine Watkins had created: a garage mechanic of no interest to anyone, including his wife. From his first words, confessing to the murder to shield her, the musical's Amos is the play's Amos. Here's Watkins, as Amos writes out his statement:

> POLICE SERGEANT (dictating): . . . "Voluntarily and of my own
>   free will—"
> AMOS: Freely and gladly!
> JAKE: Ain't he the cheerful murderer though!"
> AMOS (quickly): That ain't murder—shootin' a burglar. Why,
>   only last week the jury *thanked* a man!

The musical's version of the same moment is almost the same, with another character supplying Jake's line. What's striking is the "freely and gladly," used as a kind of personal refrain. (The musical has him say it four times.) One imagines Amos repeating it on a daily basis, or even that Watkins heard somebody use the phrase and appropriated it to characterize her plodding dullard. All the best writers steal from life.

But why did the if nothing else vital Roxie marry this shnook in the first place? The musical's script offers an explanation in that long monologue preceding "her" title song. It seems that everyone was turning Roxie down when she tried to get work as a dancer. Then she met "sweet, safe Amos, who never says no." Certain men, we learn, are "like mirrors": a woman can see what she is by how he gazes at her. And what Roxie sees is young and wonderful, before all the sex and jazz horned in. "You could love a guy like that," she tells us.

One wonders if Gwen Verdon had transmitted this notion to Fosse to add to the script as a subtext for her to play in her scenes with Amos. It does seem to be one of those secrets that only women know; we don't find it often in our popular art (though it does come up, remember, in the climax of *The Day Before Spring*).

The Matron, promoted from the simple "Mrs. Morton" of earlier *Chicago*s to "Mama Morton" (referencing Sophie Tucker and one of her theme songs, "I'm the Last of the Red Hot Mammas" [*sic*]), ended up as a musical-comedy grande dame, of a certain age and loaded with style. The role needed an old pro who'd been knocking about Broadway for years without ever quite punching out yet who radiated the confidence that comes of having worked with the best and learned from all of them.

Thus, Fosse's Mama Morton, Mary McCarty, had been identified with happy-daffy musicals since the one-week failure *Sleepy Hollow*, in 1948, and had lasted into the age of Sondheim-Prince, introducing "Who's That Woman?" in *Follies*. To veteran theatregoers, McCarty was familiar yet a bit alien, someone we're never sure of—exactly the atmosphere the Matron needs. In the hierarchy of the 1920s, every salesman has people above to buy from and people below to sell to. Thus, the Matron, a neutral figure in previous *Chicago*s, now joins the System.

As for the chorus, they were Fosse regulars, many of them *Pippin* alumni. Also among them was a future director-choreographer, Graciela Daniele, as the so-called Hunyak. It's a small but very pivotal role, the only truly sympathetic character. As I've said, Maurine Watkins named her Moonshine Maggie, basing her on one Sabella Nitti, convicted of murder simply because she was physically unattractive and couldn't speak English (though unhabilated immigrants were quite common in twenties Chicago). Consider the contradiction: Chicago's guilty women were getting off, but the one—just one—who was probably innocent was convicted and sentenced to hang.

Researching *The Girls of Murder City*, Douglas Perry came upon a document in the state university library archives arguing for Nitti's retrial because she "could not understand [her lawyer], he could not understand her, and they had great difficulty [even using] interpreters." Nitti could not sign her name except with an X—but she did notice all the pretty native girls who were getting off on murder charges. Now Perry quotes from the Chicago *Daily Tribune*, as Nitti gets out "Nice face—swell clothes—shoot man—go home." As for Nitti, "Me do nothing—me choke." Look at what became of carefree musical comedy: we see Nitti's counterpart hanged before our eyes as disembodied hands at either side of the stage applaud for this latest "act" of the vaudeville. But at least the real-life Sabella Nitti did succeed in getting a second trial, and while she was out on bail the charges, apparently based on faulty detective work, were dropped.

One *Chicago* principal was, unlike the others, professionally unknown, a South African without Broadway experience. This was the Mary Sunshine, a cross-dressed male singing in such a convincingly fluttery soprano and in such overstated attire that most theatregoers take him for a woman goofing on the blowsy opera diva. Fosse's Mary Sunshine was Michael O'Haughey, billed as "M. O'Haughey": honest yet altered, a truth designed to deceive. Ever since 1975, it has been the usage to credit whoever plays the part behind the veil of the first initial.

However, this isn't a theatrical game the way, for example, two of the Cagelles in the original production of *La Cage aux Folles* were not men in drag but women pretending to be men in drag, to appear in full true only during the curtain calls as a last charming surprise. No, *Chicago*'s Mary Sunshine is an anomaly, a "What is it?," like Baba the Turk, the bearded lady in Stravinsky's opera *The Rake's Progress*. In her skirt and fussy top, a sort of sweater studded with cotton balls, and luridly beflowered hat, Sunshine was meant to pique spectators' curiosity. To dare their suspicions. Still, as Fosse must have known, the public would assume the character was merely part of the good old musical-comedy zaniness. And the public failed the test: Sunshine's unmasking at the end of Flynn's closing argument comes as a shock, as he stripped O'Haughey to his boxers: another of Flynn's magic tricks.

Was Fosse warning us to be more alert, to take nothing for granted, especially about the reliability of the news media? We know that politicians are crooks; all that stands between them and us is a free honest press. How much of the public was willing to consider this red-button alarm from a fun-filled (if acerbic) musical comedy? It's the serious shows, from *The King and I* to *next to normal*, that get respect. A fun show is undervalued: because it's fun. Not till the Sondheim-Prince series of the 1970s, from *Company* to *Sweeney Todd*, did intellectuals even talk about musicals at all. Even then they seldom if ever get how the music fits into the conversation.

In the end, *Chicago* is extremely enjoyable but pointedly commentative, a satire in the tradition of *Strike Up the Band* and *Of Thee I Sing*—and, for that matter, the still very revivable *Finian's Rainbow* (1947). This work, too, is very attractive, yet it has a sociocultural point of view, discussing race relations, the oppression of the poor, and our high standard of living based on capitalistic credit-consumerism. The Burton Lane–E. Y. Harburg–Fred Saidy Irish-American fantasy is so political it's almost propaganda, but this is camouflaged by one of the most beguiling scores of all time. It's not a satiric score per se, though "Necessity" and "The Begat" function satirically as comic numbers using black-music models.

Chicago's score is our most satiric yet, because almost every number is presented with ironic detachment. By basing character songs on pre-existing show-biz tropes and presenting them in an out-of-story ambience, *Chicago* offers these spots within scare quotes. That way, two things occur at once: each character makes a statement about him- or herself while the show makes a statement about the character. For example, "Roxie" functions as the heroine's me-celebration, Roxie the great, even as the song's triumphalist tone ridicules the notion of a "great" Roxie. Unlike countless predecessors in the musical's tradition, Roxie is showing off in a genre she isn't entitled to. She's got the dream and the guts, yes: but she doesn't deserve success.

Or does she?

Because isn't it part of *Chicago*'s layered worldview that Roxie isn't "just" Roxie? As I've already said, she's Gwen Verdon, too—and Liza Minnelli and Ann Reinking and Sandy Duncan and so on. Star musicals are always about the talents on stage *as well as* about the characters in the plot. To separate the singer from the song is to deconstruct and discredit the entire history of the American musical, from the nineteenth century's Lydia Thompson and George L. Fox right on up to the present day.

Before looking at *Chicago*'s score, let's examine *Chicago*'s arresting book credit: "By Fred Ebb and Bob Fosse." When the first ads appeared, it looked dubious. Bob Fosse writes dialogue? Yet he had long intended to become the more or less singular auteur of his shows, to free himself from the meddling of writers.

Meddling? There wouldn't be shows without writers. Still, as far as Fosse was concerned, they did rather get in the way of things. On Fosse's final Broadway musical, *Big Deal* (1986)—another piece set in Chicago, by the way; and the subject again was crime—Fosse wrote the book and used a jukebox score. Virtually every one of the forty-six songwriters was dead. Before that, *Dancin'* (1978) was a bookless choreographic revue. And while *Pippin* did have a book writer (Roger O. Hirson) and a songwriter (Stephen Schwartz), Fosse staged the work as if the other two weren't there. In *Defying Gravity*, Carol de Giere tells us how an increasingly disheartened Schwartz would complain about the way Fosse was tilting *Pippin* toward carnality and camp. Finally, in front of the entire cast, Fosse and Schwartz got into it, as they say, over a song, leading Schwartz to cry, "I'm the one who has a record in the Top Ten!"

From then on, Schwartz was barred from rehearsals, forced to discuss his rewrites with Fosse at odd times in other places, cut off from the living production. Yet even before all this, on *Sweet Charity*, Fosse decided to write the script himself, his first chance to lock those pestiferous authors out of the process. But all he ended up with was a musical comedy without the comedy. Neil Simon could doctor it; he and Fosse had collaborated on *Little Me*. But Simon said he was too busy. In his memoirs, Simon recalled Fosse pressing him with "You owe me one."

"For what?" Simon asked.

"I'll think of something," Fosse replied.

Simon did take over *Sweet Charity*'s libretto, because, as a book writer, Fosse was a choreographer: he had the ideas, not the words. So what did an Ebb-Fosse credit for *Chicago*'s script mean? And who came up with the notion of "a musical vaudeville"? This is a key point—it's what makes *Chicago* unique. The structure is a panoply of stand-alone numbers designed to revisit the stars and song genres and catch-phrases of the golden age of American entertainment— not only vaudeville itself but nightclubs, radio serenades, and Broadway's *Follies, Scandals, Nifties, Padlocks, Artists and Models*.

Thus, the score would not be integrated naturalistically into the storyline. Instead, it consisted of a series of drop-ins because setting the action to sincerely felt plot and character numbers would emphasize the loathsome nature of these crooks and parasites. By rebooting *Chicago*'s people ironically as icons of America's bygone entertainment community, the musical could justify Watkins' vision while letting the audience identify not emotionally but intellectually, and not with any of the characters but, rather, with the show's concept.

Thus, Roxie, Velma, Billy Flynn, Amos, Mary Sunshine, and the Matron become the denizens of some never-ending variety show on the theme that everything in American life is about performance. Charisma and talent become the first virtues, and there is no morality because the whole thing is an act.

But, again, whose idea was this? In Greg Lawrence's Kander and Ebb interview book, Ebb says Fosse asked him how *Chicago* should be formatted. "So," says Ebb, "I made it vaudeville based on the idea that the characters were performers. Every musical moment in the show was loosely modeled on someone else: Roxie was Helen Morgan, Velma was Texas Guinan, Billy Flynn was Ted Lewis, Mama Morton was Sophie Tucker." Kander chimes in, citing Eddie Cantor and Bert Williams.

Further, following Ginger Rogers' ambitions in *Roxie Hart*, the heroine was given a motivation to get into show business. Rogers wanted to be a dancer, though she didn't say where, and her merry English agent, we recall, spoke of "cabarets." But in the Fosse *Chicago*, the "Roxie" monologue specifies it, as I've said: she hopes to be "a dancer in vaudeville."

This suits the show's setting, because vaudeville was a basic American thing in the 1920s, long entrenched in the culture's leisure facilities. Paradoxically, everyone inside vaudeville knew it was sinking in competition with radio and movies, yet its masters refused to consider refreshing or rejuvenating it. Douglas Gilbert's *American Vaudeville* tells us that one progressive vaudevillian tried to get through to one of the industry's titans, the vindictive and sanctimonious E. F. Albee (grandfather of the playwright), suggesting a major overhaul of the attractions on Albee's theatre chain. "To hell with your proposal," Albee replied. "I *am* vaudeville."

Albee and the rest of his art evaporated in the Depression. Still, to a Roxie Hart in the late 1920s, vaudeville was a magic word, because it was where folk of little or no talent hobnobbed with the likes of the true celebrities we see referenced in *Chicago*—the Sophie Tuckers and Eddie Cantors. A vast agglomerate of theatre circuits, each with its own policies on what could and could not be said or done on its stages, vaudeville stood below the legitimate stage and above local burlesque houses. It encompassed everything from all-star, reserved-seat bills at New York's Palace Theatre to continuous performances at a run-down neighborhood "opera house" before a public consisting largely of irritable old men wearing hats and reading newspapers.

All the same, vaudeville was a democracy. Until the talkie finally seized vaudeville's working- and lower-middle-class audience, the platform offered opportunity to virtually anyone who wanted to try his or her luck. Song and dance? A tiny dramatic playlet for a cast of two or three—or even, in a long-forgotten genre, for one person playing multiple parts through incessant exits and re-entrances in lightning-fast costume flips? Or perhaps banging out ditties on glasses filled with different levels of water?

Yes, there were wonderful talents in vaudeville. Many of the most original stars started there, from Marilyn Miller to the Marx Brothers.

But, as true democracy must allow, some of the least gifted folk were vaudevillians, too, as the cheesy opening acts in the first half on the lesser circuits of the continuous-performance programs, or, to follow the main headliner's "next to closing" spot, the "chaser," an act so spectacularly awful that everyone got up to leave, freeing seats for the next house.

Fosse saw Roxie as one of the no-talents, and, as I've said, wanted to feature her professional debut in *Chicago*'s finale as the worst act ever seen. Not campy, just...ghastly. Worthless and floppo, something even a genuine star would look terrible in. It would make a nice irony: Gwen Verdon, one of the musical's most flavorsome personalities, as a dreary disaster. The plan was for Roxie and Velma to perform an instrumental act, with Verdon blatting away on the saxophone and Rivera banging on a drum kit. It suited Fosse's sense of irony; the movies he directed, especially *Lenny*, *All That Jazz*, and *Star 80*, seemed to revel in the belief that even the most alert and intelligent people Just Never Get What Danger They're In. Moving back to Broadway, we can say that musicals use irony freely—but only the satires work entirely in irony. And *Chicago*, of course, is one of them.

However, Fosse's great ironic *Chicago* finale didn't work. It opened with "[We wanna get] It," on the aforementioned twenties term for sexual magnetism. Here was more irony, for Roxie and Velma were to be introduced as "Chicago's own killer dillers, those two scintillating sinners." Frankly, they already had It, or Something Like It. And the song's tune was prim and the lyric maidenly; it didn't match the ensuing sax-and-drums routine.

Okay, change the number. Fosse gave Kander and Ebb precise instructions: it had to be fun to hear, of course—but it must let *Chicago*'s audience know that Roxie and Velma's audience back in the 1920s would see it as a misfire, like Verdon's saxophone and Rivera's drumming. Kander and Ebb wrote just what Fosse wanted: "Loopin' the Loop," in the New Dance Sensation genre that swept Broadway from the 1910s on and, later, colonized radio and the movies. Again, this fit in with the show's program of basing song spots on the kind of music America used to listen to. "Loopin' the

Loop" was the linear descendant of "The Varsity Drag," "Charleston," and (as we remember from Ginger Rogers' *Roxie Hart* dance specialty) "Black Bottom."

But audiences hated "Loopin' the Loop." Most likely, they didn't understand why such high-powered entertainment as *Chicago* was concluding with dreck. Irony goes just so far, then it becomes puzzling. Again, in the high-strung art of the star musical, you can't separate the singer from the song.

So, while the show was still in its Philadelphia tryout, Fosse asked Kander and Ebb for yet another number, this one to set off his two divas with the élan their status required. The director was a bit sheepish about it, because he had been so demanding before; they had given him exactly what he asked for and now he wanted the opposite. Fosse was sweet but also tense, visionary yet uncertain, affable and dark and crazy, a very complex man. Yet now he was simply and completely apologetic. Would Kander and Ebb *please* write something new for the spot, something to set Gwen and Chita like rare stones in a diadem?

Putting on a fake "Well, really!" attitude, the pair marched off, wrote the replacement, "Nowadays," in an hour, then took the rest of the day off, to simulate A Heavy Session With the Muse. "Nowadays," suave and stylish, would replace "It" with a message wedded to the show's "anything goes" theme, and, dropping the sax and drums, Fosse would use "Nowadays" to generate a snappy dance finale. In the end, Roxie was vaudeville scum but Gwen Verdon was a very special attraction, for at some point in all this the irony had to yield to the show-biz handbook and let the talent overcome the story. Nobody was coming to *Chicago* to see Verdon—and Rivera as well—make fools of themselves in a chaser act.

We'll get to that last pas de deux very soon, but now let's examine *Chicago*'s score, using the occasion to slip in the plot blueprint as well. As I've emphasized, a musical satire needs an unconventional musical program, as with the extensive finalettos of the Gershwin political shows with their waggish Gilbert and Sullivan choristers. We recently heard Fred Ebb identify *Chicago*'s songs as Golden Age hommages, but in fact only major character numbers and a few situation pieces revived old forms.

Thus, "**All That Jazz**" (as we now call it) is pure Kander and Ebb up-to-date show music, despite many verbal references to the paraphernalia of twenties partying—the flapper's rolling her stockings below the knees, for comfort or daring, or the blues playing of a certain "Father Dip."[7] This is sheer scene-setting, with some plot slipped in, in that Roxie's assignation with and then murder of Fred Casely occur as two tiny dialogue scenes within the musical framework. Note, too, that, after Velma's refrain, the ensemble gets a "trio" section ("Oh, you're gonna see your Sheba . . ."), and then, in quodlibet style, Kander puts the two strophes together simultaneously.

This is a show that left some of the public ambivalent and then became one of the most popular musicals of all time, so it's interesting to note that the New York preview audiotape records an extremely avid house, all but overwhelming the show with its delight. Naturally, the first customers for a new musical by Fosse and Kander and Ebb, with Gwen Verdon and Chita Rivera, would be stoked. These spectators are the aficionados, bound to collect this latest sample of Big Broadway art without asking, May I? of critics or word-of-mouth. Still, egged on by the brisk tempo of "All That Jazz," in a realistic ambient instead of the processed sound we hear today, the public is clapping for everything.

No, not clapping. *Cheering*: for the first notes of the prelude, for the dropping of the "Chicago/Late 1920's" sign, for Rivera's entrance, Verdon's entrance. There is much laughter as well, reminding us that the Golden Age had not yet ended and the best musical comedies were, by that Age's rules, extremely *comic*, because the form favored quirky characters with a sarcastic view of life, and the performers knew how to land funny lines.

The second number, "**Funny Honey**," establishes Roxie with the first of the show-biz icon cuts. This one uses a visual mnemonic, setting

---

7. This is Ebb's creative kenning (of sorts) for Louis Armstrong, whose trumpeting was a fixture of Chicago's jazz scene in the 1920s. Armstrong was famed as "Satchmo," but his childhood nickname was "Dipper"—"short," he explained in his memoirs, "for Dippermouth, from the piece called 'Dippermouth Blues.'"

Verdon atop an upright piano, the historic perch of Helen Morgan. The original Julie in *Show Boat*, Morgan was not personally comparable to Roxie in any way. What Morgan was known for was torch songs, such as "Why Was I Born?." (And *Show Boat*'s "Bill" was a merry piece in a different show till it was rebooted for the terminally plangent Morgan.) "Funny Honey" isn't a torch song, though it does recall another genre Morgan worked in, the playful "He's not much but I love him" solo (which is in fact how "Bill" originally worked). "He ain't no sheik" is a central "Funny Honey" line, just as "Bill" 's pre–*Show Boat* lyric featured "Whenever he dances, his partner takes chances."

"Funny Honey" bears also a musical derivation, harking back to the ballad in which the A strains repeat a slightly varied melodic cell while the bass line moves steadily downward in stepwise formation. This roots Roxie's establishing number in the music of her era and gives the public its first clue that the show is going to tour through memes and clichés of the past.

Like "All That Jazz," "Funny Honey" contains a book scene that takes place in a specific location (again, the Hart apartment, where the cops are now taking Amos' "confession") while the vocal comes to us from parts unknown, something unheard of before *Allegro* invented the concept musical. For Roxie and her piano aren't "in" a physical location. Her salute to Amos (enriched by Verdon's droll mouthful of vowels on "funeeee honeeeey") atop that upright places her in a kind of portrait gallery of oldtime stars. Verdon made no attempt to suggest Helen Morgan's plaintive style, and Morgan was a soprano while Verdon sang in a very low chest register.[8] Rather, the intent was to debunk the "true to my man despite his faults" song type, as "Funny Honey" 's accompanying book scene finds Amos realizing that the "burglar" lying dead in front of him was Roxie's current flame. Amos abruptly recants his confession, and the "Funny Honey" lyrics turn venomous, regenerating the number into a "He's not much and I hate him" piece.

8. Verdon did have a soprano's head voice, at least at first, and she sang soprano in *Can-Can*'s "If You Loved Me Truly." It makes for startling listening today, as Verdon's almost hoarse—perhaps "breathless" describes it better—vocal tone was how her public knew her.

So far, so good: but Fosse directed Verdon to vulgarize the number, doing a drunk act to the point of offending the audience again. This was the underside of the Fosse-Verdon bond, *Chicago*'s war between the states. Fosse would demand and Verdon resist in a way that had seldom obtained on their previous shows together, even as he was giving Verdon the show as a present, micro-managing composition and production to be certain that she could make her farewell to Broadway in a smash. It was Fosse who made sure that Verdon got a honey contract as flattering as any yet signed, with approval of everything down to the ushers.

Yet here he was, mugging her protocols with demands for ever more vulgar behavior on her piano, for still louder glug-glug drinking noises out of her twenties hip flask. And she gave him trouble right back; the cast saw *Chicago* as a Fosse-Verdon cage match, even as he knew she was the dearest ally he had and she knew him as the greatest of the creatives she had known—certainly far ahead of that oh so self-important "Mr. Abbott," with his refusal to venture beyond the "Joke here—sing here—exit here" structure of shows that, for all she knew, dated back to Weber and Fields. But Fosse was ahead even of Jack Cole, a marvelous choreographer but a man without a shred of silly fun in him and thus a poor choice to direct a show, to tease its latent pleasures into the open as Fosse could. And what a union Verdon and Fosse had shared, fighting their way to the summit of the musical at the very height of its history, when mere "musical comedy" turned into The Musical, so protean and rich in possibilities!

Now at its second number, *Chicago* is moving at a terrific clip—hastily, really, in comparison with the Rodgers and Hammerstein model, which features an exposition on the grand scale. Fosse gives his Roxie just enough time to slip off her piano, walk over to the apartment scene, panic when she learns she faces a capital murder charge, and grab a rosary to start praying. Another announcement from a cast member brings on the "**Cell Block Tango**," a musical interpretation of Maurine Watkins' depiction of prison life. In 1926, two lengthy scenes presented the comings and goings of colorful inmates—not only the pretentious Velma but Liz, an evangelical hysteric, the hapless Moonshine Maggie, and belligerent Go-to-Hell Kitty Baxter. Of Mary Sunshine, Kitty says, "I eat children like her for breakfast."

But here, in 1975, the murderesses are characterized by not their personalities but the backstory on their own particular homicide. So six woman in prison stripes now appeared bearing life-size, lit-up jail-cell bars. The sultry tango ritornello that Kander created for the number offered something unusual: spoken key words cued to the beat, such as "Pop" and "Six." These called up each killer's crime (or, in the case of the unfortunate Hungarian, the act she has been wrongly accused of), related to the public in spoken passages cut into the singing. "Pop" referred to the aforementioned gum-chewing Bernie. ("You pop that gum one more time...") But "Six" gives us an insight into the difficulties Fred Ebb suffered in constructing interesting murder set-ups that would of necessity conclude with a punchline. As late as during the New York previews, Ebb was still tinkering with these backstories, and the "Six" tale, told by prisoner Annie (Michon Peacock), told of her liaison with a Mormon who turned out to have five wives. So she shot him six times, once for each wife "and one for good luck!"

But the driving, hectoring, inspiring yet so balefully critical Fosse wasn't content. The punchline lacked...well, punch. So the ending was changed: now Annie's "Six" referred to *six* wives instead of five, and, rather than shoot him, Annie gave him poison. "You know," she concluded, "some guys just can't hold their arsenic."

As it happens, it was not only Ebb who wrote this book material. Ruthless in his pursuit of a hit, Fosse habitually brought in doctors to cure an ailing script over the objections of the credited author, and for *Chicago* he got help from two of his best friends, Paddy Chayevsky and Herb Gardner. Fosse asked Neil Simon as well; no one could think up insert gags like Simon. But he refused to have anything to do with *Chicago*, gleefully cold and vicious as he thought it was. Gardner and Chayevsky, however, had no trouble sorting out how the show's satiric intent criticized rather than cherished the characters, and both men helped smarten up the "Cell Block Tango" speeches, along with the "Roxie" monologue.

Meanwhile, when David Rounds' plot action was folded into the Matron's role, Mama Morton became so crucial to the narration that she needed an establishing number. It was a shame to lose the snazzy "Ten Percent," but that jubilant quickstep, dancing rings around itself, wouldn't have suited the show-biz star the Matron represented, who we already know is Sophie Tucker. One of the great progenitors of the "I" song, autobiographical to a fault, Tucker maintained a grand and somewhat ceremonial persona. Here was a feminist who didn't need feminism, liberated not because they let her be so but because, like Madam Rose of a later age, Sophie knows that it's all about guts.

All of Tucker's numbers reflected that sense of absolute independence. In sex, Tucker took what she wanted, already shopping for new when the old playtoy was scarcely unwrapped. "That Loving Soul Kiss." "I'm Going To Do What I Please." "You've Got To See Mamma Every Night." "I Know That My Baby Is Cheatin' On Me [but maybe my baby don't know that I'm cheatin', too]." On one of her recordings, Sophie engages in palaver with her accompanist, telling him, "You men make me tired." He's a bit stunned at that: "Men make *you* tired?" But Kander and Ebb's Sophie Tucker number, **"When You're Good To Mama,"** is not about sex. It's about money, because money drives *Chicago*. Sex simply makes it crazy.

What is noteworthy here is the way Kander uses the vamp, and interstitial recaps of it, to lay a barbaric glow on the music, an orgasmic hedonism. The A strains and release aren't especially nonconformist, even though the first phrase is in the major and the second in the minor. No, what gives the song its wicked presence is the "Hell, break loose!" air of the sound as a whole, abetted by Ralph Burns' superb orchestration. The vamp itself is a slithery, braggy concoction; it's what *Chicago*'s soul would be like if it had one. This vamp is two measures long (then repeated), the first measure in the tonic minor and the second in the dominant seventh—except Kander has slipped the second tone of the scale into the first chord and the first tone into the second, which gives the whole thing a screwy grin. It's "Hula Lou" all over again, not least because Ebb's lyrics revel in sexual imagery even as they insistently talk about money. It's not sex *and* jazz. It's sex *is* jazz. Thus, on a line mentioning "tit for tat," McCarty blithely adjusted the hang of her right breast, as if the boodle of corruption was the Matron's personal aphrodisiac.

So the *Chicago* score is somewhat comparable to Stephen Sondheim's *Follies* in its ability to invest old forms with new attitudes—with a musical presence they didn't have when they were the soundtrack of American life. But, again, not every number is pastiche.

In fact, the next one is not even a number in any real sense, though it was listed in the program as one. Entitled "**Tap Dance**," it gives us a scene between Roxie and Amos, in which she manipulates him into raising money for her attorney's fee while four of the chorus boys dance "along" with her dialogue. Amos even calls it "your fancy footwork." But he gives in all the same.

Actually, "Tap Dance" is a set-up for the entrance of the attorney himself, Billy Flynn, in our third pop-icon number, "**All I Care About** [is love]." Here we get the typical twenties or thirties purveyor of the goodtime anthem, so often Al Jolson or Harry Richman. In this case it's Ted Lewis, a clarinetist and singer who popularized a blend of New Orleans jazz and Jewish klezmer band. Lewis was something of a joke in show business, as he favored corny numbers and even added to them corny ad libs. ("Aw, cut it out," to a cheeky trombone solo.) In his trademark battered top hat and cane, Lewis strutted and pranced, incessantly coloring and shading his notes and mesmerizing the public with fluttery hand gestures. He wasn't much of a clarinetist, though. But *Chicago* doesn't model Billy Flynn on Ted Lewis; the show invokes him because of his catalogue of numbers too absurdly ingenuous to be believable—"On the Sunny Side of the Street," say, or the winsome "Me and My Shadow," which Lewis liked to perform with a black "double."

"All I Care About" is more of the same, in its rejection of material wealth in favor of spiritual benison. Actually, Kander and Ebb might have had Harry Richman in mind, because his "Singing a Vagabond Song" aligns directly with "All I Care About" in its rejection of "your fool'ry, your jewel'ry." But Flynn's first spoken line references almost verbatim Ted Lewis' sign-in catchphrase, "Is everybody happy?," and the script specifically demands a delivery "à la Ted Lewis."

True, unlike Lewis in his clobbered high hat, Flynn is a real fashion plate, very colorfully suited up in pin stripes complete with vest, carnation, handkerchief, and—though few could see them past the fifth row, dark spats. The 1996 revival in its concert dress is so familiar that many today are unaware that, in 1975, *Chicago* was costumed (by Patricia Zipprodt) as pictorially as *The Music Man* or *Mame*. But Fosse tossed in a joke about it, for Flynn's vocal was accompanied by the ladies of the chorus bearing huge feathered fans, and at one point—who but Fosse would think to do this?—they encircled Flynn, hiding his nether quarters as if to give him a happy ending. And, lo, when we next saw his legs, his trousers were gone.

This risqué jest actually served as a scene transition, necessary punctuation in a concept musical, where, as we've seen, a lack of scenery means the creatives must use other means to let the audience know where the characters are. In this particular moment, the drum doors opened during the applause after "All I Care About" and the center winch glided downstage holding the furniture of Flynn's law office, with Amos waiting to see him and a pins-in-the-mouth tailor working on the trousers of Flynn's new bespoke suit, which Flynn then put on.

A longish book scene devoted to Flynn's fee concluded with another silken transition, as Amos and the office rolled out of sight on the winch while Roxie came up from stairs cut into the stage floor. Now Flynn had only to walk a few steps downstage to join her and create a new "geography" in another of the concept-musical "places" that are neither here nor there. Sitting on chairs, Roxie and Flynn looked up at the bandstand for the next iconic number, establishing Mary Sunshine, overhead with the orchestra.

Sunshine's number is "**A Little Bit Of Good**," a Panglossian piece with a dead-giveaway reference to Marilyn Miller and her *Sally* theme song, "Look For the Silver Lining." Oddly, the first number written for this spot, "Windowpanes of Rose," was not historically referential. It recalled the operetta heroine spinning out a descant on high while the orchestra or chorus took over the melody, but the reference was strictly generic. It did not single out a specific practitioner of the style.

"A Little Bit Of Good," on the other hand, revisits Miller and "Silver Lining" very precisely,[9] though at just one point, in the lead-in from the verse to the refrain. Back in *Sally*, Jerome Kern used an eight-note theme to link the recitative (so to say) to the aria in a droopy little tête-à-tête between two adjacent pitches. So Kander adopted this theme (slightly shortened) in Mary Sunshine's solo, thus to expose those old Pollyanna ditties to the tough love of *Chicago*'s honesty.

Now, as we've said, Miller was an achiever, a fighter. Remember, the refrain of her *Sally* establishing song began, "I wish I could be like Joan of Arc." Miller was the opposite of Mary Sunshine, that feckless devotee of spin and lies. The parallel lies in the message encased in "Look For the Silver Lining," in *Chicago*'s questioning the sincerity—or perhaps just the intelligence—of these absurd hymns to optimism. And "A Little Bit Of Good" is a very crowded text in any case. It is stacked with memes: of the drag-queen persona, of Cinderella musicals and Ziegfeld musicals, of the "sob sister" writer, of the coloratura soprano, presented here with deliberately goofy dynamics careening from pianissimo to fortissimo and an endlessly held high note just before the end.

We have traveled a very great distance since the first pages of this book, when fur trappers organized a settlement at the mouth of a river leading into a great lake and when Indians, who had already dismissed the site as untenable, were mystified when white men laid claim to something as basic and magical—really, unownable—as nature. Obviously, this nation has grown far beyond that historical

---

9. In *The Sound of Broadway Music*, Steven Suskin quotes from orchestrator Ralph Burns' instructions to Stanley Lebowsky, referencing as inspiration for his "A Little Bit Of Good" charts "the Grace Moore recordings." Moore, primarily known as an operatic soprano (and movie star), did sing popular music on Broadway early in her career, but she wasn't associated with a particular sort of number, despite having introduced two Irving Berlin standards, "What'll I Do?" (in duet with John Steel) and "All Alone" (with Oscar Shaw). Burns may have used Grace Moore as a template because there were no "Marilyn Miller recordings" for him to draw on and her films were generally unavailable at the time, whereas Moore did make recordings and some of her films were comparatively easy to screen.

moment, but my point in writing this book is that the American musical grew along with the nation. It has become ever more artistic and observant, yet it is undervalued because its innate showmanship still confounds the opinion-makers, who believe that entertainment must be self-consciously portentous to deserve respect. Yet many shows, before and after *Chicago*, have proved by their very hold on our attention that they are as analytical and philosophical as any work of art. Even a song as apparently slight of texture as Mary Sunshine's valentine to human nature reveals, on close study, a point of view on how our information may be as painted as opera, as cooked as candy, as masked as a spy.

Mary Sunshine's appearance cues in more plot, as Flynn and Roxie now face the press en masse in **"We Both Reached For the Gun,"** another number without a generic precedent in the show-biz past. It does, however, revive the now vanished usages of the ventriloquist. Dating back to the English music hall, this double act of man and doll hosted very few famous practioners, though Harry Lester and his insanely repulsive wooden partner, called not Sparky or Cranky but, ever so grandly, Frank Byron Jr., were popular in American vaudeville around the turn into the twentieth century. Not till the 1930s did the country boast of a household-name ventriloquist act, Edgar Bergen (father of Candice) and Charlie McCarthy, whose singular joke it was to appear mainly on radio, where the entire reason for "throwing" the voice is neutralized.

"We Both Reached For the Gun" takes place in a specific location, the common room of the Cook County Jail. Or so we surmise from this exchange:

MATRON: Mr. Flynn, the reporters are here.
FLYNN: Let 'em in, Butch.

The song's key visual is Flynn working Roxie as his dummy on his lap, so Jerry Orbach did the singing for both Roxie and himself, fielding the reporters' questions and maintaining Roxie's alibi, used in all the *Chicago*s, that she shot in self-defense. As so much of

Chicago's score consists of character numbers, it's notable that "We Both Reached For the Gun" is a plot number (or, more precisely, a situation number, as it doesn't actually advance the storyline but rather illustrates a moment in the action, in this case the Flynn-Roxie press conference). A venerable ventriloquist's stunt caps the music: a glass of milk was brought in for Flynn to drink during his big long-held note just before the final "gun." (The milk, of course, was fake, simply white paint applied around the bottom of the glass.)

After the number, Tony Walton's set design unveiled its coup de théâtre: a huge blow-up of a newspaper's front page came sailing down from the flies against the back wall of the stage, with that headline of "ROXIE ROCKS CHICAGO." At the same time, six of the reporters from "We Both Reached For the Gun," who had remained when the others left, phoned their scoops in to their papers, and when they, too, went off, Roxie was seen upstage at the doors of the drum, reading her "notices," all raves.

And now she stepped forward for the "Roxie" monologue, with its centrally important linking of show business and a sociopathic need for attention. It's the American dream: we seek the spotlight not for the fulfillment of talent or even to make a living, but to redeem a faulty ego system by attracting a following. "Just wanted to be noticed" is how Madam Rose explains it. Yes, of course it's a truism; in other news, the ocean is wet. Yet from *Sally* in 1920 to *Hamilton* in 2016, the musical has been telling us how basic this need is. Again, in the latter show, Aaron Burr calls it "the room where it happens": his show business is politics. Yet this needy side of celebrity keeps poking into the musical, one way or another. It's as American as...Chicago.

Kander and Ebb originally fashioned the "**Roxie**" refrain as a feverish one-step, but it was all wrong that way, because one could scarcely follow the lyrics at that tempo. Besides, Roxie now thinks she has made it. She isn't keyed-up. She's luxuriating. So, on second thought, "Roxie" was slowed way, way down, and Tony Walton sent another visitation from the flies: a big neon sign heralding Roxie's act, her name, her fame-to-blazes truth: ROXIE.

Now six of the chorus men sneaked on in clownish tights, empha-sizing the fantastical nature of Roxie's vision. But then, Fosse him-self was the fantastical director. He worked in frisky surrealism we don't find in *Oklahoma!*, *A Chorus Line*, or the rest of the short list—because of that Fosse edge, that wish to go too far. *Oklahoma!* and its fellows are realistic, even when they include a Dream Ballet. They have nothing like—for instance—*Sweet Charity*'s "Rich Man's Frug," in which Fosse *styles* the hip crowd instead of simply presenting it. This sets Fosse apart from de Mille, Robbins, Kidd, Champion: they all know that musicals are fantasies of a kind, but only Fosse wants to actualize them as bizarre and imaginary.

Now that Roxie is the queen of the prison, Velma needs to attach herself to Roxie's power. Once again, show business is the glue that bonds all of *Chicago*'s parts: Velma wants to recruit Roxie in a resus-citation of Velma's sister act, retired when Velma caught her hus-band and sister in flagrante and killed them both. Kander and Ebb got a number out of it, "**I Can't Do It Alone**," the formidable Chita's big first-act solo. Another cut with no ancestor in the show-biz past, the song found Rivera performing both parts in a double act while Verdon, at stage right, simply ate her dinner, at one point getting off an elaborate yawn.

So it's no sale, and the sequence ended in a sorrowful coda with a bit of scenery hauled in from stage right to underline Fosse's belief that everything is about sex: a bed with two holes cut in for the heads of the occupants. Thus, when Rivera poked hers through one hole, the other hole remained empty: because she simply cannot...do it...alone.

Now it was time to thicken the plot, with a rival to Roxie's infamy: Go-To-Hell Kitty, the well-known pineapple heiress.[10] The Matron narrates the backstory in dialogue to orchestral underscoring, and this "number" appeared in the playbill as "**Chicago After Midnight**."

---

10. A little joke made its debut in this episode: Kitty's last name, heretofore Baxter, was now Katz (later to be also the name of the animated cartoon cat in Kander and Ebb's 1981 musical *Woman of the Year*): Kitty Katz.

After we saw Kitty mow down her boy friend and two of his most intimate friends, the music faded and Stanley Lebowsky addressed us with "Goodnight, folks."

The press is of course thrilled with this new star:

ROXIE: Oh, Miss Sunshine...
MARY SUNSHINE: Not now, Roxie.

and the action surged toward the first-act curtain as Roxie and Velma duetted in rainwear in "[I am] **My Own Best Friend**." Fosse brought the pair far downstage to sit on the apron, back to back and unaware of each other for an anthem of egomaniacal moxie. As the number reached its climax, the ensemble joined in for some pseudo-Hollywood "heavenly choir" backup, the key jumped up a whole step, two of the chorus women appeared on the bandstand to toss confetti and, at last, Verdon and Rivera started to take a bow, pursuing the feeling of a story presented as the Great American Variety Show.

Except only Rivera bowed. Verdon fainted. And the drum doors opened to allow Flynn and the press to rush in just in time to hear Roxie announce that she was pregnant. Outfoxed again, Velma analyzed this new development with le mot juste:

VELMA: Shit.

But she was not too defeated to deliver that last bit of "All That Jazz," as the curtain fell on Act One.

Echoing Texas Guinan with the aforementioned "Hello, suckers," Velma welcomed us back for Act Two with "**I Know a Girl**," for some years *Chicago*'s least-known vocal cut, because it wasn't on the first cast album. And this led into *Chicago*'s most confusing number, because it existed in different versions: Roxie's "**Me and My Baby**." This was another vaudeville portrait, now of Eddie Cantor, noted for such frantic paeans as "My Baby Just Cares For Me" and "Yes, Yes! (My Baby Said Yes)." Cantor was permanently frantic himself, as a

milquetoast ever beset by rufftuffs. His "Baby" numbers were para-
doxes, gleeful sex cries from a creampuff who somehow or other can
wow the girls. (And writers never tired of noting that the real-life
Cantor sired five daughters on his wife, Ida.)

Fosse decided to place a sorta kinda production number here, for
Verdon and the ensemble men. The music is a zippy one-step, and Fosse
gave the dancing a slightly silent-movie feeling, with Chaplinesque
movements. (Verdon, in a man's suit, looked cute; the boys, in cross-
dressed tights, seemed a bit berserk.) However, Verdon was already
looking at a busy workout eight times a week without this heavy song
and dance as well, so Fosse put in an alternate setting, known in the
Chicago company as "The Strut." Now Verdon appeared in bombshell
tights with just two boys in a cheeky parade sort of thing: flashy but
much easier to perform. And at one performance I saw, early in the
run, a presumably exhausted Verdon reduced the entire number to
just one very slow vocal chorus, without a dance.

During "The Strut," various other principals interject dialogue on
how Roxie's "pregnancy" will influence the course of Fred Casely's
justice. Finally, Amos tries to add his little bit as "the father"—but
the music has given out. Story of his life. And now Amos gets a solo;
had we even noticed that he lacked one thus far? He must be one of
the few leads in musical history to get an establishing song halfway
through Act Two. Entitled "**Mister Cellophane**," the number is
modeled on Bert Williams' theme song, first heard in 1905,
"Nobody." Alex Rogers' lyrics, to Williams' own music, gives us the
lament of the eternal patsy:

> When life seems full of clouds and rain,
> And I am filled with naught but pain,
> Who soothes my thumping, bumping brain?
> (Spoken:) Nobody!

Though he is largely forgotten today, this sixth and last of *Chicago*'s
old-time celebrity models, Bert Williams, is an important historical
figure, the first performer to move out of the so-called "black time"

(that is, the separate world of black show business) into the "white time" (mainstream show business), when Florenz Ziegfeld hired him for *Follies of 1910*. By an odd paradox, Ziegfeld discovered all the other mainstay *Follies* stars, from Fanny Brice and Will Rogers to W. C. Fields and Eddie Cantor. Williams was the only one who was *already* famous, one of the few black people in the country whose name was well known to whites (even though, by rules of racial separatism, few if any would have seen him on stage.)

There's an arresting irony here, because while both Velma and the Matron have often been played by blacks in *Chicago*'s recent history, Amos is of necessity white, as a racially mixed marriage in twenties Chicago would haunt the story with a distracting modern resonance. Moreover, Amos is nobody because people pay no attention to him, not because he's racially invisible in a whites-only environment. Of course, the original "Nobody" song presents a "text" only we of today can read: "Nobody" was Bert Williams' ID anthem, and Williams was, in effect, the first black performer in white entertainment. As a Broadway star, he was not exactly a nobody—but, as the only black performer in the white time, not exactly anything else.

Still, *Chicago*'s interest in "Nobody" is thematic, not sociological. Kander and Ebb referenced the song not because of the racial thing but the personal isolation thing: Amos is alone in the world. Kander and Ebb adopted "Nobody" so closely that the first sixteen measures of "Mister Cellophane" correspond precisely to the scan of the verse of "Nobody" (the part I just quoted). And where Williams said "Nobody," Amos sings, "You'd notice him."

Thereafter, the new number goes off in a completely different direction, extending its verse in the mediant minor and reaching a chorus marked "Slow rag." "Nobody"'s chorus is short and straightforward, but "Mister Cellophane"'s chorus is—here's another irony—grandiose, as Amos, in a tramp outfit and a clown's oversized white collar, went into a transcendent strut of his own, a loser's apotheosis.

Roxie is *Chicago*'s protagonist; by laws established by the ancient Greeks, there can be only one—Oedipus, Hamlet, Liliom, Archie Rice. Billy Flynn would be the deuteragonist, the most crucial of the other players, as Roxie's coach, critic, and would-be savior. So Velma is the tritagonist, less influential in the action yet all the same an almost equal participant.

So now Velma gets another I-song, "**When Velma Takes the Stand**," in which she tries to pep up Flynn's flagging interest in her case with a preview of how she'll stage her courtroom performance. Fosse gave the piece a very athletic workout, with Rivera downstage dancing on and around a chair while four of the chorus men backed up her vocal with Rudy Vallee megaphones.

The concept source for the music is the now vanished parlor-piano solo, vastly popular into the 1960s, when the guitar took over as American youth's instrument of choice. Zez Confrey was the best known of the composers in this line, and each of his pieces—he published over eighty of them, from 1921 to 1959—was a little tone poem. Thus the titles: "Grandfather's Clock," with its chimes of B$^{\flat+}$ over a C octave in the bass; "Parade of the Jumping Beans"; "Phantom Cadets"; and, the most famous, and Confrey's debut publication, "Kitten On the Keys."

With the exception of a few études, all of Confrey's pieces were designed for the average accomplished pianist (unlike the work of Confrey's English rival, Billy Mayerl, whose sophisticated and more overtly jazzing solos often demanded a professional's technique). They observed the ABA structure and syncopation of ragtime, albeit with more slithery figurations. Confrey's "Dizzy Fingers" is typical: marked Presto (very fast), it races up and down the scale in the tonic sixth and then the supertonic $\frac{9}{7}$, moving on to a subsidiary section in the minor and then a trio in the subdominant, all adhering to the very busy fingerwork of the broken chords heard at the outset.

By comparison, *Chicago*'s version of Confrey, with a Charleston release and featuring the piano in Ralph Burns' zesty orchestration, gives us a slightly rudimentary ripple figuration on the keyboard, as Rivera previewed the little touches with which she would decorate her testimony. She'll tremble, cry, require a handkerchief, slump in her chair. (This last is direct from Maurine Watkins, though it was Roxie who was supposed to slump.) After the number, we got yet another show-biz meme as Rivera asked conductor Lebowsky, "May I have my exit music, please?," so she could leave the stage in style.

This is more concept-musical writing, letting a character admit that he or she is a performer in a show. But, further, isn't "When Velma Takes the Stand" another Kander and Ebb "survival" number? True, it's a variation on the formula. Now it's (energy + megalomania = success), because *Chicago* turns traditional musical comedy inside out. Wrong is right. Real is fake. Everyone's a phony because what's natural is . . . unpersuasive. It's the recipe for good salesmanship in the 1920s: lie a lot.

And yet the struggle to survive is real, for both Roxie and Velma need to stay in the headlines or Billy Flynn will put off their court date. In *Chicago*, show business doesn't create fame: fame creates show business.

A strange and even unlikely dialogue scene now finds the Matron interpreting for the Hunyak using a Hungarian-English dictionary and blithely speaking and understanding complex Hungarian sentences. This leads into a brief "vaudeville" stunt, as the Matron announces the girl's "famous Hungarian rope trick": her hanging. Of course, she was the only one of the "six merry murderesses" who was innocent, and, translating for her, the Matron actually takes her side with the girl's bored and unhelpful attorney:

> MATRON: She says Uncle Sam is just and fair and he wouldn't [penalize her] because she is innocent. . . . I think she's telling the truth.

It's disconcerting to hear the Matron being momentarily understanding given how heartless *all* the principals (except Amos) are. Then, too, this sequence criticizes not "Chicago justice" but American justice, moving this ghastly execution of the innocent out of musical-comedy black humor into something powerful, a real indictment of our culture.

And that, after one last prep between Roxie and Flynn, brings us to the trial, introduced by Flynn's **"Razzle Dazzle."** Pulling out his shirt, mussing his hair, and donning a pair of granny glasses pushed down on his nose, Orbach became Clarence Darrow, Chicago's ultra-imposing attorney for the defense—it was Darrow who successfully pleaded for the lives of Leopold and Loeb.

"Razzle Dazzle" cites theatrics and cosmetics as key in winning over any jury, committee, audience. As Orbach sang, the ensemble, in tights, came in, one by one, in a circus sideshow atmosphere. On first thought, Fosse arranged for them to stage an orgy, apparently on the notion that lawyers are whores. Once again, however, the producers—and everybody else—were repulsed, and forced him to abandon the sex stuff.

It was, Fosse thought, *New Girl in Town* all over again. But there his depiction of Anna's haunted past was simply ahead of the age. When Fosse staged the orgy in *Pippin*, after the hero's "With You," the age was ready for it, especially as it celebrated the gentle eros of flower children. The *Chicago* orgy, on the other hand, was rough and mean, for Fosse was, above all, a provocateur—not a ballet person, like de Mille and Robbins; not a barnstormer like Michael Kidd; and not a suave illustrator like Joe Layton. Fosse was an idolater of the appetitive, the addictive, the egomaniacal, and he used it in his art. Women were prostitutes and men their stooges. There was no Goethean *ewig-weibliche*, the womanly ideal "drawing us upward." To get your Ph.D. in German Literature, you must be able to recite the names and dates of Goethe's mistresses, as each in her way in-spired a poetry of the attainable perfection of man. But if there were a Ph.D. in Fosse, you'd have to memorize a little black book with notations on what they like to do and how well they do it. That's the poetry of sex and jazz.

Yet for all his determination to explode the standard cautions, Fosse lacked the revolutionary's confidence. "Razzle Dazzle" is his confession, motto, epitaph. It is a paradox of entertainment in the Golden Age that the biggest stars succeeded with a combination of content and flash. That was their brilliance, their originality. Katharine Hepburn had that affected way of speaking. Cole Porter made his characters sing in wit beyond their rightful means. The Lunts mixed a cocktail of psychological honesty and the Grand

Manner. David Merrick peeled history off the London stage for Broadway while capering like the Artful Dodger. Fred Astaire was both show-off and truth-teller.

And "Razzle Dazzle" is Fosse's guilty plea. Kander and Ebb tricked it up with finger snaps, because Fosse loved finger snaps. The song is a joke, but it's their joke, and it contains a riddle: if razzle dazzle is a swindle, why is it so satisfying?

The song's melody is short, twenty-three bars as opposed to the usual thirty-two. It has neither a verse nor a trio section. It's a cogent statement, repeated a number of times as if to emphasize its simplicity—the simplicity, really, of the art of the scam. Of course, it's a lawyer who teaches the lesson. What if it had been a politician? A college president? A chief of police? Because, once again, the word "Chicago" means all the authorities, all the crony corruption between the state and the unscrupulous, right back to the buying and selling of land when, as the Indians saw it, nature could not be owned. Can a mere musical say this? Yes. *Good News!*: "The moon belongs to everyone."

"Razzle Dazzle" leads into *Chicago*'s longest book scene, the final trial sequence. However, musical bits here and there within it remind us that the post–George Abbott format moistened the strict alternation of dialogue and music into a fluid blending of the two. Fosse wanted the trial to have the quality of a minstrel show, made of jokes and shtick, stylized and fantastical, and punctuated by the smashing of tambourines. Billy Flynn is the Interlocutor, and the roles of Mr. Tambo and Mr. Bones are taken by Roxie, Amos, and (a briefly revived) Fred Casely, re-enacting the murder while a single performer plays all of the jurymen by varying his look and manner[11] as the ensemble applauds, cries "Hallelujah" in Handelian mode, and reprises the last few measures of "Razzle Dazzle" as Flynn reaches his climax and everyone takes a bow.

---

11. Moving from chair to chair of the "jury box" brought on by the stage-left winch, this single actor deftly altered his look at moments when the audience was bound to be distracted by activity elsewhere on stage. The published text includes a prop list that gives this player's accessories as, among other things, an ear trumpet, a gray beard, mittens, eyeglasses, a false nose, a cane, and even a mask to disguise half his face.

It's time for a full-scale vocal spot, so the Matron and Velma, listening on the radio to Mary Sunshine (up on the bandstand) as she gives a play-by-play of the proceedings, rode up on the stage-right elevator. One of the show's biggest laughs—and another concept-musical, meta-theatre touch—hits in as Sunshine compliments Roxie on her outfit:

> SUNSHINE: She looks simply radiant in her stylish blue lace dress and elegant silver shoes.
> VELMA (to the radio): With rhinestone buckles?
> SUNSHINE: With rhinestone buckles.

Yes, Roxie stole Velma's shoes. Is there no justice? First it's murder, and now this!

The joke cues in "**Class**," a comedy song in Fred Ebb's characteristic conversational style. The number is marked "Quasi Franz Schubert," presumably because its simplicity of accompaniment, laying all the musical weight on the melody, is meant to suggest the great master of German Lied. More: Ralph Burn's solo violin arrangement gives the piece classical poise. But "Class"'s vocal style is too modern to be Schubertian, except in the release ("Ah, there ain't no gentlemen…"), when the key (in the published sheet) moves from D minor to B flat, descending gracefully to A minor, G minor, and C_7^9. Thus, the harmony is post-Schubert, but the sweetness of the tune favors the Meister. It's Kander's ironic joke, as the Matron and Velma are their usual coarse selves. Class is over, they lament, in music demure enough for church but wording fit for taboo.

As always with Ebb, it's the characters who make the lyrics amusing, because Velma and the Matron are utterly unaware how unfit they are to draw social distinctions. It isn't what is said: it's who says it. Thus, in the first production of *The Visit*, in Chicago, a gossipy duet somewhat comparable to "Class" called "You Know Me" featured the line "Or her ass would be on the floor." Out of context, it's virtually meaningless. But in giving us two women claiming to be above vicious snark but then indulging in it, the number brought the house down, not least because Kander banged the line home with a belted-out high note on "floor."

This is one of the identifying features of the post-*Oklahoma!* musical: unlike Lorenz Hart, Cole Porter, Ira Gershwin, and others, lyricists began to lock their fun into narrative context. Songs had to sound like the characters who were singing them. This is Offenbach's gai primitif brought up to a more sophisticated level: *Orpheus in the Underworld* plus sex and jazz.

With Roxie acquitted, Billy took his leave of the show with exit music of his own, a snippet of "All I Care About" complete with the fan dancers. Amos, conclusively rejected by his wife, now asked for *his* music. And of course there wasn't any. "Okay," he said as he exited. It's the only other element in the show—beside the "Not guilty" pleading of the Hungarian "murderess"—that arouses our sympathy.

Roxie didn't even notice. She now went into a new kind of torch song, lamenting the loss of her one great love: notoriety. Yet the disillusioned and sarcastic "**Nowadays**" then became an anthem of self-gratification as an announcer whisked us off to the theatre where Roxie and Velma were to unveil their vaudeville act bearing the ultimate Fosse regalia, top hats and canes.

This was the start of the show's finale, which in the earliest performances in 1975 built steadily to a gigantic ovation—a eulogy, perhaps, for a level of sheer musical-comedy excitement that would become all but irretrievable within a few years. To launch the sequence, the two stars moved to a measured whistling tune with a sneaky hint of wa-wa in it. Then, to arranger Peter Howard's quick-step shimmy version of "Funny Honey," called the "**Hot Honey Rag**," the pair, now stripped down to marquee couture in fringed skirts, went into what has become one of the best-known dances in the musical's history, moving as mirror images of each other. It's dazzling, the perfect capstone to an intricately exhibitionistic evening—until, during the applause, the show reached a scathing finish as the two threw flowers at the public while calling themselves "the living examples of what a wonderful country this is."

* * *

That's the continuity. Now, what of the decor? Tony Walton's layout of drum-bandstand with its three winches (left, right, and center, through the drum doors), two elevators and one stairway (through traps in the deck) left relatively little space for the dancers. But then, this show had no expansive numbers in the old sense of a stageful of people occupying a great swath of real estate, as with "The Farmer and the Cowmen" or "Get Me To the Church On Time." That sort of thing suited Fosse in the 1950s, when, not counting the principals, he could deploy some thirty choristers. *Chicago* counted a cast of nineteen in all—six principals and only thirteen in the ensemble.

Patricia Zipprodt's costumes helped to color in the somewhat stark look of the playing area, in a style that varied from the natural (in Orbach's suits) to the stylized (in Verdon's laced-up, long-sleeved beige top over long shorts cinched in by a broad belt tied with fringe, an outfit that was not likely to have been seen anywhere in Chicago in the 1920s). The murderesses were in regulation black-and-white prison stripes, but the corps in general wore bizarre tights, set off when they were reporters by fedoras (for the girls as well as the boys) with fancy-Dan banding at the brims.

And of course there were the Fosse accessories. A week before the general rehearsal period, Fosse started work with the dancers, and the first order of business was to open the famous "Fosse trunk." This was filled with goodies: capes, funny glasses, wigs, gimmick belts, what have you. Above all, there were the Fosse derbies, always to be grasped between thumb and forefinger, as if holding a gem of rare price. With the trunk opened, Fosse encouraged his people to pull out whatever attracted them, to toy with the props and work them into the staging.

This, too, set Fosse apart from his colleagues. Agnes de Mille and Jerome Robbins wouldn't have been caught dead with a trunk of gewgaws (though Susan Stroman, in the generation after Fosse, likes to build numbers around the use of props). The lone performer (Richard Korthaze) changing his ID from one juryman to another in the trial scene based his physique du rôle on the contents of the trunk, from a clown's nose to a set of piquant mustaches.

After this preliminary work with the dancers, Fosse ran the first full-cast rehearsal, and the very next day a combination of his chain smoking and "jalopy heart" (in Sam Wasson's eloquent phrasing) felled him with what may be the most famous stroke in show-biz history. It sidelined Fosse long enough for the entire production to go into limbo. Would he return? Could someone else take over? Fosse finally recovered, and rehearsals began anew. But something was very, very different about the man now. He had always been a difficult taskmaster, railing at everyone, calling dancers "stupid," snarling at any producer who dared question his taste, singling out one of the chorus girls with "Just because we fucked last night, don't expect special treatment this morning."

Well, they were almost all like that, except Peter Gennaro. De Mille could be harsh, Kidd impatient. Robbins was the worst by far. In a famous story, he's berating the ensemble of *Billion Dollar Baby* while standing at the lip of the stage apron. As he hacks away at everyone, he starts moving backward, unknowingly heading for the orchestra pit. And nobody says a word, letting him tumble head over heels. Now it's good.

However, Fosse's return to *Chicago* brought out a demonic intensity new to him, even an overtly vicious streak. Keep in mind that the ensemble he was now reviling was made up of Fosse people, hand-picked from previous Fosse shows, his stylists, his favorites. Yet at times he treated them as if they were tyros who couldn't pull off a community-theatre *No, No, Nanette*.

Fosse was rough even with Gwen Verdon, though *Chicago* was in effect his present to her as her final Broadway musical, their fifth together. In Philadelphia, when Kander and Ebb replaced Roxie and Velma's raucous amateur-night vaudeville act with the paradoxically soft-spoken Jeremiad of "Nowadays," Fosse made Verdon beg for the number. Would it be a duet? Roxie's solo? Or what if he gave the whole thing to Velma (though that would have defied dramatic sense)? As Chita Rivera told Sam Wasson, Fosse, the two stars, and Kander and Ebb met in the lounge of the Forrest Theatre as Fosse had Verdon try out the new piece.

"I want this song [as a solo], Bobby," Verdon told him. "Chita and I are very close, so this is going to be fine with her. I want that song."

Why? For one thing, it was the final vocal in the show, thus the fabled eleven o'clock spot, reserved for the star. As well, it offered an important acting opportunity, as "Nowadays," to repeat, starts with a beaten Roxie, defeated by the very system she has mastered to get off on her murder charge. Then, too, the number would be the last new one Verdon was to sing on Broadway, in a line stretching from "If You Loved Me Truly" to "I'm a Brass Band." Oddly, though all Verdon's musicals from *Can-Can* on were hits, she had introduced very few standards. Nothing from *New Girl in Town* or *Redhead* caught on for long, and even *Sweet Charity* did not give her a piece as immortally hers as "Whatever Lola Wants."

"Nowadays," however, seemed like Verdon's valentine. In the end, Fosse let her deliver the first chorus, zip into a lightning-strike dress change in the wings, and come back with Rivera to make the transition into their vaudeville act, which, we already know, was now svelte and poised and show-biz hot, a truly grand finale.

And "Nowadays" was its linchpin—the linchpin, even, of the entire show. It was Verdon's by right because it was Roxie's moment of anagnorisis, the ancient Greek "recognition," when the protagonist—and there can be only one per story, remember—realizes what the story has actually been about.

Still, Fosse wanted Verdon begging for the song. After Kander and Ebb performed it, fresh off the lead sheet, Fosse had Verdon try it out, to (as Rivera told Wasson) "an unhappy feeling in the room." In fact, Rivera asked Fosse to call a halt to the proceedings. We can do this later, Bobby, okay?

And Fosse replied, "She'll do as I say."

He wasn't acting like a man reprieved from death in the hospital, but like one surrounded by traitors in the rehearsal room. They were going to proceed without him, weren't they? With *his show*! And there was tension, too, in how the world was going to greet this latest Fosse endeavor, because he was coming off of a huge jump in career prestige, personally winning the Oscar for *Cabaret*, two Tonys for *Pippin*, and three Emmys for *Liza With a Z*, all just a bit before this. Every eye in the entertainment world was on him with extreme prejudice, so Fosse had more than personal relationships to consider, even the great relationship of his life, with Verdon. Ann Reinking, personally close to Fosse, saw what pressure he was under. As she told Sam Wasson, the director of a show like *Chicago* "has to be Henry Kissinger and Sigmund Freud and Bob Fosse." He's the one to blame if something breaks.

So Fosse was outraged in every direction. He was mad at the cast, because they got to perform and he didn't. Unlike de Mille, Robbins, and the others, who all gave up dancing when they turned choreographers, Fosse had never stopped performing. He partnered Verdon in "Who's Got the Pain?" in the *Damn Yankees* film after *New Girl in Town* had graduated him from up-and-coming to masterly. He twice took the lead in *Pal Joey* at the City Center (opposite Carol Bruce, then Viveca Lindfors) after *Redhead* stamped his credentials as a top director-choreographer. He had planned to bring *Redhead* to London with Verdon, not only re-staging it but playing the murderer. And when his production of *The Conquering Hero* was facing certain Broadway doom because of a tuneless score and a colorless cast, he proposed to jazz the show up by taking over the lead. He actually auditioned for it (but failed to persuade).

And then there was the Hal Prince thing. *Chicago*'s producers, Robert Fryer and James Cresson, could not simply abandon a major production that was capitalized and in rehearsal even upon losing their showrunner, no matter how Fosse felt about it. Yes, *Chicago* was Fosse-Verdon and Fosse-Verdon was *Chicago*. And, yes, to switch out your chief for someone—anyone—else threatened an artistic catastrophe. But what else could they do? "The show must go on" is not a bromide; it's the theatre's mission statement, because thespians' lives are built around their work, not the personal or the sentimental. What if Fosse lingered in medical support for months and then went from the hospital to the burial ground?

So the men responsible for the welfare of the *Chicago* company went shopping for a substitute, and they ended up asking Hal Prince.

This was sensible in that Prince had produced and directed *Cabaret*, with which *Chicago* bore a relationship as fellow commentative shows with Kander and Ebb scores. Prince never did assume control of *Chicago*, and when he finally saw it he felt it was not only related to *Cabaret* but an offshoot of it, an imitation.

Prince was wrong about that. It is inherent in concept musicals that each is unique, if only because the form is so out there in meta-theatricality. Rather, it is the conventional musicals that create a sameness, a series based on a single format—the Princess shows of Kern, Bolton, and Wodehouse, invariably overpraised as break-aways and, moreover, each *exactly* like the others; the Cole Porter urban frolics of the 1930s; the Big Lady vehicles pioneered by *Hello, Dolly!*.

The approach to Prince had been hush-hush, but Fosse heard about it, and he was livid. Of course, he did recover and did return to take *Chicago* to Broadway. But where the fuck did Fryer and Cresson get off offering *my* show to that puffbag Hal Prince, with his oh so artsy ghosts and his Swedish Sondheim la di da? Dear me, a reindeer ate my periwinkle.

It was the competition thing, because they all want to be King of Broadway every season. Some are worse than others—Michael Bennett, for instance. He was genuinely aggrieved at the thought that Tommy Tune, his former protégé, might have outdone him in the staging of *Nine* when Bennett's show was *Dreamgirls*. *Nine* was unique, and Bennett thought only he held the copyright on unique.

Fosse was worse, too. *Chicago* opened on June 3, 1975. Bennett's rival piece, *A Chorus Line*, moved to Broadway seven weeks later after three months at the Public Theater, where it had already pro-voked a hubbub from the bigwigs. Fosse asked his faithfuls about it, and they tried to reassure him, saying it was nothing like *Chicago*. Still, you get Preview Buzz like this only for a show that's very, very special. What if *Chicago* wasn't? What if it *was* but Public Opinion refused to deem it so? They can be like that; ask anyone in the busi-ness. They love to build you up, and then they love to tear you down.

So often, success in entertainment is not about money or fame. It's about maintaining a winner's persona, starring in everything you do because the audience can't take its eyes off you. They think you own it all.

Listen. Sylvester Stallone is on location for some film, with the usual fans thrilling and screaming behind the usual barriers. So Stallone happens to venture out a little too far, and a woman throws her cardboard container of coffee at him. Stunned, he asks her why.

"Because," she cries, *"you have what I want!"*

The stakes are high. But Fosse did reclaim his *Chicago*, to play bumper cars with everyone's ego, especially Fred Ebb's. Entering the rehearsal room, Ebb would find the actors improvising instead of speaking the lines he wrote. Or Fosse would have his writer friends create bits and he'd stage them before even showing them to Ebb— the "Roxie" monologue, for instance, as I've said. John Kander thought it "nasty," with the feeling that Fosse actually wanted it filled with hateful imagery, hateful of Verdon, hateful of the old notion of the merry musical show that brightened one's life, hateful of the Tired Businessmen in the house. Weren't they deliberately slimed in "Ugly guys like to do that"? How was that going to play to the babbitts and their wives, after all?

And for "Razzle Dazzle" Fosse created that aforementioned orgy that everyone involved with *Chicago* except Fosse saw as a manifestation of the enraged Fosse who had come back as if from the dead, a ghoul in a hockey mask blaming everyone for his many several disenchantments with show business and the people who love it. Jerry Orbach told Fosse biographer Martin Gottfried that, with everyone else intimidated by Fosse's incensed air of righteous martyrdom, Orbach was the only one who could persuade Fosse to cut the orgy.

But gently, with finesse. The uneducated Fosse was vulnerable in the matter of classy cultural memes, so Orbach pitched his spiel in lofty terms, telling Fosse that Orbach could see that the orgy was meant as Brechtian "alienation." Yes, the famous *Verfremdungseffekt*.

And Fosse is, like, "Uh . . . yeah?"

* * *

Orbach said he understood the sheer artistic blitz Fosse had in mind. Still...hmm...doesn't it veer away from the plot too much? Aren't we losing the hungadunga of the duodenum, the sheer cytoplasmic afflatus of it all? So Orbach advised Fosse to bring the spectators along with him subtly, to let them comprehend the show's message. "Then they'll alienate."

This was a "going around Robin Hood's barn" way of telling Fosse to cut the orgy, but no doubt he already knew it was a mistake and was just waiting for someone to give him a reason to cut it—which he did the very next day.

Even so, Fosse remained difficult through the making of *Chicago*. He was so resentful that, four years later, when creating the semi-autobiographical *All That Jazz* (1979), he poured into the film all the acts of sacrilege he had suffered, retitling *Chicago* as a musical called *NY/LA* (with the exact same set design, as we see in a scale model that could easily be the one Tony Walton had constructed for the stage show). We see as well a boldly erotic ballet appalling *NY/LA*'s producers—and, incidentally, a high-strung songwriter (modeled, I believe, on Moose Charlap, the composer of *The Conquering Hero*, another show that Fosse held in intense distaste). Most telling of all is a character called Lucas Sergeant, who is unmistakably Hal Prince, complete with his habitual glasses perched on his forehead as he is cajoled into taking over *NY/LA* in the event that...uh...Bobby is...well...sidelined.

Obviously he was a great holder of grudges, Fosse. He was nice except when he wasn't, and on *Chicago* he absolutely wasn't, so the Philadelphia stand gave the company three and a half weeks of the fabled Tryout Hell. Not the one where the show is so utterly terrible no amount of revision will save it; *The Conquering Hero* was like that. Not the one where the show is a potential smash with mysterious ailments such that only a doctor called in from outside can save it; *Funny Girl* was like that.

No, this was the tryout hell wherein the showrunner has become so fierce and unreasonable that the entire company is confused and hurt and paralyzed—and Fred Ebb got it the worst. John Kander said, "No show is worth dying for," and, at one point, when Fosse was getting especially aggressive with Ebb, Kander simply grabbed his partner by the shoulder, turned him away from Fosse toward the stage door of the Forrest Theatre, and propelled him straight out onto the street and back to the hotel. Kander actually considered lighting out of the tryout and heading for home. "We were in Philadelphia for twelve years," Kander told Sam Wasson. "It never ended."

On the other hand, "We'll never get out of Philadelphia" is a venerable Broadwayite's lamentation, whether over certain casualties or potential hits undergoing severe dialysis. Here's a tale: back in 1952, suffering through the tryout of *The Climate of Eden*, its author and director, Moss Hart, was going over the play's devastating Philadelphia reviews with his brother, Bernie, who was also the show's co-producer.

"Look at these death notices," Moss groaned. "They should be bordered in black. We'll never get out of Philadelphia."

"Moss," said Bernie calmly, "We got out of Egypt. We'll get out of Philadelphia."

Still, the New York previews, at the 46th Street (today the Richard Rodgers) Theatre, heading for that June 3 premiere, were more of the same, as Fosse tinkered and insulted. Some of the changes altered a line or even a word, and one huge change, as we know, dropped David Rounds' role and enlarged Mary McCarty's, with the loss of "Ten Percent" and the gain of "When You're Good To Mama."

It meant a lot of work even in the days close to opening night, but at least Fosse was mellowing somewhat. And once he had dropped "Razzle Dazzle"'s gonzo sex ballet, the show was playing with a close and confident grip on the public. One thing all the noted director-choreographers had in common was a knack for spotting the flaccid moments and getting them to pop. Seldom if ever did a Robbins, Champion, or Bennett show fail because of the staging. Only uninspired material could defeat them.

Further, the difference in the temperature of the auditorium, from Philadelphia to New York, heartened the company, for now audiences were extremely enthusiastic, whereas Philadelphians have been famously uncomfortable with "difficult" art, from *Pal Joey* to *Anyone Can Whistle*. *Chicago*'s ID in Pennsylvania had been that of a hot show, a tricky show: approach with caution. On Broadway, it was the new Fosse-Verdon show, sure to be the last word in the excitement of talent.

Finally, just before opening night, Fosse called for one more runthrough, and, after all the taunts and *geschrei* of Philadelphia, Fosse—"mean, brilliant, friend, companion," as Fred Ebb called him in the Greg Lawrence interview book—told his cast, "You're all wonderful."

And then he came up on stage (as assistant choreographer Tony Stevens recalled for the Gottfried biography) and handed to Stevens the one and only Bob Fosse derby, custom-made for him by a London hatter, and he asked Stevens to partner Verdon in a number just for the cast, then and there. "It was the best I ever danced," Stevens said. "I had to be good with the hat."

The premiere performance followed only hours later, and, strange as it may sound, the critics almost hated *Chicago*. It did get some sorta kinda good reviews among the pans, and virtually every writer conceded that the staging itself was splendid. Yet there was always an objection to the spirit of the piece—its "grotesquerie," its "acid distortion of prohibition Chicago," its "tawdriness." And nearly every review mentioned *Cabaret* as Fosse's matrix, if only to diminish, however slightly, Fosse's recent achievement in winning the three top awards that show business has to give.

It's a cliché, but, unmistakably, *Chicago* was ahead of its time. Yes, the show was cold and cruel, if one didn't understand how its satire worked. But then, no previous such musical had been this harsh. *Johnny Johnson*, though dealing with the slaughter of war, was above all wistful, and even *The Cradle Will Rock* counts some sweet-hearted characters. Besides, *Chicago* was, I repeat, Big Broadway, not an indie production playing to an adventurous public that can tolerate the manhandling of social pieties.

Further, *A Chorus Line* opened at the same time, with its irresistible verve as well as a quality that *Chicago* utterly lacked: warmth. Nothing in Fosse's piece compared to the young girls' dreams of being beautiful in "At the Ballet"; or to the intimidated drama student who feels utterly drained of emotion when her drama-teacher nemesis dies; or to the sad tale of Paul, the lost gay boy who finally finds himself in the fantasy life of the stage.

But then, as Fosse's friends kept assuring him, *A Chorus Line* was "a different kind of show." Where *Chicago* was abrasive, *A Chorus Line* was, under its high-tech finish, tender. It attracted even intellectuals who normally ignore musicals, and some of them weaponized Michael Bennett's show to bludgeon Fosse, seen as a symbol of the establishment, stooging for ruling-class prerogatives. *A Chorus Line*, by contrast, was the underdog simply because it claimed an experimental, indie origin at the Very Downtown and Therefore Insurgent New York Shakespeare Festival.

Boy, did they get that wrong. Bennett was a Big Broadway talent with the ambitions of an overdog; had he not been struck down by AIDS, he would have gone Hollywood, just as Fosse did. Indeed, it's useful to compare *Chicago*'s curtain call with that of *A Chorus Line*, because Bennett concluded his evening with an extraordinarily showy number, each cast member entering to join in a spectacular dance in flashy dress to the orchestra's almost combatively smashing accompaniment. It was pure sensuality—just what intellectuals usually resist.

At *Chicago*, on the other hand, the curtain calls were naked of exhibition. As the band played a dizzyingly fast "Razzle Dazzle," each player, from the ensemble to the support to the stars, came running on for a solo bow, introduced by name with a single word of description. Bandleader Lebowsky called out the first one, that actor bowed and introduced the next one, and so on, so that after Candy Brown took her bow she cried, "Debonair Chris Chadman!," waving at him as he came on for his turn. (The Mary Sunshine was introduced as "Mister Michael O'Haughey," in case any among the spectators still weren't sure.)

Once upon a time, a musical's curtain calls were hastily executed, with a group bow for the chorus, a group or two of minor people, then the principals one on top of the other, in an air of Let the public say thank you and leave. Even *My Fair Lady*, the show of shows of its day, released the audience from its obligations within some thirty seconds or so. But the invention of the Big Lady Show, in the 1960s, turned the calls into a production number, staged to feature the major melodies of the score one by one and to build the applause to a crescendo as the star more or less paraded in. Thus, even the audience was subject to choreography, egged on by sound and light to rise to its feet. And everyone in the business discovered, to his surprise, that the public appeared to like it that way.

Chicago, however, was not a Big Lady show. The Big Lady is a grande dame of sorts, an artist of the V.I.P. variety, gracing us with her presence. Gwen Verdon was an acting dancer, and dancers are too lithe and liquid to be grand. She came on for the gypsy segment of *Redhead*'s Dream Ballet flying headlong through the air from offstage to land in the male dancers' arms, an electrifying feat. Big Ladies don't electrify, much less fly headlong. Big Ladies promenade. Try to imagine Verdon on the *Hello, Dolly!* runway with the waiters, ever so gracefully extending the arms like this, like that; leading the knee slaps, now me, now you; in the whole grand tour of it all.

Impossible. Besides, Verdon didn't dominate *Chicago* in a Big way as Carol Channing did *Dolly!* or Angela Lansbury did *Mame*. Chita Rivera actually had greater dancing responsibilities in *Chicago* than Verdon did.

And there was this: Verdon may have lost some of her box-office booster power, for ticket sales started slipping not long after the opening. Even so, as Lorelei Lee once put it, "Fate keeps on happening"—for Verdon accidentally inhaled a bit of fluff from one of her costumes and was now to be laid up in care, and it wasn't certain when she would return. Her standby, Lenora Nemetz, took over, and Nemetz was a powerhouse. Still, you can't give the public the last Fosse-Verdon show with an alternate so early in the run, unless the alternate is prominent herself. Luckily, fate's name was Liza Minnelli. With her close relationship to Kander and (especially) Ebb, she was asked if she would be willing to—

"*Yes!*" Liza cries. "*When?*"

Now: or as soon as she can learn Roxie's lines and music and dances. And who but the young (twenty-nine and five months) and high-energy Minnelli could have stepped in on a few days' notice? She not only mastered everything Verdon had done but took on "My Own Best Friend" as a solo (as Kander and Ebb had written and wanted it) and reinstated the original "Me and My Baby" dance, with all the chorus boys costumed as infants.

Now, a few other performers might have done what Minnelli did. But they wouldn't have been as show-biz hot as she was at the time, fresh off *Cabaret* and *Liza With a Z*. Note, however, that the producers did not tout this arresting cast change in official PR. There were no ads to the effect, and no window cards were printed bearing Minnelli's name in place of Verdon's, thus to protect the latter's position as *Chicago*'s prima donna. Minnelli wasn't replacing anyone; she was just...helping out in a jam. It was smart housekeeping, no more.

Of course, all the professional know-it-alls made it the talk of the town, and ticket sales immediately picked up. Minnelli went in on August 8, 1975, and stayed for five weeks, long enough to reinvent *Chicago* as the show no one could miss even after Minnelli relinquished Roxie to a recovered Verdon. And at Minnelli's performances, the crowd filing into the 46th Street Theatre was extremely keen. So, when a voice over the loudspeaker announced "a change in tonight's program," everyone became anxious. The message went on with:

VOICE: The role of Roxie Hart ...

and the audience began to growl, till:

VOICE: ...usually played by Gwen Verdon, will be played by Liza Minnelli.

At which the house went crazy with the anticipation of fast trackers assured of a high-status experience all their very own. To recall what set and lighting designer Robert Edmond Jones said about the radioactivity in the auditorium just before the curtain rose on the Paul Robeson *Othello*, in 1943, "If a cat had walked across the footlights it would have been electrocuted."

As for Minnelli's Roxie, she was at her best—spry, quirky, adorable, irresponsible yet avid. She made no attempt to model her portrayal on Verdon's; this was perhaps the only "innocent" Roxie in *Chicago*'s history. Instead, Minnelli played the part as a wide-eyed, pre-flapper without any perspective on what's she's doing, who goes through life with a slightly unsure "Everybody's crazy but me, right?" attitude that sweeps her into and out of trouble with no price to pay: the polar opposite of the heroines F. Scott Fitzgerald invented, in a back-alley milieu Fitzgerald didn't know existed.

Still, in her own odd way, Minnelli lent the piece the warmth that few if any "correct" Roxies give off. Remember, musical-comedy heroines are likable almost as a rule—and Roxie isn't. She's hateful, in fact. Yet does the music soften her? The comedy? Is there a "Roxie charm"—from Verdon and her successors? Or is this show rich enough, even ambiguous enough, to tolerate a *pleasant* killer? Because in fact there is no ambiguity about it. There is in some shows, especially musical plays, such as *Carousel*: how do we really feel about Billy Bigelow and his violence? But *Chicago* is what it is, without excuses or apologies.

In the end, the show ran for over 900 performances,[12] some two years and three months, long enough for Verdon to need a replacement. Ann Reinking, who had just been the second Cassie in *A Chorus Line*, took over as a devilish Roxie opposite Lenora Nemetz, now a superb Velma—a racing greyhound, shimmering with power. Jerry Orbach stayed with the show, however, while his wife, Elaine Cancilla, understudied Nemetz, occasionally going on as an unusually "soft" Velma. The true Velma is not only hard but much more so than Roxie, who was created to be an opportunist boxing above her weight.

Meanwhile, the 1976 Tony Awards came along just as *Chicago* was reaching its first anniversary. It received nominations in all possible categories except for Featured Actor and Actress—from Best Musical, Book, Score, Choreography, and Direction to Best Actor

---

12. The exact figure is disputed by even trustworthy sources, giving 923, 936, or 947 as the tally.

(for Jerry Orbach) and two Best Actresses (for both Verdon and Rivera) to Best Sets, Costumes, and Lighting (for Jules Fisher).

And of course it lost them all, because this was *A Chorus Line Presents the Tonys*, with a few awards sprinkled among *Pacific Overtures* and a *My Fair Lady* revival. The Best Actor, absurdly, went to the Alfred Doolittle of George-Rose-in-a-box, who beat not only Orbach but Ian Richardson's wonderfully psychologized Henry Higgins and the versatile tour de force of *Pacific Overtures'* narrator, Mako.

To be fair, *A Chorus Line* was not only a great show but a great Tony Awards show, opening and closing the event and winning numerous ovations over the course of the evening. Michael Bennett had demanded one extra camera to capture the staging details in his show's first sequence, a seven-minute number climaxing with the almost insanely brilliant button of the auditioners striding forward as the upstage mirrors revolved in a blackout. Then, when the lights came up once more, there was the even then highly symbolic pose of them all in their line, holding up their (real-life) headshots in front of their faces.

By contrast, *Chicago's* musical selection for the Tonys was "All I Care About," amusing enough but, out of story context, inconsequential. Surely it should have been "Roxie," letting Gwen and "my boys" substantiate her Broadway farewell on the national level. At that, though, none of *Chicago's* numbers would have landed when performed away from the show's atmospheric unit set, instead to turn up in a Happy Tony Limbo of rectangles of white makeup-table lights that parted for Orbach's entrance as if on some fifties variety hour.

It looked especially feeble on the same program that showed us the wonderful way Michael Bennett used the stage floor, the mirrors, and the head shots of his *Chorus Line* applicants. Anyway, Bennett's show excerpts beautifully, while *Chicago* makes its effect as a series of concept-musical magic tricks that gradually integrate into a powerful cross-section of social power centers, dazzling the audience sensually while enlightening it intellectually. No single piece of *Chicago* "tells" the way bits of *A Chorus Line* can.

The Drama Critics' Circle Award for Best Musical scorned *Chicago*, too—even without *A Chorus Line*, ineligible because of its late opening. On the first ballot, *Chicago* got only one vote, from *Cue* magazine's Marilyn Stasio. True, *Pacific Overtures*, a very worthy rival, got six votes (and eventually won, on the second ballot). However, no fewer than nine critics abstained entirely on Best Musical, and others voted for such masterpieces as *Rex*, *The Robber Bridegroom*, and *Tuscaloosa's Calling Me...But I'm Not Going*.

After the New York run, *Chicago* went on tour, still with Jerry Orbach (later replaced by Bill McCauley) and M. O'Haughey but giving Roxie to Penny Worth and Velma to Carolyn Kirsch. There was some softening of the verbal texture; Roxie's "I gotta pee" after the murder became the ambiguous "I gotta go." During the *Chicago* stand, Verdon, Rivera, and Mary McCarty reclaimed their roles and went on with the company to San Francisco and Los Angeles, where the original lines were set back into place.

This was not, however, the New York staging. The direction and also the choreography (by original-cast chorus member Gene Foote, "after" Fosse) were new, and the physical presentation was redesigned—all, presumably, to facilitate mobility. Sometime in 1978, the production closed.

And with that, one might say, an era in the musical's history had ended. Five years later, in a book called *Broadway Babies*, I wrote an obituary for this show—not for the musical itself, but for the tradition that a Fosse-Verdon attraction represented, the tradition of splendid and unique talents collaborating on new work. That is: not just new writing, but new performing.

I said that this would never return to us, because by the late 1970s all the marvelous talents were retiring or gone, and it seemed that most of those replacing them in the leadership cadres were not as gifted. The wonderful freaks who had been the musical's marquee names, so bizarre and exciting—the kinds of headliners celebrated in *Chicago*'s iconic numbers—were to be succeeded by capable but often humdrum players. Worse, though there were still imaginative choreographers, most directors smoothed performing style down from the fantastical to the ordinary, demanding "reality-based" portrayals that scorned comic skills and grand gestures. Once, the musical was an adventure; now it was turning into a documentary. This is the approach that would later give us a revival of *Annie* without the laughs and a kindergarten *Gigi*.

True, the Sondheim-Prince musicals of the 1970s maintained the larger-than-life aspect of a musical's presentation. *Sweeney Todd* was so full of theatrical ceremony and struck-by-lightning acting that it seemed a combination of antique melodrama and the latest word in operatic *espressività*. Elsewhere, however, more and more, Broadway would be starved for a Fosse, a Verdon.

Chicago of course has rejoined us, and its spiky DNA will not let it be performed down, so to say; this is one of the most conclusive musicals of all time. It can be played correctly in only one way, and its quicksilver defiance of every caution in the moralist's handbook means its comic style is practically director-proof. There can be no *Chicago* without the laughs, no kindergarten *Chicago*, and, lo, the times finally caught up with it, so it no longer shocks. It enlightens.

9

⌒∿⌒

The Revival and the Third Movie

"If It Doesn't Fit, You Must Acquit!"

Chicago's first run didn't quite end with the closing of the national tour. The Crucible Theatre, in Sheffield, England, mounted it in 1979, and this production then moved to the Cambridge Theatre in London. Directed by Peter James and choreographed by Gillian Gregory, it featured Jenny Logan as Roxie opposite the Velma of Antonia Ellis (probably best known as the duplicitous Maisie of Ken Russell's film of *The Boy Friend*, though she was as well a replacement Fastrada in Fosse's *Pippin* near the end of its Broadway run).

Ben Cross, a serious movie actor who moonlit as a singer-songwriter, was Billy Flynn—once again, a spry matinee idol in a role Maurine Watkins conceived for a creaky character player. Hope Jackman, who with Jessie Evans had cornered the market on Tough Old Dames in London shows (Jackman created the Widow Corney in *Oliver!* in both London and New York), was the Matron. A certain G. Lyons honored the initial-only-on-the-first-name credit for Mary Sunshine, and there was an American in the cast, as Amos. This was Don Fellows, who specialized playing squish parts in West End stagings of our shows, and often replaced stars in a long run—Billy De Wolfe, for instance, London's first J. B. Biggley in *How To Succeed*.

Though *Chicago*'s original Broadway mounting was, paradoxically, a minimalistically elaborate affair, with its many costume changes, bits of scenery constantly being winched in and out, and trap-door entrances and exits, *Chicago* as a composition can easily be staged on the simple side, and that's what Sheffield went for. London's critics thought it offensively cheap-looking, but at least the cast was interesting—Antonia Ellis in particular brought a sort of radiance to the "sly and knowing" type that would read very well as Velma.

Like London, like Sydney, so an Australian production followed, two years later, led by the then reigning divas of the Sydney-Melbourne musical, Nancye Hayes and Geraldine Turner, with Terence Donovan as Billy Flynn. This version, too, was physically underwhelming, with coarse orchestrations replacing Ralph Burns' brilliant charts, though the costuming was arresting, as when the press corps for "We Both Reached For the Gun" were all in white suits emblazoned with newsprint, from headlines to tidbits.

It may be that *Chicago*'s London success—the run lasted a year and a half—prompted the creation of another (partly) American musical based on a twenties comedy about press corruption in Chicago. The source was Ben Hecht and Charles MacArthur's *The Front Page* (1928), by far the classic satire on big-city pressmanship. However, it's a poor subject for a musical, as there is nothing the characters need to sing about in any real sense, and musicals are about need: "What's the Use of Wond'rin'?," "Some People," "My Shot." Then, too, *The Front Page* is a farce, which turns on a lot of physical action but little character development. Further, the many cynical reporters would surely be an encumbrance once they start singing—and they're on stage for most of the action. Worse, there's no genuinely major woman principal (*Journey's End* and *Mister Roberts* likely would not make valid musicals, either), and the whole thing ends up starved for emotion.

Yes, so does Maurine Watkins' *Chicago*. But that's its point. It looks at a heartless world, which is why Flynn's defining statement that he cares only about love is so pointed in its irony. But how many more musicals did we want that are dedicated to sociopathic newshounds and their money-grubbing partners-in-crime?

Then, too, this *Front Page* musical, British Tony Macaulay and American Dick Vosburgh's *Windy City* (1982), was no quicksilver horror-spoof like *Chicago*. The authors tried to set the original play as a standard book musical rather than devise an innovative narrative structure and a satiric score, to accommodate the crazy story and the eccentrics peopling it. The result was frenetic yet monotonous, with too many numbers for the reporters (who, remember, form the play's background, not the play's story) and a few Hotsy-Totsy Club girls thrown in on a pretext to bring some youth and beauty into the mix.

Anton Rodgers played the tyrannical newspaper editor based on the real-life Walter Howey, editor of Watkins' home outfit, the *Chicago Tribune*. It was Howey who famously told his writers, "Don't ever fake a story.... That is, don't ever let me catch you at it." Dennis Waterman was the reporter hero and, in the built-up role of the prostitute Mollie, Diane Langton had a kind of insert number in "I Can Talk To You," one gentle moment amid the chaos.

The show didn't work even in an elaborate production featuring a working sample of Chicago's overhead Loop railroad, but, moving near to Broadway in a revision, *Windy City* appeared in 1985 at New Jersey's Paper Mill Playhouse, with Ron Holgate, Gary Sandy, and Judy Kaye as Mollie. It still didn't work, with its dutiful realism in its single boring set. (There were no Loop trains this time.) Behind the unnecessary songs, *Windy City* was still an old-fashioned spoken play; it needed the cartoon carnival of *Finian's Rainbow* or *Li'l Abner*, satires on the wild side. Or: it needed Fosse, to turn it inside out with his daffy vaudeville.

We might say that *Windy City* finally put the finishing touch on *Chicago*'s first decade. But then came a resurgence: the Long Beach Civic Light Opera in California put on an authentic replica revival of *Chicago*, in 1992. Rob Marshall directed, Ann Reinking recreated Fosse's choreography (with, however, her own version of the "Hot Honey Rag"), the original Tony Walton set design and Patricia Zipprodt's costumes (with some new ones by Garland Riddle) were used, and along with Juliet Prowse's Roxie, Bebe Neuwirth's Velma, Gary Sandy's Billy Flynn, and Kaye Ballard's Matron were Barney Martin and M. O'Haughey of the original cast. In her rave review in the *Los Angeles Times*, Sylvia Drake called it "a careful reproduction of the original." It would appear that, at long last, the public might be able to appreciate *Chicago* as a study in corruption rather than an unthinking reflection of it. And then came the O. J. Simpson double-murder trial, in 1994.

In *Outrage: The Five Reasons Why O. J. Simpson Got Away With Murder*, former Los Angeles prosecutor Vincent Bugliosi lays out an elaborate deconstruction of the trial. Weighing the evidence, Bugliosi makes it clear that Simpson was unquestionably guilty, and that he got off through "the most incompetent criminal prosecution I have ever seen." Nor does the judge, Lance Ito, come off well: "thin-skinned," the author calls him, "offended by the slightest transgression, real or perceived," while "exhibiting little common sense" and behaving in "an irrational, almost goofy way." And, to top it all, "making patently erroneous rulings, one after another."

Most relevant to us is the question of the trial's media coverage, and here Bugliosi is even more scathing. He scorns the press' servile praise of the defense's "dream team," pointing out that it consisted of "a lawyer who has never tried a murder case before ([Robert] Shapiro), another who isn't even primarily a criminal lawyer but a civil lawyer ... [Johnnie Cochran], and another who lost the last big case he tried over twenty years ago [F. Lee Bailey]." Further, Bugliosi asks, "Why should I care if these [commentator] talking heads were babbling and ranting on TV almost around the clock?" Indeed, Bugliosi feels strongly "that they contributed ... to the not guilty verdict" because they "magnif[ied] defense points far beyond their worth and mut[ed] important points made by the prosecution."

This recalls Maurine Watkins' feeling that the press was shaping the public reaction to murder trials to exculpate the guilty. But more: consider the show-biz aspect of the whole Simpson chronicle—the low-speed chase in the Bronco to the cheers of mindless crowds; Simpson's disguise kit, complete with the actor's spirit gum, for pasting on a false beard; the ridiculous charade of trying on the fatal glove, capped by Cochran's idiot melody of "If it doesn't fit, you must acquit!"

This is not to mention the telecasting of the trial in the first place, and the defense's smearing of Detective Mark Fuhrman using

America's Achilles heel, race mania. It was exactly akin to Roxie Hart's lying "pregnancy," and Vincent Bugliosi is at pains to detail proof of Fuhrman's absolutely race-neutral behavior on the job, despite the damning evidence of things he said off the job, on the infamous "Fuhrman tapes."

The lesson everyone took from this case was that high-profit justice is show business by other means: the very message of *Chicago*. With the nation more or less transfixed by this staged miscarriage of due process, the musical's lesson was at last learned. The Simpson Not Guilty verdict came down on October 3, 1995, and New York's official museum of old musicals, City Center's *Encores!*, brought *Chicago* back for reassessment in its immediately following season, in the spring of 1996.

A beloved institution in Manhattan's arts scene, *Encores!* revives musicals of the past in staged-concert form, from such resonant titles as *Pal Joey* and *The Pajama Game* to artifacts such as *Sweet Adeline* and *Out Of This World*. Most are from the 1950s, with strong showings from the 1940s and 1960s. Few are less than a generation old, however, and an Encores! *Chicago*—a show that had closed only nineteen years before—was a surprise, Simpson or no Simpson.

Ann Reinking, Bebe Neuwirth again, and James Naughton led the support of Joel Grey, Marcia Lewis, and D. (for David) Sabella. Walter Bobbie directed, Reinking choreographed "in the style of Bob Fosse," and Rob Fisher conducted. There had been a rumor floating through the chatter circuits that *Encores!* had asked Liza Minnelli to revive her Roxie; oh, but *could* I? . . . on *shtage* again, darlingsh? . . . It'sh yesh, it'sh maybe, it'sh no. In the end, Reinking (who had grown too content choreographing, as at Long Beach, to want to perform anymore) had to step in to save the day. Her participation was doubly authentic, as she had learned the Fosse style at first hand and, as the fourth Broadway Roxie (after Verdon, Nemetz, and Minnelli), established a link with the original production.

Interestingly, now that twenty years had passed, Reinking felt attuned to Roxie as never before. Speaking to *Playbill*'s Mervyn Rothstein, she said, "The show was created for [Gwen Verdon in her] late forties, for a woman of a certain age, and I am now a woman of a certain age.

So I'm more appropriate for the part now. It's for somebody who has a personal history, and when [I first played Roxie] I didn't have a personal history."

What did she mean by the last two words? A public profile as a performer? A seasoned wisdom as a living, thinking member of society? Or is this that paradox I mentioned earlier in which every star part in a musical is really two people—the character and, in the American theatre's iconolatry of talent, the actor playing that character?

Mary Martin defined stardom through something she noticed when she was on stage: when you enter, every head in the audience turns to watch you—because they have instantly sensed how wonderful you are. And, once more: wouldn't that tend to make the very ordinary Roxie extraordinary simply because that's what Gwen Verdon was? And does that magic extend to the other wonderful artists playing Roxie?

Chicago really is hot Broadway at its highest voltage. It doesn't just have (more or less) show-stopping numbers: it's a show-stopping show, period. It certainly played that way back in 1975, and when a critic friend and I took our seats for the *Encores! Chicago*, I noticed an expectant hubbub utterly unlike the mild "getting ready" noises *Encores!* audiences usually produce. They can be stand-offish with obscure titles and jaded with the familiar ones; this night, they were stoked. Again, conversing with Greg Lawrence, Kander said, "I don't think I have ever been through anything like it," and Ebb seconded him with "It was [as if] we had invited everyone in the audience.... It was like hysteria."

This is no exaggeration: every song was very thoroughly cheered. Even some of the jokes provoked gigantic responses; it is safe to conjecture that not since the very first performances in New York, when connoisseurs and devotees set the tone, had *Chicago* so elated the public. In the long run, the show alienated audiences uncomfortable with the mixture of didacticism and showmanship. But the O. J. Simpson epic—and, as many have said, the Amy Fisher case as well—educated them. Maurine Watkins' *Chicago* underlines the role of the press in shaping justice, but Fosse reinstructs the emphasis, showing us something larger in the show business of it all, with everyone, not only the media, taking a role.

Yes, the razzle dazzle: as in the decision to televise the Simpson trial, our first hype-a-gonzo, grabbag-of-crazy reality show, or the serial adventures of the "Long Island Lolita" and her Mr. Clumso paramour. Why had the public taken so long to catch up with Fosse's revelation? Was it that venerable intellectuals' belief that musicals are fluff? That no matter how densely the form has evolved over the years, all musicals are believed to be variations of *The Black Crook*, *Naughty Marietta*, and *Lady, Be Good!*? Truly, the *Encores! Chicago* played as not only the greatest show of all time, but one with slightly hidden humanist traction, a piece of persuasion. I remember thinking, through all the ovations, Where were all you people in 1975?

Encores! presents each title in its complete musical setting but an edited script, an approach that favors trim musical comedy over the more profusely delineated musical play. *Allegro* and *Golden Boy*, examples of the latter, did not go over well at *Encores!*, but *Chicago* lends itself wonderfully to this format. In charge of the book, David Thompson had little more to do than drop lines here and there to keep the pace zippy and avoid any scenes calling for complicated staging.

Thus, in 1975, in the Matron's first meeting with Roxie, she carried on the conversation while selling murderess Annie some liquor. That was cut. At one point, Chita Rivera's Velma Kelly made an exit down the center stairs, whereupon Gwen Verdon, in a nod to Rivera's Latin ID, sneered, "She sure don't look like a Kelly to me." That was cut. Billy Flynn's bit with the tailor after "All I Care About" would have posed difficulties, not least because Jerry Orbach reacted to a wayward pin prick with "Ow! Ya dumb fruit!" So that was cut.

Chicago experts lamented the loss of Fosse's devilish poker scene, which in 1975 was announced and musically underscored as if it was yet another vaudeville act: the Matron, Velma, and three of the other inmates in a sneaky ballet of surreptitious cheating, with cards slipped in from under a wig, out of a handkerchief, and so on. The women were seated throughout, so there was no motion other than the physics of deception—the sly scouting to see who's spying, the baroque palming of that extra ace, all to the slow, rhythmic pull of some secret cheaters' melody. Rivera even drew a card out of her mouth. So of course everyone ended up with a once-in-a-lifetime hand:

VELMA (to the matron): Where in hell did you get a royal flush?

MATRON: The same place you got four aces.

Critics missed the point of the show in 1975; now they understood. This "new" *Chicago* won such popular success that a Broadway transfer was all but inevitable—and a more comfortable rehearsal schedule than *Encores!* can provide gave the creatives a chance to fine-tune the instrument, making countless changes in the actors' behavior[1] and adding an elevator in the stage floor. It may seem a minor enhancement, but it got the evening off to a snazzy start in Bebe Neuwirth's entrance into "All That Jazz," comparable to Chita Rivera's in the original.

It was Barry and Fran Weissler who produced the Broadway staging, "based on the presentation by City Center's *Encores!*." They unveiled the show on November 14, 1996, at the Richard Rodgers Theatre (where, when it was still called the 46th Street, *Chicago* originally played), launching a run still in progress as I write. This is not only Broadway's longest-lasting revival but its second-longest-running attraction, period, behind *The Phantom of the Opera* but ahead of *The Lion King*, *Cats*, and *Les Misérables*.

This stripped-down *Chicago* is indeed underdressed next to the florid pop operas and Disney art I just cited. Still, the Weisslers did not infuse the *Encores!* concert with echoes of Bob Fosse's glittering *Regie* technology. This was to remain a lean and hungry *Chicago*: without the sly little wagons of scenery winched in to define locale in 1975; without those handsome visuals flying down from overhead; without Patricia Zipprodt's evocative costuming.

---

1. Just for example, at *Encores!*, right before he was shot, Michael Berresse's Fred Casely grinned at the audience. On Broadway, he was instead cold and self-absorbed: from a good-time boy, on equal terms with his dates, to a predator, thus giving Roxie stronger motivation to resent him.

Thus, the cast played in William Ivey Long's formal black—a tuxedo for Billy Flynn, a backless, skin-hugging one-piece with spaghetti straps for Velma. However, the ensemble was more provocatively attired, in shameless fetish get-ups using a lot of see-through mesh. One of the chorus women wore a bra trimmed with "let's do it" spangles over sheer leggings, as if she had been dressed directly from playing cards to be viewed only in the men's smoking car, and Fred Casely went shirtless in an open leather vest.

More notably, John Lee Beatty's set could not have been more basic. Most of the stage was occupied by a tiered, rectangular bandbox with gold trim for the orchestra, and the actors came and went through its center, along its sides, or from the wings. At times, they sat on chairs to the box's left and right, which created an arresting effect when poor, overlooked Amos made an exit past them at stage left and no one as much as glanced up at him.

So the entire show was given in a kind of black coloring dotted with flesh and lighting. It suggested something other than a musical comedy: a dark view of subterranean life forms in the form of a musical comedy. We got an authentic *Chicago* nonetheless, not only because of Reinking's use of the Fosse style but because of that *Encores!* policy of loyal reinstitution of a show's musical program.

To that point, however, it's worth noting that the 1975 play-out music—a medley of "All That Jazz," "Me and My Baby," and a very jiving "Mister Cellophane" for which the band rises, even the two pianists—was moved up to serve as the entr'acte. Further, Reinking asked for eight new bars from the clarinet during the trial scene, to punctuate the way she was staging a particular moment. Last, Ralph Burns himself retouched a few of his 1975 charts.

At that, Reinking's choreography explored a few opportunities Fosse left bare in the original production—the prelude, for instance. Fosse allowed the stage to remain empty during the playing of "Loopin' the Loop," letting the audience take in Tony Walton's twenties-era illustrations on two columns at extreme stage left and right, the band atop the drum, and of course the very theatrical lowering of the "Chicago/Late 1920's" sign. No performer took the stage till Rivera appeared to launch "All That Jazz."

However, the less eye-catching *Encores!* set might have given us a stage wait, so Reinking started bringing the dancers on as soon as the music started, even before the conductor's invigorating "*5-6-7-8!*" Rather than jump into a set routine, the ensemble seemed to wander about, occasionally posing or slithering here or there in rhythm. It was as if the show was pulling itself together, turning from a stylization of nightlife back in those dangerous neighborhoods of old anarchic Chicago into a modern-day entertainment. Then, when Bebe Neuwirth rose up on her gala little "special for Broadway" elevator and meticulously paced her way down a few steps with her patented deadpan expression and in strict time with the music, *Chicago*'s opening number finally went into its dance.

Of the cast, Reinking and Neuwirth played off against each other quite well, as Reinking's mercurial Roxie, brought off in "big" style, seemed like a defiance of Neuwirth's invincible underplaying. At times, Reinking seemed to toy with her lines, sculpting and twisting them. Much earlier, in *Goodtime Charley* (1975), as Joan of Arc, no less, Reinking gave a very consistent portrayal of serene determination: as a being so imbued with the inner light that even as a warrior she gave off a radiance, rather as we imagine saints actually do. (Coincidentally, her Joan played opposite Joel Grey, here as Charles VII and later, of course, Reinking's *Chicago* Amos.)

But Reinking's Roxie was the opposite of her Joan: unstable and lacking a context for her own behavior, as if permanently out on a lark. The role is rich in laugh lines, though some Roxies don't land them. Reinking got them all, even on "Ugly guys like to do that"— one of the very few times in the script when Roxie makes a genuine observation about how the world works.

Billy Flynn, on the other hand, is observant to the utmost, and James Naughton brought something new in his casual sense of command. Maurine Watkins had based the character on several real-life defense attorneys, incorporating within her script statements and taunts and sarcastic comebacks they had actually uttered. But her chief source was the colorful Charles E. Erbstein— "the best of all our legal bamboozlers," Ben Hecht called him in *Gaily, Gaily*, "with a repertoire of magic tricks. He could make evidence disappear, turn damning exhibits into comic props [as with Johnnie Cochran's use of O. J. Simpson's bloody glove], make monkeys out of eyewitnesses, and outwit justice as if she were a rube with mittens on."

In other words, here was another of those wayward Chicago Characters. Now, Adolphe Menjou, in *Roxie Hart*, answers the description. But Naughton launched a line of smooth-operator Billy Flynns, above all *affably* sly: which is how the role is usually played today. Back in 1975, Jerry Orbach really seized the stage, barking out his lines, taking and threatening and dismissing. Naughton, however, played it as the guy who knows he's in charge. So why shout?

The *Encores! Chicago* also revised the show's credits, giving Joel Grey over-the-title billing with the three leads, though his Chaplinesque "little guy" demeanor was far less naturalized and sympathetic than Barney Martin had been in the original production. As the Matron and Mary Sunshine, Marcia Lewis and D. Sabella were good enough without truly lighting up their scenes, but the chorus people were top-notch, as Broadway choruses are bound to be, given the intense competition for those spots.

In fact, the ensemble was thought so elemental in the show's profile that members were included in the poster photography, especially the women, in William Ivey Long's forbidden-fruit peekaboo. These pictures, shot in black and white, wore a deliberately downbeat look, as if sex and jazz were really taking their toll. A few were somewhat electrified, new on the scene. But the haggard appearance of the Sunday after the sin-filled Saturday was pervasive, and there was even a view of Roxie in the back of a squad car, next to a baleful uniformed cop.

The breakaway point for this was *Redhead*, back in 1959, when, for the first time, Fosse was absolute master of the realm as the director-choreographer. He wanted his people to pick out at random an individual in the audience and fix that person with a look of homicidal rage as if needling a helpless butterfly on an exhibition tray. This would obtain only at certain moments in certain dance numbers. At other times in the show, Fosse wanted them to show disdain or a bizarre sort of perfunctory bliss. Off in the ballet world, George Balanchine would tell his people, "Don't act, darling. Just dance." Fosse was the opposite: every moment in his musicals was about something, even about several things at once. He wanted dancers who were like himself: complicated, bossy, charmingly menacing, unknowable.

These *Chicago* revival PR photos, constantly updated with new shots in the same grimly quixotic style (both nationally and for Chicago's many stagings abroad, from Buenos Aires to South Korea) are not a mere stunt. They tell us that the show's setting is the Chicago of the Everleigh sisters and their upmarket bordello, the place where the high life meets the low life. Where Big Broadway preaches sin. Yes, David Thompson's book revisions removed those two tricky remarks, on Chita Rivera's ethnicity and the tailor's sexuality. Yet this *Chicago* is every bit as tough as the original was. The show hasn't changed: we have.

Again, like *The Day Before Spring, Allegro,* and *Love Life* back in the 1940s, some musicals deflate the public's wishful notions on how life works: but now they have the public's permission to do so. And this time *Chicago* won Tonys—for Best Revival of a Musical, for Best Director, Best Choreographer, Best Actor (James Naughton) and Best Actress (Bebe Neuwirth) in a musical, and Best Lighting (Ken Billington).

In another book, while speaking of Hollywood, I broke the moviegoing public into three audiences. First were the sophisticates. The second group liked innovation kept to a minimum. And the third wanted only stories and characters that had been well broken in: the good old stuff. Moving back to the stage musical now, one would expect *Chicago* to be strictly a first-audience proposition. Yet, judging by the revival's two decades on Broadway thus far as well as its global success, this show appeals to all three audiences.

A story: the last time I saw the show on Broadway, about five years ago, some in the Ambassador Theatre seemed so unused to theatregoing that orchestra ticket holders went up to the balcony and vice versa, while a few of the leads were bearing down heavily

on the laugh lines, virtually hectoring an uncertain crowd into re-
acting. Still, the house was appreciative, and some were keen. Two
couples sat behind my friend and me, and one of the women told
the other pair that she had never been to the theatre before. Yet she
got quite caught up in the show, and became so enthralled in following the trial that, when the multi-character jury man ostentatiously
mouthed an ad lib at the Roxie, the woman behind us all but shouted
the line along with him: "*I love your shoes!*"

No doubt the Weisslers could run the production with miscella-
neous replacements, and it is true that some of the principals over
the years have been no more than solid journeymen. However, some
fine Broadway stalwarts and even "stunt" stars have graced the staging as it moved from the Richard Rodgers (after three months) to
the Shubert (for six years) and then to the Ambassador, its present
home. Sometimes the support is more interesting than the three
leads, as when Carol Woods' Matron, as so often now cast with a
black woman, enlivened the final phrases of "When You're Good To
Mama" with some soul coloratura.

The role of Billy Flynn has been especially appealing to notables,
whether Novelty Stars making their Broadway debut such as Robert
Urich, Billy Zane, Hollywood suntan king George Hamilton, or a
Novelty Star making a Broadway return such as former Bo Duke
John Schneider (who had already sung as a replacement Baron in
Grand Hotel). Many Broadway regulars have passed through the
part: Ron Raines, Brent Barrett, Gregory Jbara, Hinton Battle,
Michael Berresse (the former Fred Casely, who went on for an ailing
Battle for so long he was given the role on tour and then transferred
to New York). The Weisslers dote on television names as well, such
as Michael C. Hall, of *Six Feet Under* and *Dexter*, who, thus encouraged by his *Chicago* gig, went on to *Cabaret*'s Emcee and the title role
in *Hedwig and the Angry Inch*. There is even a curiosity among the
lists: Louis Gossett Jr., who lasted only four days, in 2002.

Naturally, Roxie is a diva magnet, although this has necessitated
simplified routines for those with primitive dancing skills. The role
attracted even the unexpected Melanie Griffith, who wanted to be
near her husband, Antonio Banderas, while he was playing in the 2003

Nine revival, just down Forty-Ninth Street from the Ambassador, at the Eugene O'Neill. Tentative at first, Griffith grew into the part to become a charmingly enigmatic Roxie, prototypally dumb and unthinking yet at the same time strangely aware of the opportunity her crime had created for her. Even more paradoxically, she was so detached from the action that she seemed less a killer than a movie star who dreamed she was a killer, proving that Roxie is not only the work's protagonist—the fulcrum on which the tone of the performance is balanced—but *Chicago*'s only role that can be played in a number of different ways. By comparison, an actress cannot toy so with Eliza Doolittle or, for that matter, Eliza Hamilton.

Nevertheless, Griffith had fun with the staging in a very individual way. At the "Roxie Rocks Chicago" scene, after the reporters left, Griffith took control of the stage in the way that performers did in the early twentieth century, extemporizing (or appearing to) for the public's pleasure. Yet Griffith remained in character. Holding up the newspaper with Her Headline in it, she asked the audience, "Can you see?" Then, looking up at the balcony: "Can you see way up there? Yeah?" Now the orchestra, as she walked upstage: "Have you guys seen this? Did you read your paper today?" Now she asked the conductor if he'd like a look, trading her journal for his baton. As he read, she led the band (who of course were simply playing the "Roxie" vamp over and over), concluding by hitting the drummer's high-hat cymbals.

While not a Broadway pro, Griffith knew the value of thespian homebrew, of establishing a relationship with the audience on one's own terms. However, it only works if the performer has a sense of how theatre differs from the other sectors of entertainment. Mel B, of the Spice Girls, joined the revival at the end of 2016 to play a raucous and unfocused Roxie and, on her last performance, broke character several times, with asides to the spectators and to her daughter backstage. She even interrupted the "Roxie" monologue to sing a phrase of her former group's old hit "Wannabe." It was the lowest point in what was already an unhappily casual performance.

One of the revival's very best Roxies was Sandy Duncan, all agog over the fuss she had created and turned out to the nines in her flowering blond topknot and lavish fake eyelashes. A performer whose innate intelligence and effervescence shines through in every role, even if inadvertently, Duncan might have given a clever and talented Roxie, which would have deranged the character. Instead, Duncan turned Roxie from stupid to simply uncultured, albeit knowledgeable about some basic life instructions.

She was pensive, even rueful, on "I'm older than I ever intended to be." Most Roxies go for the laugh; with the right intonation, it's a very humorous line. Duncan, however, made it grave and confidential, the key to Roxie's character: because she senses that show business (in other words: the world as a whole) likes its men mature and commanding but its woman fresh and untasted. In fact, Duncan gave many ordinary lines distinctive readings, as a character completely in tune with herself where most Roxies are impulsively thoughtless and a few, following Gwen Verdon, are pure sociopaths to whom nobody else is entirely real. Duncan was unique, something of a Little Engine That Could, conquering the justice system instead of a mountain.

As the New York cast enjoyed its rotations, the Weissler production went on tour, at first with Charlotte D'Amboise, Yasmine Guy, and Obba Babatundé, and to London with Ruthie Henshall, Ute Lemper, and Henry Goodman (who sang "All I Care About" in a precise recreation of the twenties "crooner" style). In fact, *Chicago* now played virtually every theatre capital in the Western World and even became a staple of the high-school dramatic club, a far cry from the days when *Good News!* and *The Boy Friend* ruled the calendar.

However, I say again that this revival's great success has obscured how elaborate the show was written to be and supposed to be— how, in fact, it *was*, in 1975. The 1996 staging, after all, wasn't, at first, a Broadway show. It was a concert. It was tweaked when it moved to Broadway, but not significantly altered. Some shows play in a unit set—*A Chorus Line* and *Hamilton*, for instance. But this show now plays without a set at all, really.

And that, curiously, is how the public appears to accept and even welcome it. It has become a kind of *Cradle Will Rock* but with a band and dancing: a political statement, one might say. We don't need sets or costumes, these *Chicago*ans tell us. We have a superior decor: the truth.

* * *

Another consequence of the popularity of the 1996 *Chicago* was the revival of interest in a Hollywood adaptation. For years after the original staging closed, one heard rumors. At one point, Liza Minnelli was to play Roxie again, this time opposite Goldie Hawn's Velma. Larry Gelbart was writing a script, turning out draft after draft to try to satisfy the usual interference from Hollywood idiots; one told him to add in a romance for Roxie. Yes, the Fox movie did so. Still, the Fox *Chicago* was so different from Fosse's that Fox's Roxie wasn't even guilty. Gelbart eventually departed the project.

Now other writers were being mentioned, other stars. Nicholas Hytner would direct. Madonna might be Roxie—no, wait, she plans to steal the film as Velma in her patented Madonna cone bra. Other writers, this director, that. The whole business recalls Lewis Stone's repeated line in MGM's *Grand Hotel*: "People come, people go. Nothing ever happens."

Then something did happen, because while California has always loved telling New York that success on Broadway "means absolutely nothing here," the very opposite is true. From the dawn of film through the advent of the talkie and its need for fully developed dialogue right up to last Thursday, moviemakers have been very aware of the New York stage. It used to be a matter of prestige, for the cinema was humiliated by its origin as the delight of riffraff. The movies were bathing beauties and people throwing pies at one another. The stage was . . . you know, Shakespeare.

In the 1960s, the film versions of *West Side Story*, *My Fair Lady*, and *The Sound of Music* impressed Hollywood chieftains with something even better than prestige: popularity. True, the absurdly expensive *Camelot*, *Hello, Dolly!*, and other films-from-Broadway almost destroyed the movie musical altogether. Still, there was always the feeling that the form was a sleeping giant—and the vastly successful *Chicago* could awaken it.

Except: how does one film a concept musical, with its fanciful mashing of time and space? Bob Fosse himself did it with *Cabaret*, but only by banning the situation and character numbers and moving the cabaret inserts from a commentative limbo into the naturalism of performance spots. The commentary remained, but the stage show's use of a story intersecting with a theatrical conceit was gone: everything became "real life."

How could one do that with *Chicago*, whose fantasy, in true concept-musical style, so permeated the piece? I've already noted that, when Velma comes forth at the top of the show to create atmosphere *and* watch Roxie shoot Fred Casely, she isn't "in" a specific locale. She's in a concept musical.

In *Show Boat*, when the curtain goes up, everyone's on the levee. In *The Music Man*, everyone's on a train. In *The Book of Mormon*, everyone's ringing doorbells. How was a *Chicago* movie to accommodate "All That Jazz"? Or the rest of the score, for that matter? Under what circumstances would the Matron sing "When You're Good To Mama"? While being kittenish with the prison guards? Where would Amos be while singing "Mister Cellophane"? In his garage, working on a truck ignition? Then why does the music bear a grand old slow-build-to-cakewalk-finale strut in it?

In the Greg Lawrence book, John Kander reveals that Bob Fosse told him he had figured out how to film *Chicago*. Would it be something like *Cabaret*, readjusting the piece from concept musical to . . . or would Fosse resuscitate the show-biz icons, actually bringing Sophie Tucker and Bert Williams back in person in some way? Or maybe . . .

Fosse failed to tell Kander what he had in mind, and then Fosse suffered his final heart attack, in 1987. The *Chicago* film project seemed doomed to undergo Hollywood's flopsy-mopsy approach to film-making, where everyone has an opinion but nobody knows anything.

And then, just about three years into the revival's run, Rob Marshall directed a television adaptation of *Annie* that successfully reclaimed the piece from John Huston's dire movie version: so Hollywood might listen to Marshall. And he had a solution to *Chicago*'s concept-musical problem: to scrap the vaudeville presentations and the show-biz icons, instead to let the movie imagine *Chicago*'s characters as musical performers by other means, to respect the stage version's "isolation" of the song spots while retaining the "Life is show biz because show biz is life" meme that energized the work in the first place.

Thus, when Queen Latifah's Matron first appears and soon enough reaches "When You're Good To Mama," we don't get the Matron as

Sophie Tucker, as we did in the show. Rather, we get the Matron as Queen Latifah, entertaining onstage in a fringed golden gown and a tiara, with Hippodrome bust and innuendo eyes as she waves a huge feathered fan (in the first chorus) and silken green handkerchief (in the second).

Granted, in the film's very first number, it is Roxie who imagines herself as a performer (in Velma's place), through a kind of turnaround camera shot. This sets up the notion that all of the numbers are objective-correlatives of Roxie's dream of getting into vaudeville. And this is how Rob Marshall wanted it. In the "making of" documentary included in the DVD, he says that Roxie "sees her life through musical sequences." But would Roxie visualize "All I Care About" or "Mister Cellophane"? Does she have the perspective about human nature to contemplate the hypocrisy of lawyers, the inert blandness of her husband? She would know what everyone "knows"— all lawyers are shysters and a loser is a loser. But she doesn't know what Kander and Ebb know about Billy Flynn and Amos, so crediting Roxie's imagination with these two numbers is to exceed a conceit.

Rather, it is the *movie*—in effect, Marshall himself—that does the visualizing. It is as if this *Chicago*, the fifth and thus far final entry in the saga, asks us what life would be like if life were a musical— "embracing the fact," Marshall continues, "that all these numbers [originally] took place on stage rather than trying to disguise that."

Ironically, after all this concern about how the songs could be filmed, when the movie approached its release, in 2002, the trailer tried to minimize its musical component. "A flash of leg, the taste of temptation, the smell of corruption," the usual Hollywood spieler intones, to a lightning-fast array of scenes. They emphasized Fossean sex and jazz but also warned us of the rivalry of Roxie and Velma. The trailer even showed the all-important moment when Roxie, watching Velma on stage, substitutes herself and, so to say, takes over the story. Still, "All That Jazz" was the only vocal quoted, and while the deluge of shots did take in some of the dancing (and even a silhouette of "Mister Cellophane"), each of these lasted perhaps two seconds. It was a very skillful preview, but it did seem to cater to the taste of those moviegoers who don't like musicals.

At that, five of the show's numbers were dropped, partly to keep the musical segments from overwhelming the plot continuity, because most stage musicals navigate through the score but all movies, including the musicals, navigate through the plotline. In any case, "A Little Bit Of Good" would not have suited the re-gendered Mary Sunshine, with its operatic foodledoo, as Christine Baranski's reporter was sympathetic but not, as in the Fosse version, idiotic.

As for "I Know a Girl," this number imbues Velma with the authority of an omniscient narrator. This is useful in a concept musical, where certain characters strike up a kind of interlocutory relationship with the audience, half emcee and half character in the story. But it would be confusing in the realistic medium of film (even if Fosse made it work with the Emcee in *Cabaret*). To put it another way, the moment Chita Rivera sets foot on stage, her sheer professional confidence tells you she knows everything about the narrative already. But Velma doesn't. Retaining "I Know a Girl" would have crowded the movie's contents with meta-theatre.

Further, "When Velma Takes the Stand" was perhaps just one number too many for the running time, but "My Own Best Friend" and "Me and My Baby" were actually in the shooting script, dropped at the last minute. (The latter is heard on the soundtrack accompaniment when Roxie announces her "pregnancy.") And there is a sixth omission: "Class." This one was filmed, and, despite seamless editing, you see exactly where it fit into a scene in which the Matron and Velma are following Roxie's trial on the radio. In dialogue closely modeled on the stage script, Velma attacks the radio physically when she realizes that Roxie has stolen all the tricks Velma was going to use, not to mention Velma's eye-catching garter. Saving her radio, the Matron waxes philosophical:

MATRON: Well, what do you expect? I mean, these days you get a little success and it's good riddance to the people who put you there.

She then adjusts the radio dial and gets some music—the lead-in, in fact, to "Class." But in the release print, the Matron uses the dial to shut the radio off, and the scene continues, songless.

The "Class" footage is included as a bonus on the DVD, and in the optional commentary track Rob Marshall says he dropped the piece because "it doesn't come from our concept [of the numbers stemming from] Roxie's imagination." Indeed, "Class" is not a performance piece on a stage with an audience: as filmed, it's really a "book number" sung in dark lighting, like something that sneaked in from Broadway. One wonders if Marshall thought about letting the Matron and Velma put the song over in a mockup of a classical recital before an appreciative vaudeville public, savoring (in its raucous way) the gulf between the dainty melody and the coarse language of the lyrics. But perhaps that's a notch too dense for an already very rich mise-en-scène.

Kander and Ebb actually added to the score with a new number, "I [just] Move On," for Roxie and Velma to sing over the closing credits. With no connection to the pastiche pieces or even the modern character cuts such as "I Can't Do It Alone," "I Move On" doesn't suit the tone of *Chicago*'s music and has no relation to Roxie or Velma in the first place. Rather, it lends presence and can potentially attract awards activity.

But that leads us to a bizarre footnote in the matter of the *Chicago* score: Miramax's Harvey Weinstein wanted to insert something for the youth audience, and asked Kander and Ebb to consider collaborating with...oh, how about Janet Jackson? Kander sarcastically invoked a picture of him and Ebb "sitting around the kitchen table" brainstorming with Jackson.

In the end, the youth audience got their song, sung by Anastacia, but Kander and Ebb didn't write it, and, by contract, they banned Weinstein from shoving it into the movie itself, though Weinstein was legally empowered to put it on the *Chicago* soundtrack CD. A raving drivel made of a few dumb lines repeated over and over and entitled "Love Is a Crime," it is the work of Damon Sharpe, Greg Lawson, Denise Rich, and Ric Wake, ineluctably recalling Cole Porter's remark, hearing the extraordinarily tedious "Cossack Love Song" from the twenties operetta *Song Of the Flame*, whose score was jointly credited to George Gershwin, Herbert Stothart, Oscar Hammerstein, and Otto Harbach, "It took four men to write *that*?"

As if stating that the *Chicago* film is to be at once very faithful to the stage show yet rebooted for the screen, director Marshall opens his movie with a single eye (presumably Roxie's, as she visualizes the whole thing, to explain where the musical numbers are to come from) but then cuts into the neon-red lettering of the title that was used for the Broadway logo and giving us the same wawa trumpet and "5-6-7-8!" that launched the music on stage.

Yet there are crucial differences between director-choreographer Fosse and director-choreographer Marshall. For one thing, all the dancing is new, even that for the "Hot Honey Rag" at the end. And note that "All That Jazz," so "concept musical" on stage in its no-where-yet-everywhere geography, is now physically rooted in a story location, as Velma's club act—the one that Roxie sees and imagines herself taking over. There is another alteration here, as this is Velma's sister act, and various "real life" shots tell us why she's doing it without her sister, culminating in the arrival of the law during the number's final moments. The sequence thus cleverly introduces—entirely through visuals—the theme of Murder Without Remorse that *Chicago* turns on.

Then the first of the "icon" numbers, "Funny Honey," dispenses with the Helen Morgan echo to show Roxie spotlit in a glamorous front-slit pink gown, truly her dream of glory. This Roxie is not the ridiculous show-biz wannabe that Ginger Rogers played. This is Roxie thinking big. Marshall then collapses the dream and reality together, not only letting Roxie react angrily to Amos' telling the cops enough to inculpate her but directing her to fly at him in a fury, stomping out of the "Funny Honey" shot right into the adjacent "screen" of Amos and the cops, a stunning effect.

Of course, movies can show us things theatre can only stylize: the clammy isolation of your first night in jail, for instance, with the heavy tread of the guards' feet and the screams of the psychos. That's what we hear in *other* movies; Marshall gives us dripping water, as a rhythmic prelude to the implacable beat of the "Cell Block Tango."

This number, too, is different from its stage incarnation, in three ways: one, the song is intercut with real-life scenes, so that each woman's backstory functions as both song lyrics and as dish shared at the lunch table or in the laundry; two, each woman dances with the man whose murder she is charged with; and three, Marshall eventually gives us a screen packed with a chorus of murderesses, as though the city of Chicago were the very cup of crime, and it runneth over.

Culture signaling to the connoisseur, Marshall then sneaks in two hommages that most viewers might miss. Two shots in "All I Care About" deliberately "quote" the look of Tony Walton's logo art from 1975, with the Tired Businessmen gazing down upon the showgirls; and right after "We Both Reached For the Gun," we get footage of Roxie fans coming out of a beauty parlor sporting Roxie's trademark hairdo, including one woman who is the exact replica of the silent *Chicago*'s Roxie, Phyllis Haver.

So the differences between the stage and film *Chicago*s are both great and small—but now for a curious (or at least unexpected) touch: while the men in Velma's "All That Jazz" were typical Broadway dancers, the "boys" Roxie is so proud to show off in her title song are older guys in tuxedos, not the sort we usually see backing up the star in a musical number. Are they perhaps meant to be not her vaudeville partners but rather well-heeled admirers who will ply her with trophy bonbons?

Another major change lies in the trial sequence. This marked a slight lessening of dramatic tension in the stage show, as it went on too long without bringing anything new to the action. Fosse tricked it up with gadgets—Fred Casely's coming back to re-enact the night of the crime, the multi-faceted one-man jury, touches of minstrel show from the chorus, and so on. Marshall's version hews to a strict reality, albeit letting Richard Gere get far more animated in his theatrics than Jerry Orbach did.

Bill Condon uses much of the musical's stage script in his screenplay, including here, but he and Marshall emphasize the movie's trial as a tug of ego war between Gere and Colm Feore, as a District Attorney whose sedate sense of command is overwhelmed by Gere's poses and tantrums. Then, too, we get a novelty in the *Chicago* saga— Roxie's diary, creatively spiced with incriminating lines she never wrote, which gives the courtroom sequence plot power. Yes, we know Roxie will get off. But we didn't know how frenzied Gere would become, and we couldn't have anticipated the diary. And, too, Velma now puts in an appearance in court, another innovation in the stream of *Chicagos*.

In the end, the entire sequence is a tour de force and, more than ever before, a performance. This is what Maurine Watkins had in mind all along: Blind Justice presents the socko team of Flynn and Hart in the all-new extravaganza in one act, *Razzle Dazzle!*

One final small but arresting detail: "Nowadays" starts within the real-life action, then moves into the dream as a kind of consummation of the way Roxie "imagined" herself taking over "All That Jazz." The dream thus becomes the reality, as Marshall transitions from Roxie Nobody into Roxie Vaudeville Star. In a low-cut black cabaret gown, walking a runaway, she has been turned into a birthright performing avatar herself, her own Sophie Tucker or Helen Morgan. Now for the arresting detail: at the start of the song's release, a bell sounds and, right on the beat, a stage light flashes on, glowing warmly and confidently at us, another sign of how meticulously this film's music and optics are bonded.

Given the slew of players considered for the cast (including many who had no experience in musicals), it is almost shocking that everyone in the movie sings in his or her own voice. At that, this is not a famously musical crew of the Howard Keel–Kathryn Grayson model. But then, the modern musical often demands people more adept at bringing unique characters to life than at singing or dancing. By the late 1960s, movie musicals were casting Shakespeareans, cowboys, and private eyes as often as they hired Julie Andrews and Tommy Steele.

The one notable exception here (aside from Queen Latifah, though known more as a rapper than a songstress) is the Velma, Catherine Zeta-Jones, who launched her career in stage musicals in Great Britain. Ironically, her first outstanding credit was as a replacement Peggy Sawyer (the sweetheart role in *42nd Street*) at Drury Lane, where she made the character more innocent and vulnerable than had obtained in the Broadway original. The New York Peggy, Wanda Richert, couldn't hide a highly invulnerable persona; she would have made a fine Velma. But Zeta-Jones is versatile, and her movie Velma captures exactly the sarcasm and cynicism of the twenties wisecrack style that made the play *Chicago* possible.

Renée Zellweger's Roxie is an ideal foil, because while Velma seems to have been born tough, Roxie has to acquire the manner. Gwen Verdon created a Roxie who had nothing to learn; Zellweger's is studious, absorbing the lessons of the other powerful principals in how to game society's structure, from the law to the media. When Zeta-Jones strides into court in a dazzling brown ensemble with fur shoulder pompoms and matching chapeau, and when she takes the oath to tell the whole truth "and then some," we see that Roxie was out-jazzed from the start.

But note that Marshall and Condon troubled to soften—slightly—Roxie's murder of Fred Casely. The stage Casely thought he and Roxie were simply using each other for sex. The movie's Casely (Dominic West) is cheating Roxie for sex, having promised her a connection to show business that he in fact cannot make for her.

Then, too, audiences at the *Chicago* stage revival see an amusingly sporty, exhibitionistic Casely, in his tight trousers and open vest: a fantasy figure. In the movie, however, Casely wears the suit and tie customary for the sheiks of the 1920s. He's no avatar of playful sex and jazz anymore. He's a despoiler in hypocritical disguise. And, at one point, he brutally shoves Roxie to the floor, which precipitates the killing—at white heat, not in cold blood. (And for the first time since the 1926 play, Roxie turns on the gramophone first, a "jazz slayer" once more.)

Granted, abuse is not grounds for murder. Nevertheless, this is a softened Roxie, all the better to contrast her Before and After. Further, the beats of her acclimatization to the anarchy of the Chicago way of doing things are finely judged, as the prison sequence educates her very suddenly in the hierarchy of vice (Velma < the Matron < Billy Flynn), as the promise of stardom elevates her self-belief (in the "Roxie" number), as her coaching sessions with Flynn finally shave off any lingering doubts she may have had about the truth of any-thing. In Chicago, jazz is truth. The truth itself is Pilate washing his hands, futile housekeeping.

Casting Richard Gere as Flynn adheres to Fosse's view of the lawyer as a romantic lead rather than an old clunkabunk, reminding us that physically attractive salesmen are the best salesmen. The

twenties salesman, as we know, was a babbitt. But once the entertainment industry seizes a section of American life, it's never about
the smart guy: it's about the hot guy. And, to remind us of Flynn's
climactic line in the 1975 trial scene—"Things are not always what
they appear to be"—Gere got a trick entrance for "All I Care About."
Above the Fosse fan dancers, we see in silhouette a fancy Dan and a
kneeling shoeshine boy. But then the lights come up, revealing *Gere*
as the shoeshiner, grinning at our credulity.

John C. Reilly's Amos seems somehow less of a clod than Fosse's
original, Barney Martin, did, perhaps because Reilly found a paradox to play: this Amos knows everyone ignores him, yet he is always
surprised when it happens. In a bit held over from Broadway, Flynn
keeps calling him "Andy" instead of "Amos" (a reference to the radio
show *Amos 'n' Andy*, a local Chicago institution from 1928 that went
national the following year), and of course "Mister Cellophane" de-
lineates the oxymoron: Amos himself is nothing, yet the number,
like any number in a musical, has to substantiate him. In a tramp
outfit, with a big black bow tie, derby, and tailcoat, Reilly delivers
the song "onstage," to the tiniest scattering of folks in the auditorium, so unresponsive they might be dummies.

Queen Latifah as the Matron was Miramax's suggestion: Marshall
wanted Kathy Bates. However, could Bates have handled the music
as naturally as the Queen? Too, the movie Matron has more to do
than her stage counterpart, aggrandizing "When You're Good To
Mama" exponentially into a star turn of tremendous resonance yet
naturalizing the character in the dialogue scenes. We get her both
formal and casual, cocky and helpful, withering and comradely.

On one hand, there's a telling comic moment early on, when Roxie
begins her stay in jail pending her trial. The Matron takes a shine to
her, caressing her hair with a disarming "Call me Mama." Nearby
stands a surly male guard, and as he and the Matron prepare to lead
Roxie to her cell:

MATRON: Now, you'll be habilitatin' down in the East Block.
    Murderess Row, we call it.
ROXIE: Oh. . . . Is that nicer?

The Matron doesn't reply, but, as they move off, she treats the guard to an almost perfectly expressionless look that Says It All.

On the other hand, when the Hungarian has learned that her final appeal has failed—that she will be hanged despite her innocence— the Matron, leading her back to her cell, seems genuinely sympathetic. It's just a moment, but it humanizes the Matron from Watkins' starchy commando and the stage musical's merry Diva of a Certain Age. Yes, I've noted that scene in which Mary McCarty, translating with a Hungarian phrase book, took the Hungarian girl's side. But Marshall and Latifah go beyond that, letting the Matron's customary cynicism give way to a realization, however momentary, that, even in Chicago, there is good as well as evil, and goodness has no power.

The greatest change in character type from what Fosse wanted gives us a Mary Sunshine who is biologically female, Christine Baranski. Further, instead of the simpering loon of pseudo-operatic plush, Baranski sings in her normal mezzo tones and is in fact quite businesslike. She is less the "sob sister" falling for Roxie's act than a smart reporter who knows what her readers want to hear.

In an interview with Christopher Rawson for the Pittsburgh *Post-Gazette* during the filming, in Toronto, Baranski called Mary Sunshine "wily and powerful"—the very opposite of Watkins' and Fosse's character. "She's a Roz Russell type," Baranski went on, "a Barbara Walters—those ladies with their high-gloss sincerity."

Invoking Russell (who played the star reporter in the first *Front Page* film remake, *His Girl Friday*) is shorthand for rooting Sunshine in early feminism, when bold women took on jobs previously held only by males. And of course this is exactly what Maurine Watkins herself did on the *Chicago Tribune*.

In fact, the notion of a woman reporter—of hard news and crime scoops, not social occasions—was so tender in the 1920s that Watkins had to avoid using such a figure in her play, lest it distract from the main narrative and become the story itself. Watkins' topic was not gender but the whoring of the press. So her Mary Sunshine had to be inconsequential, while Marshall's version shows a quiet authority.

In truth, he treats all his reporters that way. They aren't fly-by-nights or lackeys. They're grim professionals, with the near-deadpan manner of television's old series *Dragnet*, as in the brief shots in which Baranski quietly describes events in real time into a radio microphone. Marshall uses the reporters fantastically only in their dream number, "We Both Reached For the Gun," wherein Billy Flynn not only works a Roxie dummy but handles the journalists as his personal marionette theatre, puppets of spin.

As for the Hungarian girl, she is more prominent here than in the stage show, as Marshall wants us to see The Jungle from the bottom looking up, just as Upton Sinclair did. In an extremely unnerving sequence, views of the Hungarian's vaudeville turn, announced as a "disappearing act," are interspersed with real-life shots of the girl praying pitiably in her cell, then meeting the rope (around her waist in her act but around her neck on the gallows). Marshall thus makes us look at the hanging in full true, with a theatre full of dressy enthusiasts leaping to their feet in appreciation.

The actress playing the Hungarian in the film is actually Russian, Yekatyerina Shchelkanova (transliterated in the credits as "Ekaterina Chtchelkanova"). She's a dancer and very attractive, unlike Watkins' aforementioned model for the character, Sabella ("Me choke") Nitti, who did at least eventually get off. As in the stage *Chicago*, Shchelkanova's lines are in Hungarian (except for "Not guilty"), but at one point, for unknown reasons, she breaks into her native Russian, with "Pomogitye, pomogitye, pazhalusta!" (Help [me], help [me], please!)

The movie's casting in general is not only fitting but luxurious. Lucy Liu plays Go To Hell Kitty, though it's only a bit, and Chita Rivera turns up for an under five as a fellow prisoner when Roxie is incarcerated. Even the singing and dancing ensemble takes in people we've seen in leading roles on Broadway—Sara Ramirez, Jerry Mitchell, Willy Falk, Deidre Goodwin, Darius De Haas, Capathia Jenkins, Billy Hartung, and Scott Wise, among others.

At that, Taye Diggs, at the keyboard, embodies an important linking device between the real-life scenes and the musical numbers, announcing the "acts" yet also turning up in the continuity. He's the accompanist near the very end of the action, when an exculpated Roxie auditions in a cheap-date nightclub for two whoever-they-ares.

They're not impressed. "Didn't she kill a guy a while back?" one asks the other.

In all, the *Chicago* film was a huge production even for a musical, with hundreds of names in the closing credits (along with a dedication to Fosse, Verdon, and a co-producer in 1975, Martin Richards). On some days during the shoot it seemed as if every one of them was on the sets. (There were two major ones, for the prison and the courtroom.) The budget was $45 million and the gross $307 million, and *Chicago* ended up as one of the few musicals ever to win the Best Picture Oscar.

We should note a cute agents' war over the billing, for while *Chicago* is Roxie's story, Catherine Zeta-Jones' deputy felt his client was of equal prominence. Ah, but Richard Gere's agent said *his* client was the most established of the three. In a compromise, Renée Zellweger's name stood in first place at left while Zeta-Jones' name, at the right, created an alternate first place on a higher line, while Gere, below them, got a prestigious "and."

Though it hasn't rivaled the almost psychotic success of *The Sound of Music*, a film whose devotees attended it twenty, fifty, a hundred times, *Chicago* has become middle-class common knowledge, so much so that a 2017 *Saturday Night Live* spoof with "Jake Tapper" (Beck Bennett) interviewing "Kellyanne Conway" (Kate McKinnon) could explode into a pre-taped production number using "Roxie" as a template, with a precise duplication of the sequence as staged in the film (complete with a crowd of tuxedoed chorus men and Renée Zellweger's silvery-white dress). It worked only because SNL could make the assumption that everyone would get it. *Chicago* might well become the new *Oklahoma!*—the piece Americans think of when they hear the word "musical."

They may instead think of *Hamilton*, not only because of its phenomenal popularity but because its oddly post-racial racialism suits the current age. Yet *Chicago*'s twenties setting looks back on a time when the attitudes and manners of American show business were amplified by the growing prominence of minority-group performers, as in the Ted Lewis lawyer, the Sophie Tucker Matron, the Bert Williams husband. We so take for granted the cosmopolitan nature of modern American art that we cannot imagine how innovative these figures seemed when they first appeared—Fanny Brice with her odd little songs about how the wide world looked to a Jewish girl of narrow cultural frontiers (ballet and modern dance! courtship technique! subversive politics!), Ethel Waters and her merry anthems of ghetto life, or even Will Rogers, whose cowboy ethnicity and well-known part-Indian ancestry were equally alien.

In 1975, when the Fosse-Verdon *Chicago* was new, the memory of the show biz it referenced was dimming; by now it is all but extinguished. Even some of the show's cast and creatives—Fosse, Verdon, Orbach, Fred Ebb—are gone, though they left vivid souvenirs of various kinds and remain integral in the American arts catalogue. Eddie Shapiro's *Nothing Like a Dame* records a touching meeting between Verdon and Donna McKechnie after Verdon's Fosse and McKechnie's Michael Bennett died within two months of each other. Thus, each had lost what we might call her "inner light of art": the irreplaceable person, as I've said, who understands you the way no one else can.

McKechnie asked how Verdon was doing, and she replied, "I'm fine and I'm so sorry [about Bennett]. We keep them alive inside." McKechnie had been preparing a revival of *Sweet Charity* under Verdon's supervision, and McKechnie then shares with author Shapiro the wonder of spending such a "privileged time, really working with an artist on that level. . . . Certain things pop up as highlights [in one's life,] and this is one of them."

We keep them alive inside. Part of that is through revivals of their work, whether transcendent or scathing, even if it may take the form of a warning about the corruption of the Pinocchio press— especially timely today. The American newspaper, said Chicago's fictional Irish bartender, Finlay Peter Dunne's Mr. Dooley, "comforts th' afflicted [and] afflicts th' comfortable." More broadly, the political right needs the left to curb its excesses, and the left similarly needs the right. But both need impartial news-gathering organizations to monitor their tendencies toward moral and cultural imperialism.

The politically independent pollster Pat Cadell, noted (in Accuracy in Media) that "the tragic death of a U.S. ambassador in Libya . . . was covered up for nine days because the press and the [Obama]

administration did not want to admit that it was a terrorist attack."
Cadell was warning that, when the news media choose "what truth that
you may know, as an American, and what truth you are not allowed to
know, they have...made themselves the enemy of the American people."

Comparably, in The Intercept, Glenn Greenwald—no one's idea
of a right-winger—warns against our believing evidence-free eruc-
tations from American intelligence agencies, which he calls our "un-
elected deep state overlords."

This is strong language to jump to from an analysis of a Broadway
musical. But this historically liberated form, as I've said, is a kind of
town crier, a buffer between the authorities and us, ever recalling
Americans to a worldly tolerance—of feminism, in the nineteenth
century; of racial and ethnic minority integration, in the early twentieth century—along with assaults on the warrior state and the
fascism of the money bosses, as we saw in the satires of the 1930s.

Then, more recently, we have had Compassion Musicals treating
runaway children and people with special needs. The musical is entertainment but also advocacy, commentary, investigation. O. J.
Simpson's day in kangaroo court made Chicago timely, but the events
of 2016 have done so again. Greenwald observes that "Democrats,
still reeling from...a systemic collapse of their party...are willing—
eager—to embrace any claim, cheer any tactic, align with any villain"
in countering what Greenwald calls "the serious dangers posed by a
Trump presidency."

But who are we to believe? Every few minutes there's another
"scandal" in which an organ of the Pinocchio press launches another
attack using fantasy data and speculation, only to be counter-attacked
with "alternative facts." It is as if we now live inside Maurine Watkins'
worldview, helpless to separate propaganda from revelation.

Is that perhaps why we have treasured our national art of the
musical, because of its independence and its wish to tell us who we
are as a people? Intellectuals scorned it as cotton candy, but they're
wrong. It's the art by which we comprehend ourselves, and that is
why we keep bringing those wonderful old shows back, and why we
mourn the passing of the people who created them: because they
were the friends who understood us. We keep them alive inside.

FOR FURTHER READING

It's almost poetry: "To the east were the moving waters as far as the eye could follow. To the west a sea of grass as far as wind might reach."

Thus Nelson Algren, in his book-length essay *Chicago: City On the Make* (Doubleday, 1951). He called the place "an outlaw's capital," but it's not clear whether "outlaws" means gangsters or people who scoff at too much direction by the state. And his chapter titles—"Are You a Christian?," "Love Is For Barflies," "Nobody Knows Where O'Connor Went"—bespeak Algren's wide-stance observations. This is one of best examples of travel writing ever published, pulling past even Jan Morris. Something as low as a poolroom inspires Algren, as "the sullen evening's earliest torpedo slips the long cue silently from the shadowy rack...and turns on the night." Heck, it *is* poetry.

For conventional history, try *Chicago: Growth of a Metropolis* (University of Chicago Press, 1969), by Harold M. Mayer and Richard C. Wade, profusely illustrated with black-and-whites—and Chicago is, for all its emphasis on the industrial and the expedient, a very photogenic locale, once far-famed for its architecture. Dominic A. Pacyga's *Chicago* (University of Chicago Press, 2009) is livelier in tone, but the key work is Donald L. Miller's *City of the Century* (Simon & Schuster, 1996), so detailed and richly thematic that the author had to end with the 1893 World's Fair. Miller binds his chronicle to the lives of Chicago Characters—Old Settlers, industrialists, politicians, writers—and he sees the city as instrumental in the making of American business and culture. Truly, Miller finds so much sheer *there* in the place that one understands why Maurine Watkins moved to Chicago to find material for her play. All in all, a great read.

If the epic of Chicago is the epic of America, a work on the city's beginnings should fascinate, but Ann Durkin Keating's *Rising Up From Indian Country* (University of Chicago, 2012) is flatly written, conveying none of the historical wonder of the very center of a continent disputed by antagonistic elements, especially the Indians' understanding of the land and the settlers seeking to master and reinvent it. Worse, Keating brings present-day race mania to her treatment of the Fort Dearborn Massacre of 1812.

It's a central myth among Chicago boosters even today, though all three of the histories cited above treat it virtually in passing: fifty-five soldiers, twelve militiamen, nine women, and eighteen children peacefully retreating from the fort were slaughtered by Indians, some on the spot and some a few hours later in the methodical barbarism practiced in those parts. Keating, however, insists it wasn't a massacre, euphemizing it as "a planned attack." Armed men murdering women and children in the most grisly ways imaginable is not a massacre? Yeah, right.

Meanwhile, Douglas Perry's *The Girls of Murder City* (Viking, 2010) explores the models for Roxie and Velma, along with the rest of the rogues' gallery that inspired Maurine Watkins' dramatis personae. The book's cover art combines a photograph of the press flashbulbing away with a second shot of a Shady Lady on the witness stand in some old film noir, exactly the air of rotten news that Watkins made tangible and Perry deconstructs, in lively fashion. He includes as well a Whatever Happened To as an epilogue, to detail everyone's further adventures. Surprise!: *Amos* was convicted of beating a woman to death, though he got a second trial and the case was dismissed. Those interested in reading Watkins' *Tribune* pieces on Beulah and Belva— Roxie and Velma—will find them in the Southern Illinois Press's photo-offset reprint of the original Knopf text of the play *Chicago*.

On the 1920s, Frederick Lewis Allen's *Only Yesterday* (Harper & Row, 1931) is the classic, but J. C. Furnas' *Great Times* (Putnam, 1974) gives us a much more vivid look at the way people were thinking about America. For one thing, Furnas starts in 1914, thus to set up the transformational aspect of the era; there really could not have been a Roxie or Velma in earlier times. Furnas knows a lot, too (to put it mildly). He likens Chicago gangster funerals to "the lineup of the USSR brass at May Parades in Moscow—vehicles of economic and diplomatic information." It was, as the old joke runs, a "who's still who" in the Party, and, in Chicago, the grandeur or paucity of the flower banks sent by rival gangsters told everyone present if the decedent's "mob was losing clout."

The 1920s wouldn't be the 1920s without Prohibition—a cornerstone in Americans' belief that an oppressive and hypocritical law freed them from respecting laws in general. Thus, Velma's litany of nightly escapades in "All That Jazz" mixes up the new grooming and dance styles and the jazz tooting of "Father Dip" with the thrill of lawbreaking. Daniel Okrent's *Last Call* (Scribner, 2010) supersedes the many earlier works on Prohibition with a vivid and freshly researched chronicle. (Full disclosure: Okrent edited my first book.) Wading further into the 1920s, we find Joshua Zeitz's *Flapper* (Three Rivers, 2006) explaining why women were shuffling off authoritarian control. "Real money," Zeitz writes, "could buy real freedom," so no wonder homemaking began to feel stifling. Of course, Roxie Hart is after something even money can't buy: fame. But fame buys money, doesn't it?

Scott Eyman's excellent biography of Cecil B. DeMille, *Empire of Dreams* (Simon & Schuster, 2010), is drenched in moviemaking. It's almost a history of Hollywood's first half-century. Eyman doesn't say much about DeMille's *Chicago* film, but this is a fascinating story overall, revealing a man of crusty temperament but generous nature. His current reputation suffers from DeMille's fervent anti-Communism, though why a public figure opposed to the enslavement of entire populations in Stalinist jail countries should be anathema to anyone has never been explained.

For William A. Wellman, who directed the second *Chicago* film, *Roxie Hart*, William Wellman Jr. offers *Wild Bill Wellman* (Pantheon, 2015), on obviously privileged acquaintance with the subject, who comes alive as well in his own *A Short Time For Insanity* (Hawthorn, 1974). This title is like Wellman himself, brusque and honest. It could not have been ghosted—it's as candid as a deathbed confession. Oddly, it lacks most of the famous Wellman anecdotes. Wellman's threatening of Ronald Colman for trying to sabotage Ida Lupino's big scene in *The Light That Failed* (which you can read in these pages) is missing, though his son includes it.

On the man who made the fourth *Chicago*, the best by far of several books is Sam Wasson's *Fosse* (Houghton Mifflin, 2013), given authority by Wasson's expertise in the milieux in which his subject worked. Too many show-biz biographies today command little or no understanding of how the art and the business work from era to era, leading authors to make absurd generalizations and getting all the telling details wrong. That is not so here— and Fosse emerges as an artist obsessed with the vulnerable, the wounded figure, because of his own unstable ego system. *New Girl in Town*, *Redhead*, *Sweet Charity*, *Lenny*, and *Star 80* all follow the adventures of people unsure of their place in the world. (And Fosse was originally to have directed *Funny Girl*, another tale of a troubled soul.) Wasson is as well a vivid writer. When he speaks of "the little inward jerks and isolations" that give the *Kiss Me, Kate* movie's "From This Moment On" a "louche sizzle," you know that Wasson understands exactly what made Fosse the most individual of all his colleagues.

Peter Shelley's *Gwen Verdon* (McFarland, 2015), her only biography, is written in a flat and choppy style with no sense of flow in the paragraphing. Nevertheless, Shelley unveils many a tidbit: Broadway's *Damn Yankees* producers offered Lola first to Mitzi Gaynor, Jeanmaire (who had just thrilled the critics in *The Girl in Pink Tights*), and (so said Verdon) even Marilyn Monroe; and Fosse, when working on *Funny Girl*, tried to put Verdon into the lead.

There are some odd statements, too, such as George Abbott's supposedly changing the rock beat of *Damn Yankees*' "Two Lost Souls" to make it sound like *The Pajama Game*'s "There Once Was a Man" (which title Shelley gets a bit wrong), the arrangement reverting to the original rock only ten years later, in Verdon's summer *Yankees* tour. In fact, there is no way the sultry "Two Lost Souls" could be made to sound like the country rave-up "There Once Was a Man," and, as one can hear on the *Damn Yankees* cast album, it was performed with the rock beat from the start. But Shelley does include the sad tale of Verdon's leaving after taping a segment of *Broadway: The Golden Age*. When the producer offered to call her a cab so she wouldn't be mobbed on the street, she said it wasn't necessary anymore. After reigning as the theatre's greatest dancing star, Verdon was now, she said, no more than "one of the old ladies from the *Cocoon* movies."

James Leve's *Kander and Ebb* (Yale University Press, 2009) is a dreary academic slog, but *Colored Lights* (Faber and Faber, 2003) allows the team to narrate their own history, guided by the unseen hand of co-author Greg

Lawrence. The format is a book-length conversation between Kander and Ebb as they review their career, discussing how they work and what happened on each show, along with more general reflections on the entertainment world, as when Kander, speaking of a stunt Frank Sinatra pulled during the pre-recording session for a television special, notes of "superstars" that their singing, as they age into national treasures, "become[s] more superstarish and powerful...more about them [than about the songs], so that everything begins to sound the same." Typically, for this very personal book, Kander first warns us that he might be "too harsh," and Ebb replies, "Oh, go on. I like when you're harsh."

One book I wish I could discuss is a history of the satiric component in the musical: but there isn't one. Many elements distinguish our "light" music-theatre form from that of Europe, but the crucial one is the form's determination to challenge unwritten laws (such as the racial separation that broke down gradually from the 1910s to the 1930s and more thoroughly from the 1940s on) and assorted hypocrisies that kept government elites happy. The musical was not thought of as an engine of revolutionary power when *Strike Up the Band*, in different wording, said that America joined World War I to make the rich richer. Yes, that moral imperialist Woodrow Wilson had his own reasons. But George S. Kaufman may have thought of him as a tool of his own messiah complex. Beyond that is the simple image of a musical comedy with information to impart to the thinking man or woman, because it was thinking authors who developed the musical in its Golden Age, from Oscar Hammerstein to Stephen Sondheim, and thinkers don't make fluff. Their form is poetic and enlightening, and above all independent.

A SELECTIVE DISCOGRAPHY

Let's get our bearings on the musical satire with the first one, *Strike Up the Band*. The Roxbury series of Gershwin restorations (Elektra Nonesuch), funded by Ira's widow, Leonore, offers both the 1927 and 1930 versions. The earlier one is the better deal, for the two CDs give us the 1927 score and then six new songs inserted into the revision, as a bonus. Brent Barrett, Rebecca Luker, Jason Graae, and Juliet Lambert (as the First and Second Couples) lead a worthy cast under John Mauceri, but the key thing here is the way the music conspires with the spoofy action. The Gilbert and Sullivan chorus, so keen on the doings that it becomes a principal itself, was a breakaway in 1927: choruses in other musicals were merry and helpful, but this chorus takes sides and gets obstreperous. "The Man I Love" turns up here (though not in 1930), but the true find is the "Meadow Serenade," in 1927 only, with a jumpy lilt of great charm.

While not satires per se, *Johnny Johnson* and *The Cradle Will Rock* have satiric elements, and like *Strike Up the Band* they precede *Chicago* in making baleful commentary. There are two *Johnny Johnsons*, both studio casts. MGM's, made in the wake of the label's hit recording of the "Lotte Lenya *Threepenny Opera*," gives little more than the core numbers (Lenya sings the one Paula [Miller] Strasberg laid an egg with on stage), but it's a colorful reading with, at times, the feel of the theatre. Erato's CD is complete in a sparkless performance, utterly missing the feeling of a forthright everyman surrounded by lunatics. A more pertinent *Johnny Johnson* would be—just for instance— Hank Stratton as Johnny, worried by Kristen Chenoweth's Minny Belle; Mary Testa as her bizarre mother; Christian Borle as the insinuating Captain Valentine; Christopher Fitzgerald as Private Harwood, the cowboy soldier; and Nathan Lane as eerie Doctor Mahodan, jungle drums punctuating his sermonette on that modern-day witch doctor the psychiatrist.

The Cradle Will Rock's 78 set (Musicraft; American Legacy; Pearl) is often cited as the first American original-cast album—but the orchestra is missing. Yes, the show was piano-accompanied in its improvised stage premiere. But don't we need to hear the work as Blitzstein wrote it, with his own scoring? Those original 78s are of historical interest, especially as they reveal how director Orson Welles had the villains playing in exaggerated verbal delivery. Junior Mister, in "Honolulu," proves that he is indeed "far-fetched" (as Yasha and Dauber call his kind in "The Rich"). The great *Cradle*, however, is a 1960 New York City Opera revival (Cantus Classics), sung by a combination of company people and Broadway ringers. This two-CD set gives us the scoring that went unheard in 1937 (and almost invariably thereafter, in a *Groundhog Day* view of *Cradle* that never lets it move past its original sabotaged, piano-only production), and the source tape, presumably from the City Center's sound system, is in excellent sound, though John Mauceri, in the *Kurt Weill Newsletter*, thinks the performance runs a half-step or so sharp. Ruth Kobart, soon to be the original Broadway Miss Jones (in *How To Succeed*) and Domina (in *A Funny Thing*) plays a superb Mrs. Mister, not the usual harpy but, as the wife of the town boss, a woman used to getting her way simply by asking. Operetta baritone David Atkinson is the unionist hero and, lo, Tammy Grimes, just before her big breakout role in *The Unsinkable Molly Brown*, is Moll, the prostitute.

So the performance is theatrical and well sung. "The Freedom of the Press," for instance, has never sounded so evil before, as Mr. Mister (Craig Timberlake) bullies Editor Daily (Jack Harrold, his surname misspelled in the Cantus packaging) in a fierce delineation of master and slave. Most important, the music emerges as more powerful and imaginative than on piano, with many raucous explosions and crazy little doodads—the "Hawaiian" effect in "Honolulu" (with a staging that has the audience in an uproar), for example, or the way Beethoven's *Egmont* blams out of Mrs. Mister's automobile horn.

On the musical's heroine figure: Marilyn Miller preserved *Sally* in 1929 (Warner Archive DVD), somewhat faithful to the original 1920 show's plotline but retaining only two of the Jerome Kern numbers, with inserts by others. Miller's looks aren't movie-starish, but her animated interaction with all the other characters and her one-of-a-kind hoofing style (her ballet is conventional) tell us why she was so enchanting on stage. Shot in two-strip Technicolor, the film survives only in black and white, though three minutes of the color (integrated into the DVD continuity) have been found, luckily of the best sequence in the film, the "Wild Rose" number, from the stage show and presumably filmed in replica, to honor the elfin Cinderella aura that Miller exemplified. The matrix for Mary Sunshine's "A Little Bit Of Good" is here, too, in the show's standard, "Look For the Silver Lining."

Altogether new for the film, however, is an odd low-comic sequence in which a ridiculous "Santa Claus" (the old term for a much older man who dates young women: "Ugly guys like to do that," as Roxie says) slips and fumbles getting up a ladder to an intimate table in a restaurant. This represents a now lost feature of the musical, absurd physical comedy expected at least once in virtually every show short of operetta or the musical play. The usage lasted long enough to show up in *Gypsy*, when Rose cries rape against a landlord, though it's often cut in revivals.

Speaking of *Gypsy*, Ethel Merman popularized a new style of heroine in the generation after Miller, perhaps best caught in the movie of her stage show *Call Me Madam* (Fox DVD). Where Miller sings soprano and captivates the chorus men who dance with her in "Wild Rose," Merman belts and orders men around. If you can find it, an audio capture of Merman's last night in *Gypsy* reveals what a sharp comic she was.

Coming in a few years after Merman, Mary Martin reconciled the Miller and Merman wings of the heroine edifice: Martin sang low but commanded a coloratura-soprano extension. (When she started out, her audition piece was

Luigi Arditi's "Il Bacio," the sort of thing you'd expect from Lily Pons.) Then, too, Martin began as a sweetheart type (like Miller; Merman was always a hard-edged broad) but eventually became more of a tomboy. Hear Martin's suave, rather detached vocalism on two cast albums from the 1940s combined on a single CD, *One Touch of Venus* and *Lute Song* (MCA). The one's seductive waltz "Foolish Heart" and the other's metaphorical "Mountain High, Valley Low" are songs fit for a somewhat distant figure—respectively, the goddess of love and the heroine of a mannered Chinese pageant.

But then came the national tour of *Annie Get Your Gun*, liberating Martin's playful side, and we meet a much more exuberant star in the television versions of her Peter Pan (VAI DVD) and her marvelous Annie Oakley (GI DVD). As these artifacts of Martin's theatre reveal, she was a superb and nuanced actress under the comic facade. It would have been fascinating, had Martin been a generation younger, to see what she would have made of Mrs. Lovett.

Gwen Verdon completely revised the heroine persona. In *Can-Can* (Capitol; Angel), on her one cut, she must sing soprano. And, yes, she does have the notes—but the true Verdon emerges in *Damn Yankees* (Victor), for this is Fosse's Verdon, the devil's Verdon, somewhere between mischievous and homicidal. (When her boss asks how her trip was, she replies, "Wonderful. The plane crashed in Cleveland.") Along with most of the stage cast, Verdon filmed her Lola (Warner DVD), but the film is useful mainly for preserving Fosse's choreography and its sampling of mid-fifties Broadway comic style from Ray Walston and the male support. Co-directed by George Abbott (with Stanley Donen), this *Damn Yankees* has all of Abbott's bad qualities, especially his love of hoary stage tradition over character honesty. It's worth noting that, in *Tab Hunter Confidential* (FilmRise DVD), Hunter tells us how contemptuous Abbott was of the Movie Star plonked down among the theatre folk, and how, as always, Abbott refused to discuss motivation and gave Hunter line readings.

His subjects called him "Mr. Abbott" and bowed low to the king, because he had a musical or two going up every season and no one wanted to end up on his blacklist. But he was arrogant and limited and, by the way, used Verdon in her one leading movie role so badly that, except for "Whatever Lola Wants," which was really Fosse's job, Verdon was unflatteringly directed and photographed and simply doesn't project the way she did on stage. And while Tab Hunter wasn't one of the great thespians of his day, he knew his way around a sound stage and, as the work's naive baseball hero, was perfectly cast to boot. It's a testament to Hunter's talent that everyone in the film but him and two supporting women (Shannon Bolin and Rae Allen) comes off as phony.

A more persuasive (though unseen) Verdon can be found on the *New Girl in Town* cast album (Victor), where we hear her fashion an individual, from the biting "On the Farm" through the "love awakens" number, "It's Good To Be Alive" to the love duet of chaste physical attraction (with George Wallace) "Did You Close Your Eyes [when we kissed]?" Verdon's breathy, word-centered delivery suggests someone in a hurry to get somewhere, as if impatient with the contours of musical-comedy storytelling. If she hadn't been such an accomplished dancer, would she have become a straight actress?

During her stay with Victor, Verdon recorded not only cast albums but a "personality" disc. It was a staple of the 1950s; even tone-deaf cowboy stars released them. Verdon's was *The Girl I Left Home For*, published with a cover shot of Verdon lounging on a bench with a Mona Lisa smile. The aim was to present Verdon as a sex icon, and the mixture of show and movie tunes sets forth a "naughty" ID: "It's a Hot Night in Alaska," "Find Me a Primitive Man," "Daddy." Where the fifties vocal style favored the velvety, the undramatic, Verdon tries to find a character in her numbers. So when Dick Haymes is singing, we always know it's Dick Haymes. But when Verdon is singing, we ask, "Who is she now?"

The naughtiest of the numbers is Cole Porter's "Mister and Missus Fitch," from *Gay Divorce*, on Society's latest chichi couple; Verdon sings it as one of the in-crowd but not a Fitch intimate. Note that Victor had to euphemize Porter's use of "bitch" (with "witch" and "[son of the] rich"). Even the original show (and Porter was known for naughty) had to finesse the word. In *The Complete Lyrics of Cole Porter*, Robert Kimball reports that the percussion part in *Gay Divorce*'s original charts directed the drummer to drown out Luella Gear whenever she reached the expletive.

As for Fosse's work, a look at his movies, perhaps especially the grisly *Star 80* (Warner Archive DVD), in which Mariel Hemingway's *Playboy*-centerfold heroine is set into a Passion, as if she was too beautiful to be allowed to live, reveals his versatility. I wonder if Agnes de Mille or Michael Kidd, to name two other director-choreographers, could have brought a comparable script to term with Fosse's power.

For his choreography itself, *Fosse* (Image DVD), the 1999 Broadway retrospective, gives us some classic routines from *Damn Yankees*, *The Pajama Game*, *Sweet Charity* (the "Rich Man's Frug" and the back-alley Cleopatras of "Big Spender"), and *Chicago*, with other stage and television work. In the second cut, from *Big Deal*, Fosse's last show, watch the ensemble, in their Fosse derbies, strike the Fosse pose, commedia dell'arte on hallucinogens. The grand finale, "Sing, Sing, Sing!," offers alternate Fosse body language, with the torso hunched over and arms dangling as the dancers travel on their toes or jump into the air with their upper body thrust to one side.

Now for Kander and Ebb. The former got to Broadway first, with *A Family Affair* (United Artists; DRG-EMI), written with James and William Goldman. (The billing is sphinx-like on who actually did what.) Here we find Kander in very basic musical-comedy mode, having no purpose other than creating joy, even if, in the Rodgers and Hammerstein era, there will be some realistic character conflict, here between the uncle of the bride (Shelley Berman) and the mother of the groom (Eileen Heckart). Note the Novelty Stars, not as persuasive musically as the betrothed (Larry Kert and Rita Gardner), but flavorsome, Heckart digging into "My Son the Lawyer" with surprising gusto and Berman very funny in "Revenge," an hommage to Ravel's *Bolero* (a reminder of Kander's strong identification with classical music) as he plots to even the score with Heckart. The song's centerpiece is a spoken bit, in Berman's trademark phone-conversation shtick, here with a bakery's impedient answering tape.

The *Family Affair* score as a whole has its share of such specialty cuts, as when Morris Carnovsky, a third Novelty Star as Heckart's husband, tries a touch of hula in a Hawaiian shirt in "Kalua Bay." Still, the air of a composer balancing tradition with innovation is strongly felt, as when the sweethearts' "There's a Room in My House" counters his confidential A strain with her intermediary theme and finally brings them together—marries them, as that's what the show is about. But note that *her* music supplies the song's coda...till he gets the last word, on three notes of *his* music.

Flora, the Red Menace (Victor), Kander's first show with Ebb, has a much more consistently narrative score, and the album boasts the young Liza Minnelli in her awkward, wondering persona, irresistibly *pow!* in the Heroine's Wanting Song, "All I Need (Is One Good Break)." Note the casual naturalism of the intro, as Flora fills out an employment application, the more theatrical transition ("I'll be glad to tell you...") to the refrain, and then the inevitable Kander vamp, syncopated with anticipation as Minnelli launches a slow build to a thrilling climax, true musical comedy.

Let's single out also the young Mary Louise Wilson (later celebrated as the senior of the two recluses in *Grey Gardens*) as a communist agitator, recounting feats of revolutionary zeal ("short-circuited a Duesenberg...") in "The Flame." If one of the musical's strengths is the richness of its character songs, another is the use of musical pastiche, to avoid monotony of tone with a palette of styles, and "The Flame" makes its point in a strikingly Slavic-sounding refrain, as if Wilson were taking her orders direct from the steppes.

The Kander and Ebb career mirrors the history of the musical: light entertainment growing ever more observant of life till it attains to serious purposes, even as it preserves its roots in Offenbach's genre *primitif et gai*. *Cabaret* got a complete two-disc studio reading of the original score (Jay), with the movie songs, other bits, and Gregg Edelman preserving a number he introduced in the 1987 revival, "Don't Go." This is a cosmopolitan cast, each principal working in a different style—Maria Friedman's Sally coming from the musical play, Judi Dench going Restoration Komödie as Frau Schneider, and ebullient Fred Ebb himself as Herr Schultz.

We hear Ebb (and Kander) also on a CD release of the original cast (Columbia; SONY), in demos of three cut numbers, showing us how songwriters approach the utter truth of their shows by writing and then replacing incorrect character numbers first: thus to come to recognize exactly who their people are, even what their story is. So Sally's "It'll All Blow Over" states, very simply, that she cannot see the problem in a Nazi takeover. And, true, most people in Germany in 1933 thought Hitler's appointment as Chancellor was a temporary matter, as had obtained with so many previous such appointments. However, it isn't that Sally doesn't get it. She *does* get it: and simply doesn't care. She's an amoral figure in a necessarily moral climate. That's why she's dangerous, and why she needed a different song explaining her policy: the title song, a salute to hedonism at all costs. In the original production, a curtain of streamers came down behind her before the number's last refrain, in effect cutting her off from everything outside the "cabaret": the place of make-believe.

So we see Kander and Ebb attain the commentative musical, not by abandoning musical comedy but, rather, by re-empowering it. This leads to musical plays with a strong sense of fun built into them. In one way of looking at it, Liza Minnelli is the Kander and Ebb mascot for the early, merry part of their career while Chita Rivera is the later, more serious mascot, even if the two met on equal terms in *The Rink* (Jay), a serious show, after Minnelli's *als Gast* stint in *Chicago*. Hear the Kander and Ebb Rivera in *Kiss of the Spider Woman* (Victor) and *The Visit* (Yellow Sound) as angels of death, a good long walk from the musical-comedy Rivera of *Seventh Heaven* (Decca) and *Mr. Wonderful* (Decca). Just to absorb, on the former, Rivera's playful oomph when she pronounces her name in "Camille, Collette, Fifi" is to slip back into the guiltless pleasure of absolute musical comedy, even if Ricardo Montalban did end up blinded at the show's end.

John Kander: Hidden Treasures, 1950–2015 (Harbinger) reviews music both famous and virtually unheard, performed by Kander and Ebb along with various guests. Ebb is definitely the star here, outgoing and effervescent where Kander, despite a forceful piano style, is somewhat self-effacing in his vocals. Neither is a singer per se, but they know how a Broadway score is supposed to sound, making them somehow even more vivid than the professional singers on the two discs.

I wish, though, that there were fewer famous numbers here. Do we really need the authors' "So What?" when we have Lotte Lenya's version on the *Cabaret* cast album? The program does emphasize the rarities—five numbers from the *Skin of Our Teeth* musical, and, from the unproduced *Tango Mogador*, the very clever "Seven O'Clock," as Kander supplies the traditional Arabic wailing while Ebb recounts the dramatic arrival of a Foreign Legion officer for an amatory rendezvous, though in the event he gets there as a corpse.

Most relevant to the present volume, here we can sample "Windowpanes of Rose" and "It," cut from *Chicago*, as well as the early one-step version of "Roxie"—and with all these numbers new to our ears, the accompanying booklet offers first-rate notes by Jesse Green, to site each song in the evolution of Kander's art. For me at least, the outstanding cut (once Green explains its context) is the aforementioned "You Know Me," a comic piece from *The Visit* in an excellent reading by Alix Korey and Barbara Walsh. Though heard in earlier *Visit* stagings, it was cut by some idiot for the New York production, because it's "too" entertaining—that touch of Kander and Ebb musical comedy slipping into a fable of betrayal and revenge. Yes, next time let's drop "Gee, Officer Krupke" from *West Side Story*, too.

Exploring the iconic figures referenced in *Chicago*, let's start with Sophie Tucker: *Jazz Age Hot Mamma* (Take Two), fourteen late acoustic and early electric 78s along with six vocals from Tucker's (lost) talkie, *Honky Tonk*, right off the soundtrack. This last group includes the irresistible "I'm Feathering a Nest [for a little bluebird]," a man's song that Tucker sings without changing a word. They did that in the old days; dance-band discs of "Can't Help Lovin' Dat Man" and others such routinely featured a vocal refrain by a male. The *Honky Tonk* cuts are all nightclub floor numbers, complete with audience applause to greet

Sophie's entrances. This makes the film a story peppered with vaudeville solos: very much the feeling of *Chicago,* though *its* vaudeville takes in not just songs but spoken set pieces and the poker pantomime that the 1996 revival omitted.

Take Two's "Mama" number, from 1923, is "You've Got To See Mamma [*sic*] Ev'ry Night," because Sophie has no use for a man "who does his sheiking once a week." Note the vamp at the very start of the cut, a venerable show-biz practice that directly anticipates the melody of the verse and was often used to cover stage business. The orchestra would quietly repeat the vamp while the star got through a spoken intro, so when he or she started singing the verse, the two measures of vamp fit right in as the beginning of the accompaniment. The John Kander vamp, on the contrary, usually anticipates the *rhythm* of the *refrain,* and is too industrious to serve as underscoring (though it is used thus in the "Roxie" monologue).

Take Two's Sophie Tucker disc includes also her best (of several over many years) "Some of These Days"—and, lo, it is accompanied by Ted Lewis and his band, sounding like a klezmer group wailing through a wedding reception. As Lewis was as well known for his clarinetting as his singing, one wonders if Kander and Ebb ever considered letting Jerry Orbach fake a bit of "All I Care About" on the licorice stick.

A cornucopia awaits on *The Ziegfeld Follies* (Living Era), as we get three of *Chicago*'s icons, Helen Morgan, Bert Williams, and Eddie Cantor. Williams even gives us "Nobody," the matrix of Amos' "Mister Cellophane." Note the paradox: "Nobody" is about a nonentity, but Williams is very personable. Even the trombone on the downbeat of the refrain's A strain is full of presence, and in the second strophe Williams imitates the instrument himself. He also makes a little banquet out of the song's title, as "Nohbohdeh."

Cantor gives us "If You Knew Susie" and "You'd Be Surprised," the latter being Irving Berlin's salute to a wan little nerd who turns into a couch artist when the lights are low. For a Cantor "baby" number, you might turn to the early talkie based on a Ziegfeld-Cantor stage hit, *Whoopee!* (Warner Archive). In early Technicolor and featuring most of the original stage principals, this is a splendid preservation of what musicals used to be like before they got commentative, with librettos functioning less as narrations than joke books. Note that, except for the love songs, the numbers tend to veer around the plot rather than connect with it; the "baby" piece, "My Baby Just Cares For Me," leaps in out of nowhere—and don't miss the ridiculous smile on mean Sheriff Bob's face as Cantor sings.

Returning to the *Ziegfeld Follies* CD: Helen Morgan's "What Wouldn't I Do For That Man?" is a sweet and happy cut in a lush arrangement featuring solo violin and guitar, not in any way a precursor of "Funny Honey." That song references instead another Morgan number, *Show Boat*'s "Bill" (not on the disc)—or, for that matter, Fanny Brice's "My Man" (which *is* on the disc): I love him, flaws and all. Most singers of these numbers were low-voiced, like Gwen Verdon, but Morgan is a soprano, which gives her style a caressing quality.

The Ziegfeld Follies is a solid investment in general, as it includes much of the top talent of the day, for Ziegfeld always hired the best. John Steel brings on the beauties in "A Pretty Girl Is Like a Melody," sounding like John McCormack at some opera diva's birthday party. Marilyn Miller drops in, too, in a snippet of the soundtrack from her third and last film, *Her Majesty, Love*, and there's a two-sided twelve-inch 78 medley of numbers from *Ziegfeld Follies of 1927*, with original-cast members backed by a Victor house band. This is the rich treasury of hot Broadway that authors of musicals have been pastiche-ing in countless shows—Gallagher and Shean in their "Absolutely? Positively!" patter duet, Van and Schenck in "Mandy" (a minstrel-show tintype)...and it was John Steel and his "girls" anthem that led to the invention of Roscoe and "Beautiful Girls" in Sondheim's *Follies*.

Those curious about Zez Confrey, the progenitor of the piano pieces inspiring "When Velma Takes the Stand," can find an informative sampling by Eteri Andjaparidze (Naxos), so bright and facile in "Kitten on the Keys" that you'll sign up for piano lessons. One caveat: Andjaparidze is apparently playing from the 1982 Belwin-Mills Confrey compendium, a photo-offset of the original sheets that accidentally printed the jangly rag of "Mississippi Shivers" under the title of "Kinda Careless" and the shuffling "Kinda Careless" under the title of "Mississippi Shivers." The disc includes both pieces under these wrong names; a number of YouTube cuts make the same error.

For *Chicago* itself, the original cast (Arista) of course gives us Fosse's company, an obviously authentic reading. "Roxie," interestingly, starts with the reporters and the monologue before reaching the song itself. The first London cast was not recorded, but the Australian (Polydor) was, following the Arista text, with its complete "Roxie," the slow and short version of "Me and My Baby," "Nowadays" without the whistling and rag-dance sections, and a non sequitur finale of "All That Jazz." It's a terrible performance. The pianist has to carry the downsized band, even unto replacing the mandolin effect in "When You're Good To Mama," which is taken too slowly in any case. The Billy Flynn lacks the big high note near the end of "All I Care About," and the two women leads are shrill. An unnecessary disc.

Aside from Lee Konitz's jazz interpretations (GM) and Ben Bagley's *Contemporary Broadway Revisited* (Painted Smiles), both with the cut "Ten Percent" and "Loopin' the Loop," there was no more *Chicago* till the 1996 revival and its London version (both on Victor). They are equally valid, with dashing playing by the orchestras in Ralph Burns' original scoring (though London does give us more of the score). Still, other than Ann Reinking's roughhewn and Ruthie Henshall's elegant Roxies, the casts don't match the 1975 people for sheer élan.

A real surprise in the *Chicago* cast-album sweepstakes is a Viennese cast (Reverso-BMG) taken down live at the Theater an der Wien, the house where Beethoven's *Fidelio* was first performed: a noble hall, a holy site of Western Civilization. And Beethoven's heroine, Leonore, is a Goethean *Ewig-weibliche* ("Eternal womanhood," in David Luke's translation), inspiring and thrilling us. Yet the Viennese delighted in *Chicago*'s depraved heroine and ate the whole show with a spoon. This is unusual for an Austrian audience; they don't cheer like this for *Fidelio*. Frederike Haas, Anna Montanaro, and Rainhard Fendrich (the suavest of Billy Flynns) head the lively cast, with a Mary Sunshine (billed as Ch. Maxwell) who sounds like a real opera soprano. The disc provides a very full reading, with dialogue bits and the occasional English—"Okay," "Das ist show business," and, for the finale, an intro for "Chicagos einzige [own] killer girls!"

The translation inevitably fails to pull all of Ebb's imagery into focus, though German versions of American shows are generally more precisely rendered than those of other European languages. But then, what would the Viennese know of "Father Dip" (whose reference is reduced to a generic mention of "Der alte Blues" [the old blues])? Further, "Class" is sung (and much too smoothly, as if it really were Schubert) as "Moral" (accented on the second syllable, the German word for "morality"). This throws the number out of sync with itself: Velma and the Matron aren't lamenting the loss of virtue but the rise of vulgarity, and that creates the joke, because the music is so polished. Then, too, "Razzle Dazzle" becomes "Hocuspocus," invoking fairy-tale witches instead of slick production values.

Still, it's such an energetic performance that it rivals all other *Chicago* discs. Note that, even across the ocean, the Weisslers seem to have hit on exactly the right note to strike in their heralds, making everyone look like his or her own Wanted! poster, as in the 1996 PR photography used in New York.

In video, YouTube offers various *Chicagos* from near and far, complete and in snippets, going back even to its week at *Encores!*, and including productions in various Latin American theatre capitals that remind us that "Broadway" remains a guarantee of professional authority sometimes elusive elsewhere. There is as well a BBC/Bravo "making of" documentary, nearly an hour long, on the London revival, notable mainly for its paucity of event. Someone appears to have wanted to ridicule the Weisslers, by showing them blithely touring London to seek a venue for the cast party, this interpolated with scenes of the cast exhausting itself in rehearsals. But what are the Weisslers supposed to do, don sweats and strike Fosse poses with the corps? There's also a touch of fake news when the Velma, Ute Lemper, is shown threatening to quit the production for no apparent reason; this is an exaggeration of what actually happened. Anyway, the documentary comes alive only when music director Gareth Valentine, with his back to us, shows some of the cast women his Prince Albert. The ladies burst into amazed giggles. "Does that hurt?" one of them cries.

As so often with these "rehearsals and reflections" tapes, we don't learn all that much about the show, though Ruthie Henshall reminds us that *Chicago's* undertext is the rivalry of Roxie and Velma. "The two of them," she observes, "are in competition the whole way through." The work's *point* is to disclose the vulnerability of our right to a free and responsible press. But the work's energy resides in its War of the Divas. In the American musical, from *Naughty Marietta* to *Gypsy* to even *Hamilton*'s tableau vivant of our Founding Fathers, everything is personal.

INDEX